The SIOP® Model for Teaching English-Language Arts to English Learners

MaryEllen Vogt

California State University, Long Beach

Jana Echevarría

California State University, Long Beach

Deborah J. Short

Center for Applied Linguistics, Washington, DC
Academic Language Research & Training, Arlington, VA

With contributions by Karlin LaPorta and Lisa Mitchener
Downey Unified School District,
Downey, California

PEARSON

Boston   Columbus   Indianapolis   New York   San Francisco   Upper Saddle River
Amsterdam   Cape Town   Dubai   London   Madrid   Milan   Munich   Paris   Montreal   Toronto
Delhi   Mexico City   Sao Paulo   Sydney   Hong Kong   Seoul   Singapore   Taipei   Tokyo

Vice President, Editor-in-Chief: *Aurora Martínez Ramos*
Series Editorial Assistant: *Amy Foley*
Vice President, Marketing and Sales Strategies: *Emily Williams Knight*
Vice President, Director of Marketing: *Quinn Perkson*
Marketing Manager: *Danae April*
Production Editor: *Gregory Erb*
Editorial Production Service: *Nesbitt Graphics, Inc.*
Manufacturing Buyer: *Megan Cochran*
Electronic Composition: *Nesbitt Graphics, Inc.*
Interior Design: *Nesbitt Graphics, Inc.*
Photo Researcher: *Annie Pickert*
Cover Designer: *Linda Knowles*

For Professional Development resources visit www.pearsonpd.com.

Copyright © 2010 Pearson Education, Inc.

Between the time website information is gathered and then published, it is not unusual for some sites to have closed. Also, the transcription of URLs can result in typographical errors. The publisher would appreciate notification where these errors occur so that they may be corrected in subsequent editions.

Cataloging in Publication data is on file at the Library of Congress.

Printed in the United States of America

10 9 8 7 6 5 4 3 2   BRG 13 12 11 10 09

Photo Credits: p. 1, PhotosToGo; pp. 16, 29, 76, 95, 119, 142, Bob Daemmrich Photography; p. 57 Lindfors Photography

www.pearsonhighered.com

ISBN-10: 0-205-62760-9
ISBN-13: 978-0-205-62760-8

Dedication

*This book is dedicated to the reading, language arts, and
English teachers who are committed to the SIOP® Model . . .
but who on a daily basis wonder what the heck the difference
is between content and language objectives
in the English-Language Arts!
This book is for YOU!*

contents

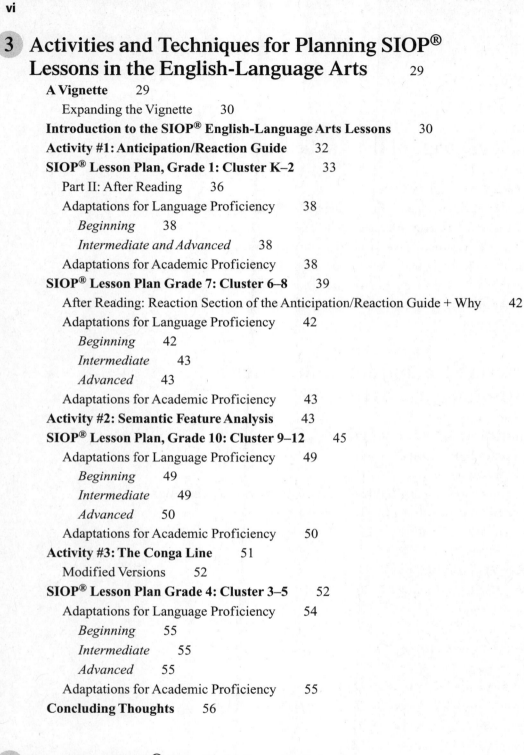

5 Sample SIOP® English-Language Arts Lessons and Units (Grades 3–5)   76

6 Sample SIOP® English-Language Arts Lessons and Units (Grades 6–8)   95

preface

We have written this book in response to the many requests from teachers for specific application of the SIOP® Model to English-language arts. During our nearly 15 years of working with the SIOP® Model, we have learned that both the subject you teach and the students comprising your classes are major considerations in making effective lesson plans. Showing a SIOP® social studies lesson plan to an Algebra teacher and asking him to "adapt it" has resulted in rolled eyes and under-the-breath comments like, "You've got to be kidding." A similar reaction occurs if we show a physical science lesson video clip to elementary reading teachers and ask them to modify the techniques in their classes. Whatever our subject area, we teachers know what we need and we know what we want.

So, this book is intended specifically for teachers of the English-language arts (ELA), including literacy coaches, intervention teachers, and reading specialists. If you teach in grades K–2, 3–5, 6–8, or 9–12, you'll find information about teaching ELA written specifically for your grade-level cluster. If you are an elementary teacher, obviously you teach multiple subjects and you may want to check out our companion books for teaching mathematics, social studies, and science within the SIOP® Model.

We offer an important caveat. This book is intended for teachers who have familiarity with the SIOP® Model. Our expectation is that you have read one of the core texts: *Making Content Comprehensible for English Learners: The SIOP® Model* (Echevarria, Vogt, & Short, 2008), or either *Making Content Comprehensible for Elementary English Learners: The SIOP® Model* (Echevarria, Vogt, & Short, 2010a) or *Making Content Comprehensible for Secondary English Learners: The SIOP® Model* (Echevarria, Vogt, & Short, 2010b). If you have not read one of these books or had substantial and effective professional development in the SIOP® Model, we ask that you save this book for later. We want this book to be just what you've been looking for, a resource that will enable you to more effectively teach English-language arts to your English learners (and other students). Therefore, the more familiar you are with the philosophy, terminology, concepts, and teaching techniques associated with the SIOP® Model, the better you will be able to use this book. We also encourage you to review the lessons and units from the grade-level clusters other than the one in which you teach. Throughout all of the lesson plans in Chapters 3–7, you will see many teaching techniques and activities that truly span all grade levels and content areas, so please don't overlook them.

The SIOP® Model is the only empirically validated model of sheltered instruction. Sheltered instruction, or SDAIE (Specially Designed Academic Instruction in English), in general, is a means for making content comprehensible for English learners (ELs) while they are developing English proficiency. The SIOP® Model distinctively calls for teachers to promote academic language development as they provide comprehensible content. SIOP® classrooms may include a mix of native English-speaking students and English learners, or just English learners. This depends on your school and district, the number of ELs you have in your school, and the availability of SIOP®-trained teachers. Whatever your context, what characterizes a SIOP® sheltered classroom is the systematic, consistent, and concurrent focus on teaching both academic content and academic language to English learners.

Organization and Purpose of This Book

We have specifically written this book for elementary and secondary educators. In the book, you will read about a wide variety of instructional activities, many of which are effective for any grade level when teaching the English-language arts. The readability of the literature selections will change over the grade levels, of course, but nearly all of the meaningful activities were selected to provide practice and application of key concepts, vocabulary, and academic language, and they work well with all students, including English learners in grades K–12. This book includes the following sections:

Chapter 1: The Academic Language of English-Language Arts (ELA)

Chapter 1 focuses on the academic language that students need to develop to be successful in school in the English-language arts. In this chapter we also explain the academic reading, writing and oral discourse skills (such as classroom conversation and discussion) that ELs need to master. We provide specific examples of academic language culled directly from K–12 English-language arts content standards.

Chapter 2: SIOP® Lesson Planning and Unit Design

In Chapter 2 we provide specific recommendations for planning SIOP® literacy lessons and units, including an explanation of the SIOP® lesson plan format that is used throughout this book. We also provide a brief overview of how English learners develop reading, writing, and vocabulary and how this knowledge guides SIOP® English-language arts lesson planning.

Chapter 3: Activities and Techniques for Planning English-Language Arts SIOP® Lessons

Chapter 3 is written by two English-language arts teachers who are also reading specialists and SIOP® trainers in their district, Karlin LaPorta and Lisa Mitchener. In this chapter, you will find three elementary, middle school, and high school reading and literature lesson plans that demonstrate how effective instructional techniques are applied in sample SIOP® lesson plans across grade level clusters. Suggestions are provided for differentiating the lessons for students' varied levels of English proficiency.

Chapters 4–7: Sample SIOP® English-Language Arts Lessons and Units (Clusters K–2, 3–6, 6–8, 9–12)

Within Chapters 4–7, you will find four comprehensive SIOP® English-language arts units that all focus on Character Development. The units were designed for the following grade level clusters: K–2 with grade 1 lessons; 3–6 with grade 4 lessons; 6–8 with grade 7 lessons; and 9–12 with grade 10 lessons. Even though the lessons focus on a particular grade level, the unit and lesson plans can be adapted to the other grade levels within the cluster.

In these chapters, our contributors, Karlin and Lisa, describe their planning process for the SIOP® lessons in each unit presented, and discuss objectives and the standards they derive from, the SIOP® techniques and activities they have chosen, and other goals they have. You will find several "think-alouds" and self-directed questions throughout the units in which the writers convey their decision-making process. For those of you unfamiliar with think-alouds, they are structured models that teachers use to show how readers, writers, and learners, think about language and learning tasks (Baumann, Jones, & Seifer-Kessel, 1993; Oczkus, 2009). Further, you will notice "Planning Points," comments that clarify and provide additional information, including tips for lesson and unit design. You will also find the three lessons from Chapter 3 embedded in a comprehensive unit. Being familiar with the topic and one lesson should allow you to envision the delivery of the unit more fully. The lesson plans and units also include sample handouts the teacher will use with students, such as specific graphic organizers, guides, and charts.

Chapter 8: Pulling It All Together

In this chapter, we conclude with our final thoughts about lesson and unit planning, and what we have learned from working with the SIOP® Model over the years. Our contributors for this book then add their comments, insights, and final recommendations about teaching English learners with the SIOP® Model.

Appendixes

In the Appendixes, you will find several useful resources. If you need a refresher on the SIOP® Model, you will find a brief overview of each of the eight components of the model and a discussion about why it is especially important for English learners. Additionally, you will find the SIOP® Protocol, many examples of academic language in ELA across the grade levels, a chart that illustrates how the SIOP® components map onto the various activities in the lessons and units, and blackline masters for a variety of graphic organizers that are used throughout the units.

If you are an elementary teacher, you may wish to read the other books in this SIOP® content series including those on using the SIOP® Model to teach mathematics, science, and history/social studies to English learners. Although you will find a few similarities in the books, each provides lessons and unit plans for the specific content and academic language of the respective discipline.

Acknowledgments

We acknowledge and appreciate the suggestions offered by the educators who reviewed this book. They include Lisa deMaagd, Wyoming Elementary; Karen Fichter, Wilburn Elementary; Andrea Honigsfeld, Molloy University; and Minda Johnson, St. Anthony's Elementary.

We would also like to thank elementary teachers Jennifer Toledo, Patricia Martinez, and Stephanie Blanco for their ideas and suggestions for activities, and for keeping us grounded in the realities of the classroom.

To our Allyn & Bacon team we express our gratitude for keeping us focused and on task. To Aurora Martinez, our incredible editor who never sleeps, we know that it has been through your understanding of the academic and language needs of the English learners in our schools that this series of books has been written on the SIOP® Model. Thank you, Aurora.

We have been most fortunate to have as our contributors to these content area books eight content specialists and SIOP® experts. Their insights, ideas, lesson plans, and unit plans across the grade level clusters clearly demonstrate their expertise not only in their content areas but also in the SIOP® Model. With deep gratitude we acknowledge the significant contributions to this book by our colleagues, Karlin LaPorta and Lisa Mitchener. Their deep understanding of the SIOP® Model is evident in their teaching techniques, ELA lesson plans and units, and we thank them for their belief in and commitment to English learners and the SIOP® Model.

Finally, we acknowledge and express great appreciation to our families. The SIOP® Model wouldn't exist if it hadn't been for their support and encouragement over all these years.

mev   je   djs

MaryEllen Vogt is Distinguished Professor Emerita of Education at California State University, Long Beach. Dr. Vogt has been a classroom teacher, reading specialist, special education specialist, curriculum coordinator, and university teacher educator. She received her doctorate from the University of California, Berkeley, and is a co-author of fourteen books, including *Reading Specialists and Literacy Coaches in the* Real *World* (2ⁿᵈ ed., 2007) and the SIOP® book series. Her research interests include improving comprehension in the content areas, teacher change and development, and content literacy and language acquisition for English learners. Dr. Vogt was inducted into the California Reading Hall of Fame, received her university's Distinguished Faculty Teaching Award, and served as President of the International Reading Association in 2004–2005.

Jana Echevarría is a Professor Emerita at California State University, Long Beach. She has taught in elementary, middle and high schools in general education, special education, ESL and bilingual programs. She has lived in Taiwan, Spain and Mexico. Her UCLA doctorate earned her an award from the National Association for Bilingual Education's Outstanding Dissertations Competition. Her research and publications focus on effective instruction for English learners, including those with learning disabilities. Currently, she is Co-Principal Investigator with the Center for Research on the Educational Achievement and Teaching of English Language Learners (CREATE) funded by the U.S. Department of Education, Institute of Education Sciences (IES). In 2005, Dr. Echevarría was selected as Outstanding Professor at CSULB.

Deborah J. Short is a professional development consultant and a senior research associate at the Center for Applied Linguistics in Washington, DC. She co-developed the SIOP® Model for sheltered instruction and has directed national research studies on English language learners funded by the Carnegie Corporation, the Rockefeller Foundation, and the U.S. Dept. of Education. She recently chaired an expert panel on adolescent ELL literacy. As the director of Academic Language Research & Training, Dr. Short provides professional development on sheltered instruction and academic literacy around the U.S. and abroad. She has numerous publications, including the SIOP® book series and five ESL textbook series for National Geographic/Hampton-Brown. She has taught English as a second/foreign language in New York, California, Virginia, and the Democratic Republic of Congo.

Karlin LaPorta has been an educator for twelve years. After starting her career as a fourth-grade teacher, she learned her true calling was at the middle school level. She taught English and reading to struggling learners in the sixth, seventh, and eighth grades while also coordinating the school's Title I program. She is currently the EL Teacher Specialist for the Downey Unified School District and provides SIOP® professional development for teachers in her district. She has also served as SIOP® National Faculty and has facilitated SIOP® Institutes all over California. She earned her masters degree in Curriculum: Reading/Language Arts along with a Reading Specialist Credential from California State University, Long Beach.

Lisa Mitchener is an elementary teacher at Gauldin Elementary School in Downey, California. She has been teaching for fifteen years and has experience with all elementary grade levels. She holds a Specialist in Reading credential and has earned two master's degrees, one in Multicultural Education from California State University, Dominguez Hills, and one in Curriculum: Reading/Language Arts from California State University, Long Beach. She was selected as a SIOP® National Faculty and has provided training in her district for the past three years.

Academic Language of the English-Language Arts

Introduction

If we were to survey the general population, we would most likely find that English-language arts teachers are some of the most: (1) prodigious readers; (2) preeminent writers; and (3) articulate speakers with sophisticated vocabularies. For example, have you ever driven your friends crazy at a cocktail party when you corrected their grammar, answered questions in complete, elaborated sentences, used synonyms to paraphrase what someone has just said, or, most annoying of all, gave the etymology and derivation for a word a friend just used? If so, you are indeed part of a very special group of educators, those who love the English language, treasure great literature, and recognize the turn of a good phrase, whether delivered orally or in writing.

However . . . how did you feel when you purchased your most recent BlackBerry/fancy cell phone/digital camera/new computer . . . and you had to figure out how to turn it on? It's amazing how highly educated, literate people, including educators, can turn into mush when trying to navigate today's technology. As an example, perhaps you have run across words and phrases in a product's manual such as:

- *glog* (hmm . . . like a blog?)
- *e-cycle center* (a store where you can buy e-cycles?)
- *dynamic smart cooling* (something to aid menopausal women?)
- *chiller* (an especially cold smoothie?)
- *in-row cooling* (like an ice cube tray?)
- *drexting* (texting while wearing a dress?)
- *conficker* (we don't even want to try . . .)
- *influencer* (we've got it . . . the suffix "er" means "one who . . .")

While *one who influences* is a good guess here, the actual technological definition for *influencer* is: *In the blogosphere, an influencer is a person who blogs about a specific subject and is highly recognized online as an expert. An influencer differs from an a-list blogger in that they are often able to sway another's opinions and thoughts on the subject matter.*

Okay, but what's an *a-list blogger*? And, were you able to resist the temptation to correct the definition to read, "An influencer differs from an a-list blogger in that he or she is . . .?" Further, if one of your students used the word *influencer* in an essay, how quickly would you circle it in red and jot, "No such word . . ."?

We have all had experiences where, as knowledgeable, well-read, educated people, we became lost when we listened to or read about a new and unfamiliar topic. We're often tripped up by the terminology, phrases, and concepts that are unique to the subject matter. When this happens, we most likely become frustrated and disinterested, and we may tune out and give up. Every day, many English learners sit in classrooms where both the topic and the related words and concepts are totally unfamiliar to them. Other ELs may have familiarity with the topic, perhaps even some expertise, but because they don't know the English words, terminology, and phrases—that is, the content-specific academic language— they are also unable to understand what is being taught.

What Is Academic Language?

As an elementary reading/language arts teacher or secondary English teacher, you may be wondering how it is possible to separate "academic language" from all the other types of language within our content area. This is similar to the dilemma frequently expressed by language arts teachers that it's especially challenging to write language objectives because as language arts teachers, all we "do" is language! However, within our particular content area, academic language plays a critically important role, and for English learners (as well as struggling readers and writers), academic language can provide serious challenges. In this chapter, we will define academic language (also referred to as "academic English"), discuss why academic language is challenging for ELs, and offer suggestions for how to effectively teach academic language. We also include an overview of academic language specifically for teachers of English-language arts (ELA).

Although definitions in the research literature differ somewhat, there is general agreement that academic language is both generic and content specific. That is, although many academic words are used across all content areas (such as *demonstrate, estimate, analyze, summarize, categorize*), others pertain to specific subject areas (*idioms, characterization, symbolism* for Language Arts; *angle, ratio, dispersion* for Math). It is important to remember that academic language is more than specific content vocabulary words related to particular topics. Rather, academic language represents the entire range of language used in academic settings, including elementary and secondary schools.

When you reflect on the previous examples for Language Arts and Mathematics, you can see that academic language differs considerably from the social, conversational language that is used on the playground, at home, or at cocktail parties (see Figure 1). Social or conversational language is generally more concrete than abstract, and it is usually supported by contextual clues, such as gestures, facial expressions, and body language (Cummins, 1979; 2000; Echevarria & Graves, 2007). To further clarify academic language, the following definitions are offered by several educational researchers:

- Academic language is "the language that is used by teachers and students for the purpose of acquiring new knowledge and skills . . . imparting new information, describing abstract ideas, and developing students' conceptual understandings" (Chamot & O'Malley, 1994, p. 40).
- Academic language refers to "word knowledge that makes it possible for students to engage with, produce, and talk about texts that are valued in school" (Flynt & Brozo, 2008, p. 500).
- "Academic English is the language of the classroom, of academic disciplines (science, history, literary analysis), of texts and literature, and of extended, reasoned discourse. It is more abstract and decontextualized than conversational English" (Gersten, Baker, Shanahan, Linan-Thompson, Collins, & Scarcella, 2007, p. 16).
- Academic English "refers to more abstract, complex, and challenging language that will eventually permit you to participate successfully in mainstream classroom instruction. Academic English involves such things as relating an event or a series of events to someone who was not present, being able to make comparisons between alternatives and justify a choice, knowing different forms and inflections of words and their appropriate use, and possessing and using content-specific vocabulary and modes of expression in different academic disciplines such as mathematics and social studies" (Goldenberg, 2008, p. 9).
- "Academic language is the set of words, grammar, and organizational strategies used to describe complex ideas, higher-order thinking processes, and abstract concepts" (Zwiers, 2008, p. 20).

Some educators suggest that the distinction between conversational and academic language is somewhat arbitrary and that it is the *situation, community,* or *context* that is either predominantly social or academic (Aukerman, 2007; Bailey, 2007). For purposes of this book, we maintain that academic language is essential for success in school (the *context*), and that it is more challenging to learn than conversational English, especially for students who are acquiring English as a second or additional language. Although

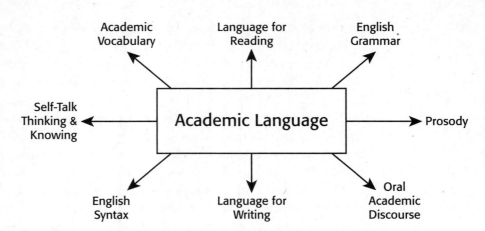

FIGURE 1. *The Spectrum of Academic Language*

knowing conversational language assists students in learning academic language, we must teach English learners (and other students, including native speakers) the "vocabulary, more complex sentence structures, and rhetorical forms not typically encountered in nonacademic settings" (Goldenberg, 2008, p. 13).

How Does Academic Language Fit into the SIOP® Model?

As you know, the SIOP® Model has a dual purpose: to systematically and consistently teach both content and language in every lesson. Once again, sometimes English-language arts teachers feel that "This is what we always do, so why do we need a demarcation between content and language?" The simple answer to this question is that although content and language objectives help focus the teacher throughout a lesson, these objectives also (perhaps even more importantly) focus students on what they are supposed to know and be able to do during and after each lesson as related to *both* content knowledge and language development.

English learners especially need to understand that they should be concentrating not only on acquiring content (such as learning the difference between a simile and a metaphor) but also on learning how to correctly use figurative language in written and spoken English. You might be thinking, "Well, of course! That's what teaching English, reading, writing, grammar, and spelling is all about!" And, to a degree, you're right. But because we also have specific content in our field (such as teaching roots, base words, prefixes, affixes, and figurative language), we must provide opportunities for English learners (and other students) to develop their English proficiency by using and producing language through reading, writing, listening, and speaking. And, that's what the SIOP® Model is all about.

A critical aspect of academic language is academic vocabulary. Within the SIOP® Model, we refer to academic vocabulary as having three elements (Echevarria, Vogt, & Short, 2008, p. 59). These include:

1. Content Words. These are key vocabulary words, terms, and concepts associated with a particular topic. Key vocabulary can come from literature and expository texts (such as *character, setting, rising action, conflict, denouement, falling action, resolution, cause and effect, main idea, supporting details, generalization*); from writing analysis (such as *imagery, sentence structure, writing process, thesis statement,*

conclusion, sentence fragment); from grammar (such as *action verbs, noun clauses, subjects, predicates, homonyms, antonyms, imperative, declarative, interrogative*); as well as from other components of the curriculum. Obviously, you will need to introduce and teach key content vocabulary when teaching poetry, biography, plays, and other genres related to both reading and writing.

2. Process/Function Words. These are the words and phrases that have to do with functional language use, such as *how to request information, justify opinions, state a conclusion, uncover an author's message, "state in your own words," identify multiple perspectives, summarize, persuade, question, interpret*, and so forth. Tasks that students are to accomplish during a lesson also fit into this category, and for English learners, their meanings may need to be taught explicitly. Examples include *list, explain, paraphrase, debate, identify, create, write a five-paragraph essay, define, share with a partner,* and so forth.

3. Words and Word Parts That Teach English Structure. These are words and word parts that enable students to learn new vocabulary, primarily based on English morphology. Although instruction in this category generally falls under the responsibility of English-language arts teachers, we also encourage teachers of other content areas to be aware of the academic language of their own disciplines. While you teach past tense (such as adding an *-ed* to regular verbs) as part of your ELA curriculum, a history teacher might reinforce past tense by pointing out that when we talk or write about historical events, we use the past tense of English. Similarly, as part of an ELA curriculum, you are responsible for teaching about English morphology (base words, roots, prefixes, suffixes). However, science teachers use many words with these morphemes as part of their key vocabulary (such as *arthropod, ecosystem, anaerobic respiration*). If English learners (and other students) have an opportunity to read, write, and orally produce words with complex parts during their English/language arts class as well as their history and science classes, English development is doubly reinforced. And, if this reinforcement occurs every school day, one can assume that English learners' mastery of English will be accelerated, as happens with repeated practice in any new learning situation. For a usable and informative list of English word roots that provide the clue to more than 100,000 English words, refer to pages 60–61 of *Making Content Comprehensible for English Learners: The SIOP® Model* (Echevarria, Vogt, & Short, 2008). This is a must-have list for both elementary and secondary teachers in ALL curricular areas.

Picture a stool with three legs. If one of the legs is broken, the stool will not be able to fulfill its function, which is to hold a person who sits on it. From our experience, English learners must have instruction in and practice with all three "legs" of academic vocabulary (content words, process/function words, and words/word parts that teach English structure) if they're going to develop the academic language they need to be successful students.

Of course, academic English also involves reading and writing. As you most likely know, the National Reading Panel (National Institute of Child Health and Human Development, 2000) defined the components of reading as phonemic awareness, phonics, fluency, vocabulary, and reading comprehension. Research suggests that high-quality instruction in these five components generally works for English learners as well, although additional focus on oral language development and background building are called for to enhance comprehension (August & Shanahan, 2006; Goldenberg, 2008).

Although English learners are able to attain well-taught word-level skills such as decoding, word recognition, and spelling that are equal to those of their Native-English speaking peers, the same is not typically the case with text-level skills such as reading comprehension and writing. The reason for the disparity between word-level and text-level skills among English learners is oral English proficiency. Well-developed oral proficiency in English, which includes English vocabulary and syntactic knowledge plus listening comprehension skills, is associated with English reading and writing proficiency. Therefore, it is insufficient to teach English learners the components of reading alone; teachers must incorporate extensive oral language development opportunities into literacy instruction. Further, English learners benefit from having more opportunities to practice reading, check comprehension, and consolidate text knowledge through summarization. They also need instruction on the features of different text genres, especially those found in subject area classes—such as textbook chapters, online articles, laboratory directions, math word problems, and primary source materials. Because reading is the foundation for learning in school, it is critical that teachers use research-based practices to provide English learners with high-quality instruction that will lead to the development of strong reading skills.

Academic writing is an area that is affected significantly by limited English proficiency. Whereas oral skills can be developed as students engage in meaningful activities, skills in writing must be explicitly taught. The writing process (involving planning, drafting, editing, and revising written work) allows students to express ideas at their level of proficiency with teacher (or peer) guidance and explicit corrective feedback. However, for English learners, it is critical that a lot of meaningful discussion take place prior to asking students to write because such dialogue leads to writing and provides students with the English words they will use. Writing is also facilitated by such things as teacher modeling, posting of writing samples, providing sentence frames, and even having students occasionally copy words or text until they gain more independent proficiency (Graham & Perin, 2007). This kind of constant exposure to words and sentence patterning allows ELs to become familiar with the conventions of how words and sentences are put together in the language (Garcia & Beltran, 2003).

English learners should be encouraged to write in English early, especially if they have literacy skills in their native language, and they should be provided frequent opportunities to express their ideas in writing. Errors in writing are to be expected and should be viewed as part of the natural process of acquisition. Providing scaffolded writing tools, such as partially completed graphic organizers for pre-writing and sentence frames for organizing key points and supporting details, will help ELs write in the content classroom.

How Is Academic Language Manifested in Classroom Discourse?

Our teachers come to class,
And they talk and they talk,
Til their faces are like peaches,
We don't;
We just sit like cornstalks.
(Cazden, 1976, p. 74)

These poignant words come from a Navajo child who describes a classroom as she sees it. Teachers like to talk. Just observe any classroom and you'll find that the teacher does the vast majority of the talking. That might be expected because the teacher, after all, is the most expert English-language arts person in the classroom. However, for students to develop proficiency in language, interpret what they read, express themselves orally and in writing, participate during whole-group and small-group instruction, and explain and defend their viewpoints and answers, they need opportunities to learn and use academic language. To promote more student engagement in classroom discourse, the Interaction component is included in SIOP® Model. The features of the Interaction component include:

- Frequent opportunities for interaction with and discussion between teachers and students and among students, which encourage elaborated responses about lesson concepts
- Grouping configurations that support language and content objectives of the lesson
- Sufficient wait time for student responses consistently provided
- Ample opportunities for students to clarify key concepts in L1 (native language) as needed

These features promote balanced turn-taking both between teachers and students and among students, providing multiple opportunities for students to use academic English. Notice how each feature of Interaction encourages student talk. This is in considerable contrast to the discourse patterns typically found in both elementary and secondary classrooms. Most instructional patterns involve the teacher asking a question, a student responding, the teacher evaluating the response (IRE: Initiation/Response/Evaluation), or providing feedback (IRF: Initiation/Response/Feedback), followed by another teacher-asked question (Cazden, 1986; 2001; Mehan, 1979; Watson & Young, 1986). A typical interaction between a teacher and her students following the reading of a short story is illustrated in the following example:

T: Who is the main character in the short story we just read?

S1: The boy.

T: Yes, you're right. But what's the boy's name? Who can tell us?

S2: Billy.

T: That's right. Billy is the main character. Very good. Now, what is the setting of the story? Remember that the setting is where and when the story takes place.

S3: A farm in summer.

T: Great! Now, what do you think is the problem in this story?

And so it goes, often for a good portion of the lesson. Notice that the teacher asked questions that had one correct answer with no reasoning or higher level thinking required, the teacher controlled the interchange, and the teacher evaluated student responses. Also note that the only person in the interchange to actually orally produce academic language (*main character*, *setting, problem*) was the teacher. The students didn't need to use more than one or two words in response to the teacher's questions in order to participate appropriately. Only three students were involved, while the others sat quietly.

The IRE/IRF pattern is quite typical and it has been found to be one of the least effective interactional patterns for the classroom (Cazden, 1986; 2001; Mehan, 1979; Watson & Young, 1986). More similar to an interrogation than to a discussion, this type of teacher-student interaction stifles academic language development and does not encourage higher level thinking because most of the questions have a straightforward, known answer. Further, we have observed from kindergarten through high school that most students become conditioned to wait for someone else to answer. Often it is the teacher who ultimately answers his or her own question, especially when no students volunteer.

In classrooms where the IRF (Initiation, Response, Feedback) pattern dominates, the teacher's feedback may actually inhibit learning because she changes students' responses by adding to or deleting from their statements, or completely changes a student's intent and meaning. Because the teacher is searching for a preconceived answer and often "fishes" until it is found, the cognitive work of the lesson is often carried out by the teacher rather than the students. In these classrooms, students are seldom given the opportunity to elaborate on their answers; rather, the teacher does the analyzing, synthesizing, generalizing, and elaborating.

Changing ineffective classroom discourse patterns by creating authentic opportunities for students to develop academic language is critically important because as one acquires language, new concepts are also developed. Think about the previous example of trying to understand technology terms. Each new vocabulary word you read and understand (e.g., *influencer*) is attached to a concept that in turn expands your ability to think about technology resources. As your own system of word-meaning grows in complexity, you are more capable of understanding the associated concepts and generating the self-directed speech of verbal thinking: "Now that I know what twittering is, I can give it a try." Without an understanding of the words and the concepts they represent, you would be incapable of thinking about (self-directed speech) or discussing (talking with another) your newest electronic gadget.

Why Do English Learners Have Difficulty with Academic Language?

Developing academic language has proven to be quite challenging for English learners. In fact, in a study that followed EL students' academic progress in U.S. schools, researchers found that the ELs actually regressed over time (Suarez-Orozco, Suarez-Orozco & Todorova, 2008). There are myriad influences that affect overall student learning, and academic language learning in particular. Some factors, such as poverty and transiency, are outside of the school's sphere of influence, but let's focus on some of the influences that are in our control, namely what happens instructionally for these students that facilitates or impedes their learning.

Many classrooms are devoid of the kinds of supports that assist students in their quest to learn new material in a new language. Since proficiency in English is the best predictor of academic success, it seems reasonable that teachers of English learners should spend a significant amount of time teaching the vocabulary required to understand the lesson's topic. However, in a study that observed 23 ethnically diverse classrooms, researchers found that in the core academic subject areas only 1.4% of instructional time was spent developing vocabulary knowledge (Scott, Jamison-Noel, & Asselin, 2003).

The lack of opportunity to develop oral language skills hinders students' progress in all subject areas. Passive learning—sitting quietly while listening to a teacher talk—does not encourage engagement. In order to acquire academic language, students need lessons that are meaningful and engaging and that provide ample opportunity to practice using language orally. Successful group work requires intentional planning and giving students instructions about how to work with others effectively; teacher expectations need to be made clear. Grouping students in teams for discussion, using partners for specific tasks, and other planned configurations increase student engagement and oral language development.

Another related influence on language development is access to the language and the subject matter. Think about a situation in which you hear another language spoken. It could be the salon where you get a manicure or your favorite fast food place. Just because you regularly hear another language, are you learning it? Typically, not. Likewise, many English learners sit in class and hear what amounts to "English noise." It doesn't make sense to them and thus, they are not learning either academic language or the content being taught. Without the kinds of practices that are promoted by the SIOP® Model, much of what happens during the school day is lost on English learners.

Finally, some teachers have low expectations for EL students (Lee, 2005). They are not motivated to get to know the students, their cultures, or their families. Poor performance is not only accepted, but expected. Rather than adjusting instruction so that it is meaningful to these students, these teachers attribute lack of achievement to students' cultural background, limited English proficiency and, sadly, ability.

How Can We Effectively Teach Academic Language in English-Language Arts?

In a recent synthesis of existing research on teaching English language and literacy to ELs in the elementary grades, the authors make five recommendations, one of which is to "Ensure that the development of formal or academic English is a key instructional goal for English learners, beginning in the primary grades" (Gersten, Baker, Shanahan, Linan-Thompson, Collins, & Scarcella, 2007, pp. 26–27). Although few empirical studies have been conducted on the effects of academic language instruction, the central theme of the panel of researchers conducting the synthesis was the importance of intensive, interactive language practice that focuses on developing academic language. This recommendation was made based upon considerable expert opinion, with the caveat that additional research is still needed.

Because you are already familiar with the SIOP® Model, you know that effective instruction for English learners includes focused attention on and systematic implementation of the SIOP® Model's eight components and 30 features. Therefore, you should use the SIOP® protocol to guide lesson design when selecting activities and approaches for teaching academic language in the English-language arts.

Jeff Zwiers (2008, p. 41) notes that "academic language doesn't grow on trees." Rather, explicit vocabulary instruction through a variety of approaches and activities provides English learners with multiple chances to learn, practice, and apply academic language (Stahl & Nagy, 2006). Teachers must provide comprehensible input (Krashen, 1985) as well as structured opportunities for students to produce academic language in their content classes. This will enable English learners to negotiate meaning through confirming and disconfirming their understanding while they work and interact with others.

In addition to explicit vocabulary instruction, we need to provide a variety of scaffolds, including context. Writing a list of new terms on the board or pointing out sentences that are bolded in the textbook only helps if students know what they mean. To create a context for learning academic English, teachers must preteach terms and sentence patterns (e.g., interrogative and declarative), and explain them in ways that students can understand and relate to, followed by showing how the terms and sentence patterns are used in the textbook. Scaffolding involves providing enough support to students so that they are gradually able to be successful independently. Another way of scaffolding academic English is to have word walls or posters displayed that show academic language (such as literary terms with definitions) or processes (such as a strategy poster for decoding unknown words). Certainly, older learners can work in groups to create these posters with mnemonics, including cartoons or other illustrations. As English learners refer to and use these posted academic language words and phrases, they will internalize the terms and begin to use them independently.

In the lesson plans and units that appear in Chapters 3–7, you will see a variety of instructional techniques and activities for teaching, practicing, and using academic language in the English-language arts classroom. As you read the lesson plans, note the box on the lesson plan that is labeled "academic vocabulary." Reflect on why particular activities were selected for the respective content and language objectives. Additional resources for selecting effective activities that develop academic language and content knowledge include: Buehl's *Classroom Strategies for Interactive Learning* (2009); Vogt and Echeverria's *99 Ideas and Activities for Teaching English Learners with the SIOP® Model* (2008); and Reiss's *102 Content Strategies for English Language Learners* (2008). Secondary teachers will also find the following books to be helpful: Zwiers's *Building Academic Language: Essential Practices for Content Classrooms (Grades 5-12)* (2008), and *Developing Academic Thinking Skills in Grades 6–12: A Handbook of Multiple Intelligence Activities* (2004).

The Role of Discussion and Conversation in Developing Academic Language

As mentioned previously, researchers who have investigated the relationship between language and learning suggest that there should be more balance in student talk and teacher talk in order to promote meaningful language learning opportunities for English learners (Cazden, 2001; Echevarria, 1995; Tharp & Gallimore, 1988; Walqui, 2006). In order to achieve a better balance, teachers need to carefully analyze their own classroom interaction patterns, the way they formulate questions, how they provide students with academic feedback, and the opportunities they provide for students to engage in meaningful talk.

Not surprisingly, teacher questioning usually drives the type and quality of classroom discussions. The IRE or IRF pattern discussed previously is characterized by questions to which the teacher already knows the answer and results in the teacher unintentionally expecting students to "guess what I'm thinking" (Echevarria & Silver, 1995). In fact, researchers have found that explicit, "right there" questions are used about 50% of the time in classrooms (Zwiers, 2008). In contrast, open-ended questions that do not have quick "right" or "wrong" answers promote greater levels of thinking and expression.

Something as simple as having students turn to a partner and answer a question first, before reporting to the whole class, is an effective conversational technique, especially when the teacher circulates to monitor student responses. Speaking to a peer may be less threatening; in addition, this method actively engages every student. Effective SIOP® teachers facilitate discussion by following up with open-ended questions and probes that stimulate divergent thinking and language development.

Rather than responding to student answers with "Very good!", teachers who value conversation and discussion encourage elaborated responses with comments like, "Can you tell us more about that?" or "What made you think of that?" or "Did anyone else have that idea?" or "Please explain how you figured that out."

Zwiers (2008, pp. 62–63) has classified the types of comments you can make to enrich classroom talk. By using comments like those that follow (adapted from Zwiers), you can create a better balance between the amount of student talk and teacher talk. Further, classroom interactions are less likely to result in an IRE or IRF pattern. Try using some of these comments and see what happens to the interaction patterns in your own classroom!

To Prompt More Thinking

- You are on to something important. Keep going.
- You are on the right track. Tell us more.
- There is no right answer, so what would be your best answer?
- What did you notice about . . .

To Fortify or Justify a Response

- That's a good probable answer . . . How did you get to that answer?
- Why is what you said so important?
- What is your opinion (impression) of . . . Why?

To See Other Points of View

- That's a great start. Keep thinking and I'll get back to you.
- If you were in that person's shoes, what would you have done?
- Would you have done (or said) it like that? Why or why not?

To Consider Ethical Ramifications

- Should she have . . .?
- Some people think that . . . is [wrong, right, and so on]. What do you think? Why?
- How can we apply this to real life?

To Consider Consequences

- Should she have . . .?
- What if he had not done that?
- Some people think that . . . is [wrong, right, and so on]. What do you think? Why?
- How can we apply this to real life?

A conversational approach is particularly well suited to English learners who, after only a few years in school, frequently find themselves significantly behind their peers in most academic areas, usually because of low reading levels in English and underdeveloped language skills. Students benefit from a conversational approach in many ways because conversation provides:

- A context for learning in which language is expressed naturally through meaningful discussion
- Practice using oral language, which is a foundation for literacy skill development
- A means for students to express their thinking, and to clarify and fine-tune their ideas
- Time to process information and hear what others are thinking about
- An opportunity for teachers to model academic language, use content vocabulary appropriately, and, through think-alouds, model thinking processes
- Opportunities for students to participate as equal contributors to the discussion, which provides them with repetition of both linguistic terms and thinking processes and results in their eventual acquisition and internalization for future use

A rich discussion, or conversational approach, has advantages for teachers as well, including the following:

- Through discussion, a teacher can more naturally activate students' background knowledge and assess their prior learning.
- When working in small groups with each student participating in a discussion, teachers are better able to gauge student understanding of the lesson's concepts, tasks, and terminology, as well as discern areas of weakness.
- When teachers and students interact together, a supportive environment is fostered, which builds teacher-student rapport.

When contemplating the advantages of a more conversational approach to teaching, think about your own learning. It probably takes multiple exposures to new terms, concepts, and information before they become yours to use independently. If you talk with others about the concepts and information you are learning, you're more likely to remember them. English learners require even more repetition and redundancy to improve their language skills. As they have repeated opportunities to improve their oral language proficiency, ELs are more likely to use English, and more frequent use results in increased proficiency (Saunders & Goldenberg, 2009). Discussion and interaction push learners to think quickly, respond, construct sentences, put their thoughts into words, and ask for clarification through classroom dialogue. Discussion also allows students to see how other people think and use language to describe their thinking (Zwiers, 2008).

Productive discussion can take place in whole class settings, but it is more likely that small groups will facilitate the kind of high-quality interaction that benefits English learners. Working to express ideas and answers to questions in a new language can be intimidating for students of all ages. Small group work allows them to try out their ideas in a low-stress setting and to gauge how similar their ideas are to those of their peers. Working with partners, triads, or in a small group also provides a chance to process and articulate new information with less pressure than a whole class setting may create.

Earlier in this chapter, you read an interaction between a teacher and her students in which the IRE (Initiation/Response/Evaluation) pattern prevailed. In contrast, read the following transcript from a tenth grade literature discussion, and reflect on the differences in the two classroom interaction patterns (Vogt, 1996, pp. 182–183):

SARA: In the book *The Count of Monte Cristo,* what caused Eugenie to flee?

JUAN: She was going to marry Benedetto . . . is that wrong? I'm wondering . . .

TRAN: It's not right . . . she wanted to run away from her parents, I think.

TEACHER: Look at Sokea because she has the answer to this, I think. Sokea seems to think there's a little bit more to this.

SOKEA: Yeah . . .

ALEX: Wait, I know! Benedetto was convicted as a criminal, so you know the cops were going to arrest him so he was shamed. In other words, Eugenie's family was shamed 'cause they were supposed to, uh, marry the count . . . so that's why she ran away . . .

TEACHER: Are you satisfied with that?

SOKEA: Yeah, that's kinda like what I was thinking . . . .

SARA: Yeah, okay, good, but I'm still wondering why Madame Danglars and Duprey met in secret at the hotel . . .

TEACHER: Interesting thought. They had been meeting in secret for a long time . . .

ALEX: Okay, they're meeting and she brought Duprey a letter that Monsieur Danglars left her and he told her that he was leaving town . . .

CARLA: Yes, but I also think . . . (the conversation continues . . .)

Now, your students may not sound exactly like these students or speak English as fluently. However, this is a regular tenth grade classroom with diverse students, including English learners. Note how the teacher facilitates this discussion with very few words— just probes and careful listening. Sharing conversational control with students involves some risk-taking on the part of the teacher and practice on the part of students who may prefer to answer questions with monosyllabic words. Simply telling students to "discuss" will likely have poor results. We need to teach students how to engage in meaningful conversation and discussion and provide the support they need to be successful. Rather than sitting as "quiet cornstalks," students, including English learners, can learn to express themselves, support their viewpoints, advocate their positions, and defend their beliefs. When this occurs, we establish a classroom environment in which conversational control is shared among teachers and students alike.

What Is the Academic Language of English-Language Arts?

There are myriad terms that are used in academic settings. Some of these are used commonly across content areas and others are content-specific. The metaphor of bricks and mortar is helpful here as we think of some words representing bricks, such as English-language arts content-specific words such as *imagery, symbolism, narrative,* and *nonfiction.*

The mortar refers to general academic words such as, *describe, represent,* and *approximate* (Dutro & Moran, 2003). Understanding both types of terms is often the key to accessing content for English learners. For example, although most students need explicit instruction in the terms related to literary analysis, English learners (and struggling readers) also require that general academic words be included in their vocabulary instruction.

As you plan for lessons that teach and provide practice in both English-language arts content words and more general academic language, take a look at your teacher's guides from your reading series and/or literature anthologies. Note the highlighted vocabulary. Also, identify other terms and phrases that are included in the student texts, but are not necessarily highlighted for teaching. This latter group of words may be precisely the academic vocabulary that is unfamiliar to your English learners (and struggling readers).

Other resources include the "1,000 Most Frequent Words in Middle-Grades and High School Texts" and "Word Zones™ for 5586 Most Frequent Words," which were collected by Hiebert (2005) and may be found online at *www.textproject.org*. For those of you who are high school teachers, you might also want to take a look at the Coxhead Academic Word List (Coxhead, 2000).

In addition to your teacher's edition and other word lists, use your state English-language arts content standards, and, if they exist, your state English language development standards for ELs to help you select academic language for writing and teaching accompanying language objectives. Let's take a look at several ELA content standards taken from the *English-Language Arts Content Standards for California Public Schools (K–12)* (1998). The words that are English-language arts content-specific are **bolded** and general academic words are underlined.

Examples from Standards for Grades K–2

- Match **oral words** to **printed words**.
- Identify and describe the elements of **plot, setting,** and **character(s) in a story**, as well as the **story's beginning, middle and ending**.
- Distinguish between **complete and incomplete sentences**.

Examples from Standards for Grades 3–5

- Ask questions and support answers by connecting prior knowledge with **literal information** found in, and **inferred** from, the text.
- Identify and use **past, present, and future verb tenses** properly in writing and speaking.
- **Make and confirm predictions** about text by using prior knowledge and ideas presented in the text itself, including **illustrations, titles, topic sentences, important words,** and **foreshadowing clues**.

Examples for Standards for Grades 6–8

- Determine the adequacy and appropriateness of the **evidence for an author's conclusions**.
- Support all statements and claims with **anecdotes, descriptions, facts** and **statistics,** and **specific examples**.
- Analyze the relevance of the **setting (e.g, place, time, customs)** to the **mood, tone,** and **meaning** of the text.

Examples for Standards for Grades 9–12

- Critique the logic of **functional documents** by examining the **sequence** of information and **procedures** in anticipation of possible **reader misunderstandings.**

- Describe with **sensory details** the **sights, sounds, and smells of a scene** and the specific **actions, movements, gestures,** and **feelings of the characters**.

- Discern the meaning of **analogies** encountered, analyzing specific comparisons as well as **relationships** and **inferences**.

As you can see, many of the underlined words may be used in other content areas as well, but students need to be explicitly taught their meaning. Some of these words are common, but have a specialized meaning in the English-language arts. And, as mentioned previously, for those of us who teach ELA, it's sometimes difficult to separate "academic language" from "content language" (and you might even wish to argue some of our examples above in terms of which is which!). For students who speak a Latin-based language such as Spanish, cognates may help in teaching some words. For example, *predict* in English is *predecir* in Spanish; *justify* in English is *justificar* in Spanish; *communication* in English is *communicacion* in Spanish.

What is important is that academic language is taught so that English learners and struggling readers can be successful throughout the school day. In the English-language arts, academic language enables students to read, write, and speak like writers, literary critics, and knowledgeable and informed readers.

In Appendix B you will find a comprehensive list of ELA and academic words and phrases across several domains in the grade-level clusters used throughout this book (K–2, 3–5, 6–8, 9–12). The words and phrases were culled from the California State Content Standards for the English-Language Arts. Your state's standards and domains will differ a bit, but we hope this extensive list will assist you in your lesson and unit planning, and in the writing of your content and language objectives.

Concluding Thoughts

Proficiency in English is the best predictor of academic success, and understanding academic language is an important part of overall English proficiency. In this chapter we have discussed what academic language is, why it is important, and how it can be developed. In ELA, teachers need to explicitly teach both content area terms and general academic terms as well as provide opportunities for students to develop academic language, so that English learners can fully participate in lessons, meet content standards for the English-language arts, and increase their academic language proficiency. An important way to provide opportunities for students to learn and practice academic language is through classroom conversations and structured discussions. When you teach students how to participate in classroom conversations, you not only improve their English skills but also prepare them to understand the type of language used by historians, scientists, mathematicians, authors, literary critics, and other scholars. You will give them the tools they need to practice language skills that will enable them to back up claims with evidence, be more detailed in their observations, use persuasive language compellingly in arguments, and compare events or points of view.

SIOP® Lesson Planning and Unit Design in the English-Language Arts

Introduction

When we as teachers attend any new professional development training, our first thought is, "How can I adapt this to what I'm already doing?" The reality is, you may already be incorporating many of the SIOP® features into your daily teaching, but the key to effective implementation is to be cognizant of doing so consistently and systematically. Teaching a stray SIOP® lesson here or there may be a starting point for many teachers, but the eventual goal is to be able to modify your current teaching to reflect all eight components and thirty features of effective sheltered instruction in your lessons. We usually define "lesson" as the time frame during which lesson objectives (content and language) can be taught, practiced, applied, reviewed, and assessed. For grades K–2, a lesson may range from fifteen minutes to thirty or more. In the upper grades, a lesson may extend over a couple of days, depending on the length of your class periods. Although initial SIOP® lesson planning does take additional time and lots of practice, we think you'll find the more you use the SIOP® components and features to plan and create your lessons, the easier it will become to internalize the model and adopt it as your natural teaching style.

Our overall goal for this book is to help you master SIOP® lesson planning and delivery in the English-language arts, which will enable you to incorporate the components and features of the SIOP® Model consistently in the classroom. We expect that you are well-grounded in the theoretical background of the SIOP® Model, perhaps from taking a university methods course or attending a series of inservice workshops, and by reading one of the core SIOP® texts (Echevarria, Vogt, & Short, 2008; 2010a, 2010b). This book is a companion to the core text, and as such it is an important resource designed especially for English-language arts teachers.

At this point, some of you may be wondering why we're referring to these lessons and units as "English-language arts (ELA)," and to you as teachers of the English-language arts. If you are currently an elementary classroom teacher in K–5 or 6, you probably have a language arts block during which you teach phonics, comprehension, writing, spelling and grammar from an adopted reading series or another set of materials.

If you are teaching in grades 6–8 (or 7–8) in a middle school, you probably have reading, literature, English, or language arts periods during which you teach from a grammar and/or spelling book and a literature anthology. If you are teaching in grades 9–12 in a high school, you probably have periods of reading, American literature, English, and whatever else you're assigned, and you teach from anthologies and other resources. Therefore, to make it easier for all who teach these topics and subjects, in this book we're simply referring to the whole range of possibilities in K–12 as "the English-Language Arts" (ELA).

When we were discussing how we wanted to approach the SIOP® ELA lessons for this book, we made a decision to select an ELA content standard that is continued throughout the grades from kindergarten to grade 12, so that you can see how SIOP® ELA lessons "grow" within a particular standard. We decided to write the lessons and units on Character Analysis within narrative texts because nearly all elementary and secondary reading/language arts and English teachers teach to this important literacy standard. Our expectation is that you learn how to write SIOP® lesson and unit plans through this particular ELA content standard, and that this knowledge will extend into other aspects of the curriculum, including specific lessons on writing and the writing process, grammar, oral language and speech, phonemic awareness and phonics, literary criticism, and so forth. It is important to remember that the SIOP® Model is curriculum- and resource-neutral. All elements of the English-language arts and any effective instructional resources can be used when planning SIOP® lessons and units.

Getting Started with SIOP® Lesson Planning

We recommend that you to think of SIOP® lesson planning as a process that develops over time. For example, begin planning for one subject if you're an elementary teacher, or one period if you're a secondary teacher. We also suggest that you implement the SIOP®

components one at a time, perhaps one per month (all eight in one school year's time), or one per quarter (four the first year; four the second year). Of course, the addition of new components is cumulative. As you implement SIOP® components for the subject or class you've selected, continue teaching as you usually do for the rest of your subjects and/or classes throughout the day. We have learned that when teachers take this slow and steady approach to SIOP® lesson planning and teaching, writing the more detailed lesson plans for only one subject or period, they are able to accomplish the task of "SIOP-izing" their lessons in a more controlled and efficient manner. Eventually, you'll begin implementing the SIOP® components in your other subjects and/or classes as well.

Technology and SIOP® Lessons

The increasing use of technology in the classroom is an exciting trend, filled with many possibilities. A growing number of teachers use interactive white boards (I-boards) as replacements for traditional whiteboards, overhead transparencies or flipcharts or video/media systems such as a DVD player and TV combination. A number of interactive software programs such as Inspiration, Kidspiration, and Language Learner are available as are interactive websites (as of this writing). Some interactive whiteboards allow teachers to record their instruction and post the material for review by students at a later time, providing much-needed opportunities for repetition for English learners. Other technologies include hand-held devices that can be used in many ways such as recording student responses, learning about concepts in measurement, practicing multiplication tables, and taking notes in class.

Not all schools have these resources available for teachers due to a lack of funds or low commitment to technology use. Unfortunately, it is often the schools with high numbers of English learners that are the most disadvantaged. In order to be sensitive to teachers of ELs who lack access to more advanced technologies, the lesson plans presented throughout this book are fairly "low tech." If you are one of the fortunate teachers who have these resources at your disposal, when the lesson plan calls for use of an overhead transparency or worksheet, you would use an interactive white board; when the lesson plan suggests showing a picture, you might project a website.

SIOP® Lesson Plan Formats

At present, there are numerous SIOP® lesson plan formats that teachers are using in schools and districts throughout the country. Some have been created by teachers, others have been adapted for the SIOP® Model from district lesson plans, and still others have been created by SIOP® National Faculty and the SIOP® authors. You may recall that four lesson plan formats are included in the core SIOP® texts (Echevarria, Vogt, & Short, 2008; 2010a; 2010b), and eleven other lesson plan formats are included in the SIOP® implementation book (Echevarria, Short, & Vogt, 2008). You will find four of the lesson plans in writable electronic lesson plan formats at *www.siopinsitute.net*. While we do not endorse any particular lesson plan format, we advocate that you select or create one that works well for you. Not surprisingly, commercial lesson plan notebooks with 3 × 3 inch boxes for planning do not lend themselves to SIOP® lessons, especially in the beginning stages of learning the model.

The SIOP® lesson plan that is used throughout this book was adapted from a plan created by Melissa Castillo and Nicole Teyechea, members of the original group of SIOP® National Faculty. Additional sample lesson plans using this format are found in Echevarria, Vogt, and Short (2008; 2010a; 2010b), and Vogt and Echevarria (2008). Our English-language arts contributors selected this particular format because it is one that includes attention to all eight components and thirty features of the SIOP® Model, and once you know the format and have practice with it, lesson planning becomes much easier.

If you have a Teacher's Edition that accompanies your anthology or other ELA resource, don't hesitate to use it when planning SIOP® lessons. Keep your SIOP® protocol with its list of thirty features handy, so you can remind yourself of what must be included to meet the needs of English learners. Especially in the beginning, it is helpful to plan your lessons in this order: (1) Content Standards; (2) Content Objectives; (3) Language Objectives; (4) Content and Academic Vocabulary; (5) Building Background and Links to Past Learning; (6) HOTS (although these may change as your lesson plays out); (7) Meaningful Activities: Lesson Sequence; (8) Review & Assessment; (9) Supplementary Activities. Of course, after you've planned your lesson sequence, you may need to go back and adjust the lessons as necessary (see Figure 2.1).

FIGURE 2.1 *Lesson Plan Format Used in This Book*

Key: SW = Students will; TW = Teacher will; SWBAT = Students will be able to . . . ; HOTS = Higher Order Thinking Skills; SF = Student Friendly (for primary grades)

Unit Title: *Indicate the unit title, if appropriate. Not all lessons will be part of a larger unit, especially in the elementary grades.*

Grade: *Indicate grade level of students who will be taught this lesson.*

SIOP® Lesson: *Indicate your specific lesson topic. You can also include the estimated timeline for this particular lesson (e.g., 45 minutes or 2 days)*

Content Standards: *Indicate the standards that guided the writing of your content and language objectives.*

Key Vocabulary:	*Supplementary Materials:*
Content: *Carefully select the critical content vocabulary you will introduce, teach, reinforce, and assess for this particular lesson.* **Academic**: *Carefully select any academic vocabulary that ELs will need to know in order to practice, apply, and master the content and language objectives.* *Note: As you read through the lesson plans in this book, you may think the number of vocabulary words in some lessons are excessive for English learners. When you select vocabulary for SIOP® lessons, consider your ELs' language proficiency levels and select accordingly. If you teach heterogeneous classes (with both native-English and English learners), you may need to differentiate vocabulary words for each group. Generally, for English learners, 10–15 new*	*List any supplementary materials that you will include in the lesson to scaffold students' understanding and provide opportunities for practice and application.*

(continued)

FIGURE 2.1 *Lesson Plan Format Used in This Book (continued)*

Key Vocabulary:	Supplementary Materials:
vocabulary words per unit are appropriate, depending on the length of the unit and the English proficiency of your students. **HOTS:** *Write higher order thinking questions here, along with any tasks that require critical thinking. Make sure ELs have the language to be able to respond and participate fully.*	

Connections to Prior Knowledge/ Building Background Information

Links to Students' Background Experiences: *Indicate how you will explicitly activate students' prior knowledge, and then build background where gaps in knowledge and/or experience may exist. How will you assist students in making connections to what they already know and have experienced?*

Links to Prior Learning: *Indicate how you will link explicitly the content learning from past lessons to the specific content that is being taught in this lesson. How will you assist students in making connections to the content taught in these past lessons?*

Content Objective(s):	Meaningful Activities/ Lesson Sequence:	Review & Assessment:
SWBAT: *Write content objective(s) that can be taught, practiced, and assessed within this particular lesson. It's not necessary to use "SWBAT. . . ." You may choose "We will. . .," "You will . . .," "Students will . . .," etc.* **SF** (if needed): *Younger children and beginning English speakers will benefit from content objectives that are written in simple, "student friendly" language.* **Language Objective(s):** **SWBAT:** *Write language objective(s) that can be taught, practiced, and assessed within this particular lesson. It's not necessary to use "SWBAT . . . ." You may choose "We will . . .," "You will . . .," "Students will . . .," etc.* **SF** (if needed): *Younger children and beginning English speakers will benefit from language objectives that are written in simple, "student friendly" language.*	*In this section, write your lesson sequence, beginning with the oral presentation of content and language objectives, and what you will do for the features of Building Background (links to students' backgrounds, past learning, and introduction of vocabulary). Continue to briefly write the sequential steps of the lesson, including meaningful activities that provide practice and application of key content concepts and key content and academic vocabulary.*	*As you are writing your lesson sequence, indicate where and when you will have an opportunity to review content concepts and vocabulary with students, and assess their progress in meeting the content and language objectives for this lesson. For the most part, these assessment opportunities will be spot-checks, teacher observations, and questioning as students practice and apply. If you find that students aren't making progress related to the objectives, back up and re-teach a small group or the entire class if necessary. Remember that all of the activities you choose to include in the lesson should provide opportunities for assessment.*
Wrap-up Activity: *Write a quick wrap-up activity to provide closure to the lesson.* **Final Review:** *Orally review key content concepts, key vocabulary, and content and language objectives with students.*		*Your wrap-up activity provides you with additional assessment information that can serve as the basis for tomorrow's lesson. Your final assessment is of students' responses to whether they have met the lesson's content and language objectives.*

At the end of each lesson plan in this book, you will see a checklist of additional SIOP® features on which the teachers have indicated which of the features are incorporated into the particular SIOP® lesson plan (see Figure 2.2). By carefully reviewing the lesson plans in Chapter 3, we hope you will see how SIOP® lessons can be successfully developed. This will assist you in understanding the lesson plans and units developed for your particular grade level cluster in Chapters 4–7.

There are many wonderful activities and techniques in the lesson plans throughout this book that are especially effective for English learners when teaching ELA. Some have been drawn from *99 Ideas and Activities for Teaching English Learners with the SIOP® Model* (Vogt & Echevarria, 2008), whereas others were suggested or created by our ELA contributors. For each activity, you will find a description of the technique and its purpose, an explanation of how the activity is applied, a list of the SIOP® components the activity reinforces, and a step-by-step method for engaging students in the activity.

There is no doubt that implementing the features of the SIOP® Model to a high degree requires careful, detailed planning, as shown in Figure 2.3. However, as you practice including the features in ELA lessons, you will find that the SIOP® Model becomes a way of teaching and, eventually, less detailed lesson plans are required.

Writing Content and Language Objectives in the English-Language Arts

If you have been working with the SIOP® Model in your ELA classroom for some time, you've probably discovered that writing content and language objectives can be difficult. There are several reasons for, this including that it's sometimes tricky to determine how to distinguish between content and language in the English-language arts. As we

FIGURE 2.2 *Additional SIOP® Features*

The following chart is added to each lesson as a reminder to consider the other SIOP® features that are not included in the plan.

Additional SIOP® Features

Preparation	*Scaffolding*	*Group Options*
☐ Adaptation of content	☐ Modeling	☐ Whole class
☐ Links to background	☐ Guided practice	☐ Small groups
☐ Links to past learning	☐ Independent practice	☐ Partners
☐ Strategies incorporated	☐ Comprehensible input	☐ Independent

Integration of Processes	*Practice/Application*	*Assessment*
☐ Reading	☐ Hands-on	☐ Individual
☐ Writing	☐ Meaningful	☐ Group
☐ Speaking	☐ Linked to objectives	☐ Written
☐ Listening	☐ Promotes engagement	☐ Oral

FIGURE 2.3 *SIOP® Lesson Planning Over Time*

Detailed SIOP® Lesson Planning

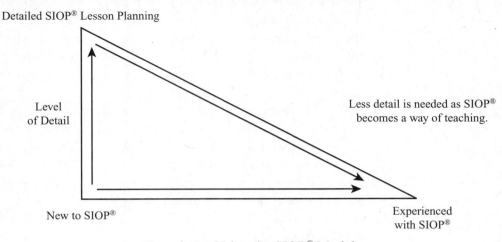

Level
of Detail

Less detail is needed as SIOP®
becomes a way of teaching.

New to SIOP®

Experienced
with SIOP®

Experience Using the SIOP® Model

have frequently advised, don't get all tangled up in the differences, but do continue to have separate objectives for both content and language. Your ELs need to be reminded in every lesson that they are learning ELA content as they are gaining English proficiency. Appendix C, the comprehensive list of words and phrases for ELA that is related to both content and language, should be helpful to you as you write objectives. In addition, you can review the six types of language objectives in the core SIOP® texts (Echevarria, Vogt, & Short, 2008, pp. 29–30; 2010a, pp. 32–33; 2010b, pp. 32–33). The content and language objectives included in the lesson plans in Chapters 3–7 will also help define the ELA content and academic language English learners must practice in order to be able to meet the content standards.

In Chapter 1 we suggested that you can use your state's ELA content standards for selecting academic vocabulary, and writing content and language objectives. As an example, let's revisit a few of the standards from Chapter 1 (see pages 14–15) and generate some examples of content and language objectives derived from them. Keep in mind as you read these examples that while the objectives represent the key content concepts and targeted language, how students (ELs and native speakers) meet these objectives may differ considerably. That is, while the objectives stay the same, we can differentiate the process, such as ELs using sentence frames while English proficient students create their own sentences without the frames. The product can also be differentiated. For example, to meet an objective, beginning English speakers may be given a minimal phrase that needs to be turned into a complete sentence with a simple subject and predicate. Proficient English speakers may be provided with a more elaborated phrase that needs to revised into a complex and complete sentence. Also notice that there are many ways to begin objectives, such as "You will . . . ," "We will . . . ," "We can . . . ," "Students will . . . ," or "Students will be able to . . . ." What you choose as a stem depends on your own personal preference and the age of your students.

For those of you who are struggling with distinguishing between ELA content and language objectives, we hope the following examples will help.

- *Kindergarten Standard*: Match oral words to printed words.
  Content Objective (stated in student-friendly terms): Today, your job is to point to words as you say them out loud.
  Language Objective: Another job will be to practice with a partner saying the words out loud as you both point to them.

- *Grade 2 Standard*: Distinguish between complete and incomplete sentences.
  Content Objective: You will tell the difference between a complete and incomplete sentences.
  Language Objectives: (1) In writing, you will turn an incomplete sentence into a complete sentence. (2) You will also orally explain the changes you made to a partner.

- *Grade 4 Standard*: Identify and use past, present, and future verb tenses properly in writing and speaking.
  Content Objective: We will identify past, present, and future verbs in the story we will read today.
  Language Objective: Using correct verbs and sentence frames, we will tell a partner about something that happened last night, something that is happening today, and something we think will happen tomorrow. (Note: Students who are able to create their own sentences without the frames should be encouraged to do so.)

  1. Yesterday, something that <u>happened</u> to me <u>was</u> _____ .

  2. Today, something that <u>is happening</u> to me <u>is</u> _____ .

  3. Tomorrow, I hope that _____ <u>will happen</u>.

- *Standard for Grade 6*: Determine the adequacy and appropriateness of the evidence for an author's conclusions.
  Content Objective: Students will identify the author's conclusions in a science article and the evidence for those conclusions.
  Language Objective: Students will read an article, paraphrase in writing the conclusions, and orally state the evidence for the conclusions. (Note: This is another example of where differentiation in process and product may occur. For ELs and struggling readers, the readability level and length of the article might differ from what is provided for native English speakers who are capable readers. Also, the required length of the writing assignment may differ, especially for beginning English speakers.)

- *Standard for Grade 8*: Support all statements and claims with anecdotes, descriptions, facts and statistics, and specific examples.
  Content Objective: Students will determine a position on the topic of capital punishment, and provide evidence for the position with anecdotes, facts and statistics, and specific examples.
  Language Objective: In teams, students will informally debate the topic of capital punishment, providing clear evidence for the positions they take.

- *Standard for Grade 10*: Students will be able to critique the logic of functional documents by examining the sequence of information and procedures in anticipation of possible reader misunderstandings.
  Content Objectives: (1) Students will be able to compare and contrast two candidates' positions in a published voter's guide by examining the sequence of the information provided. (2) Students will use the information provided by the candidate to predict what voters may question and critique. (Note: These two objectives are loaded with academic vocabulary that must be reviewed if students are to understand what they're to do.)

Language Objective: Based on the examination of the two candidates' positions, with a partner, students will be able to rewrite one of the candidate's statements for clarity and accuracy.

- *Standard for Grade 12*: Discern the meaning of analogies encountered, analyzing specific comparisons as well as relationships and inferences.
Content Objective: Identify the analogies used in a printed version of the President's weekly address to the Nation.
Language Objective: For each analogy, provide a written explanation of its meaning, and suggest why the President chose this particular analogy to make her point.

Some of you high school teachers may be thinking that your English learners would not be able to meet the grade 10 and 12 objectives as presented here. However, remember what the SIOP® Model is all about: providing English learners with access to complex content concepts and vocabulary. If you plan your lesson with focused attention on the SIOP® features and include the techniques and methods that are advocated, your English learners who are developing each day both English proficiency and ELA content knowledge can be successful in meeting challenging objectives such as these.

We have found that it is helpful to occasionally vary how content and language objectives are introduced to students prior to a lesson and reviewed following the lesson. Figure 2.4

FIGURE 2.4 *Techniques for Sharing Objectives with Students (adapted from Castillo, 2008)*

Read the objectives as a shared reading piece with your entire class. Then ask students to paraphrase the objective with a partner, each taking a turn.

Ask students to read the objectives on the board and have them paraphrase them in their English notebooks. Have students read their paraphrased objectives to each other. This could be done as a warm-up activity at the beginning of class.

Present the objectives and then do a Timed Pair-Share activity, asking students to predict some of the things they think they will be doing in class that day.

Ask students to do a Rally Robin (taking turns), naming things they will be asked to do that day in the particular subject or class.

Ask students to find important words in the objectives and highlight them (e.g., action verbs, nouns, adjectives), or important content or academic vocabulary.

Give students important words to "watch" and "listen" for during the lesson, and call attention to that part of the objective when you mention the academic vocabulary in the lesson.

To re-focus your students during a lesson, revisit the objectives using shared reading.

Ask students to rate themselves as to how well they are understanding and meeting the objectives, using finger symbols that can be shown in class or hidden under their desks. Thumbs up = I get it! Thumbs down = I am lost! Flat hand tilted back and forth: I understand some of it, but I'm a bit fuzzy. At the end of the period, say: "Rate yourself. How well did you meet the objectives today?"

Ask students to write one or two sentences explaining what they learned in class today, and show an example. This can be done in a learning log or on a post-it note left on the desk.

Rally Robin: Students take turns and talk for a specified time with a partner about how they can prove they met their learning objectives for the lesson.

Tickets-Out: Students write a note to the teacher (or a letter to parents/caregivers) at the end of each day telling what was learned and asking any clarifying questions as needed. You can begin the next day's lesson by responding to questions students wrote on the Tickets-Out papers.

provides several options for orally sharing and reviewing objectives so that students are involved in internalizing what is expected and what has been accomplished. Some options are more appropriate for teaching younger children, some are ideal for older students, and some work well for all students; none should take a great deal of instructional time. In addition to identifying a lesson's objectives, these options provide students with opportunities for interaction, self-assessment, and critical thinking.

Planning for In-Class Reading of Grade-Level Texts

One of the greatest challenges of teaching students with diverse literacy skills and language proficiencies is determining how to provide access to challenging grade-level texts, both narrative and expository. If we truly believe that all students should be taught with the same rigorous academic standards, then we must provide access for all students to grade-level text that may be very difficult for some students. But we cannot meet this goal with the ubiquitous practice of round-robin reading, named after the common practice in the elementary grades of calling randomly on students to read passages aloud. The major problem with this practice is that virtually no one is paying attention during the read-aloud. The person reading is worrying about sounding like a good reader, the good readers are reading ahead, the average readers are counting paragraphs and practicing in case they're called on next, and the poorer readers are doing just about anything to avoid being called on, which is bound to cause public humiliation. You, as the teacher, are avoiding at all costs the one student in your class with hand held high who reads poorly, but *loves* to read aloud. Each time you call on him or her to read, you hear audible groans from the rest of the class.

So, what to do? In the section that follows, we offer a variety of options for helping all students, but especially those who struggle to read. We hope you will refer to this list frequently during your SIOP® lesson planning, so that the reading task is not so onerous for those students who seriously dislike and conscientiously avoid reading.

Alternatives for Text Reading

The first group of reading alternatives is teacher-led.

Teacher Read-Aloud

It is good practice to read aloud to students at all grade levels, and occasional read-alouds can be particularly helpful for ELs and struggling readers who need to hear standard English inflection, pronunciation, intonation, and nuance. You'll find in the following SIOP® lesson plans that several times the teacher begins by reading aloud to start everyone off. However, it is problematic when a teacher reads everything aloud. This prevents struggling students from practicing reading with grade-level texts, and for your very proficient readers, it's frustrating. Select carefully the text you'll read aloud, think about the purposes of the read-aloud, and be judicious in the frequency with which you choose this option.

Teacher: Page and Paragraph

This option begins with the teacher reading a page or paragraph aloud; students then read the next page or paragraph silently. The task can be differentiated so that some students (e.g., ELs or struggling readers) might just read a few sentences silently with the teacher helping them by reading the next section orally in a small group. The rest of the class could be reading the paragraph or page silently.

Teacher Chime-In Reading

This is great for fluency practice in the elementary and middle school grades, but it is not appropriate for a "cold" reading (the first time through the text). After students have been exposed to a text (either through silent or oral reading, or by listening to the teacher read it), do a repeated reading as a "chime-in." Begin reading the passage orally while walking around the room. As you are reading and walking, tap the desk of a student, who then chimes in with you, and together, you continue reading the passage aloud. While reading with that particular student, tap additional students who join the group read-aloud. Eventually most of the class members will be orally reading the passage together. This is fun and it's beneficial because students silently follow along until they're "tapped," and then they begin to practice oral reading along with others. Even though your advanced students may not need fluency practice, all students seem to enjoy it.

Teacher: Choral

This is essentially the same as the previous option except there's no "chime in." Different groups (e.g., half the class or table groups) orally read together a passage or page. If the teacher or lead student sets an appropriate pace for reading, the students who are struggling have an opportunity to hear themselves as fluent oral readers, perhaps for the first time.

Teacher: Rehearsed Oral

Prior to any whole-class oral reading (e.g., taking turns reading throughout a selection), the teacher asks for volunteers who want to read aloud. While the rest of the class is engaged in a preview/survey of the text, a quickwrite, or another type of pre-reading task, the oral readers who volunteered take five minutes to practice what they'll be reading. You'll be surprised at the difference in the students' oral reading fluency if they are able to practice first. When it's time for the oral reading of the text, it becomes a "performance," and everyone (good readers, poor readers, and the student who is reading) are much more attentive to comprehending the text because they're not waiting to be called on, reading ahead, and so forth. Anxiety about who will read next disappears and the problems with "poor readers listening to poor readers reading poorly" are considerably reduced (e.g., increases in eye regressions, sub-vocalization, and a decrease in comprehension).

The second group of reading alternatives are encouraged or assigned when students are reading on their own.

Students: Page, Paragraph, Pass

The students read aloud in small groups (3–4) and they may choose to read a page, a paragraph or today they may choose to pass. Teachers can also assign "Page or Paragraph" if they want to have students reading with no passes. The issues with unrehearsed read-alouds by students don't seem as pronounced when students are reading in safer, smaller groups.

Students: Equal Portions

This option is the same as the previous one except all students read a paragraph (or page), rather than choosing one or the other. This is also a small-group activity.

Students: Small Group Turns

Again, students are reading together in small groups, but they rotate turns and read the amount they want. This option is less teacher-controlled in terms of the amounts of oral reading students do.

Students: Partner Choral (or Buddy Choral for Younger Students)

Two students read aloud together, orally, throughout the assigned text. We suggest that you don't pair a top reader with your weakest reader because it results in too much frustration for both. Instead, top readers can read with average readers; average readers can pair with poorer readers, and so on. Poorer readers should not be paired with other poor readers. You might think that high school students would not participate in an activity such as this. In reality, they will if they understand the purposes: fluency building, comprehension, and team work.

Students: Oral Self-Assisted

As students are reading orally with partners or in small groups, they jot down questions, note confusing spots, and/or copy unknown words on sticky notes that they stick in the troublesome spots in the text. These are then shared later with the whole class and confusing spots, words, and concepts are clarified.

Students: Silent Self-Assisted

This is the same as the previous option, except students are all reading silently, using sticky notes to locate areas of confusion, unknown words, and so forth. These are discussed later with the whole class.

Students: Reader-Writer-Speaker-Triads

Reader-Writer-Speaker Response Triads (Vogt & Echevarria, 2008, p. 109) provide students the opportunity to read, write, listen, and speak to each other while working in a small group. Each triad uses one piece of paper and one pencil/pen/marker during the reading activity. Everyone in the triad helps the other team members: The reader reads an article, chapter, or adapted text; the writer (recorder) writes or draws the group's response; the speaker (reporter) shares the group's responses with the other class members. This activity can be used for brainstorming (e.g., naming all the proper nouns they can think of), for review (e.g., reviewing academic vocabulary/definitions), or even for drawing (e.g., illustrating a 4-Corner Vocabulary Chart). The technique also works well for test preparation. Barbara Formoso (Gunston Middle School, Arlington, VA) makes simple construction paper "tents" in three different colors. Each group of three students has one

Reader tent, one Writer tent, and one Speaker tent. The tents are rotated among the students during the lesson as their roles change.

When you first glance at the lessons and units in your grade-level cluster that follow, you may be a bit overwhelmed by the length and depth of the plans. These are very detailed—more detailed than you will need for your own planning. In order for you to follow the plan and understand what's going on in the lesson, it was necessary for our contributors, Lisa and Karlin, to include as much detail as possible. As an experienced teacher, you know how to be cryptic in your own planning, so your SIOP® unit and lesson plans need not be this lengthy.

Concluding Thoughts

We know that the relationship between literacy proficiency and academic achievement grows stronger for students as they progress through the grade levels. As students move up the grade levels, language use becomes more complex and more content-area specific (Biancarosa & Snow, 2004). English learners must develop literacy skills for each content area *in* their second language as they simultaneously learn, comprehend, and apply content-area concepts *through* their second language (Garcia & Godina, 2004). We want them to receive a strong foundation in academic English if they are enrolled in our elementary schools, and we want teachers to have the skills and knowledge base to continue that academic language and literacy development throughout the secondary school years. This is manifested in SIOP® English-language arts lesson plans and units that are designed specifically to help English learners simultaneously develop ELA content knowledge and academic vocabulary.

We want this book to be about possibilities. We hope you will gain knowledge and ideas so you can design and deliver dynamic, engaging English-language arts SIOP® lessons that promote content and language learning among your students. We also hope you will put to use a range of techniques and activities that will advance your students' academic English skills and make the curriculum topics of ELA comprehensible. These are our goals for you as you read through the remainder of this book.

Activities and Techniques for Planning SIOP® Lessons in the English-Language Arts

By Karlin LaPorta, Lisa Mitchener, and MaryEllen Vogt

A Vignette

Teacher Patricia Toledo arrived early at school after having been away for three days of SIOP® training. She had left the inservice feeling excited and inspired about all she had learned, and she had promised herself that she would try to implement at least one or two of the SIOP® features in her classroom that day. But when she arrived at school, she started to feel a bit overwhelmed.

As Patricia placed all of her SIOP® materials on her desk, she briefly read through the substitute's report. Ugh! It looked like the kids had NOT been on their best behavior while she had been gone. She would need to open the day with a discussion

● ·

30

of appropriate behavior when there is a substitute teacher. That would take away time from the rest of the content she needed to cover for the day. Just as she opened her lesson plan book to see how she could modify her language arts lesson to fit in some of the Building Background features, her phone rang. It was the RSP teacher, reminding Patricia of the IEP meeting she needed to attend this morning for one of her students. Despairingly, she moved her SIOP® training materials to her bookshelf and resigned herself to teaching the lessons she had previously planned.

As she walked to the office for her IEP meeting, Patricia wondered how in the world she was going to fit the SIOP® Model into her daily teaching when she already had so much on her plate.

SIOP® Planning Considerations

1. What are the first steps Patricia can make toward successfully implementing the SIOP® Model into her daily instruction?

2. What adjustments or modifications must be made to adapt the current language arts curriculum to fit within the SIOP® Model?

3. How can Patricia differentiate for her students' varied levels of language proficiency?

Expanding the Vignette

As Patricia Toledo wrapped up her day, she guiltily looked at the SIOP® training materials sitting untouched on her bookshelf. She was disappointed that she hadn't been able to incorporate anything she'd learned from the training into her lessons today. One of the things she remembered from the inservice was how helpful collaboration could be when first starting SIOP® implementation. She decided to call one of her fellow grade-level teachers who had been through SIOP® training last year, and ask for some support. Patricia and her colleague scheduled a SIOP® lesson planning session during their mutual prep time the next afternoon. Patricia left school feeling like she wasn't alone in the process of SIOP® implementation, and she was excited at the prospect of modifying one of her current Language Arts units to better meet the needs of her EL students.

Introduction to the SIOP®
English-Language Arts Lessons

First off, let us say that as classroom teachers who have been able to successfully implement the SIOP® Model into our own teaching, we felt just like Patricia Toledo when we returned from our first SIOP® inservice. Many teachers today already feel overwhelmed by the number of daily meetings and school-related commitments they have, as well as the immense pressure to cover all the content standards. The daily rigors of teaching are challenging enough without the diverse professional development that is also required. We understand that and trust us, we have been there. We have all seen professional development initiatives come and go, and often teachers feel they just have to "ride it out" until another great idea comes down the line. The SIOP® Model is different. We promise. One of the most important things teachers can remember when embarking on SIOP® Model implementation in their own classroom is that it's *not* about changing everything you do

. . . the SIOP® Model is about *refining* your current teaching to meet the needs of your EL students.

With that in mind, it is still a challenge to implement something new in the classroom because of all the structured curriculum and schoolwide programs already in place. The purpose of the next five chapters is to help teachers see that it is possible to incorporate SIOP® features into existing language arts programs and lessons while still staying true to the SIOP® Model and your adopted curriculum. What follows are specific SIOP® teaching techniques and entire SIOP® language arts units that illustrate how the two separate entities can become one. It is our hope that this book serves as a collaborative lesson planning resource from our classrooms to yours to help you achieve success on your way to consistent and systematic language arts SIOP® implementation.

In this chapter, you will find four detailed lesson plans using three effective techniques for teaching within the SIOP® Model: (1) Anticipation/Reaction Guide (Buehl, 2009; Ruddell, 2007; Vogt & Echevarria, 2008); (2) Semantic Feature Analysis (Fisher & Frey, 2008; Pittelman, Heimlich, Berglund, French, & Heimlich, 1991); and (3) Conga Line (Kagan, 1994; Vogt & Echevarria, 2008). Figure 3.1 illustrates how these activities are included in lesson plans for the particular grade levels indicated in bold type.

Within this chapter, we describe the planning process for these lessons and how it varies across the grade levels. We also address issues of how to adjust lessons and differentiate instruction to accommodate students at different levels of academic and language proficiency. We highly recommend that you read through all of the lessons, even if you are not teaching at a particular grade level.

In Chapters 4–7, you will find four complete, five-day English-language arts units across the grade bands of K–2, 3–5, 6–8, 9–12. Both the completed plans and excerpted sections of the lessons found in this chapter are also shown in the expanded units in Chapters 4–7. We have tried to demonstrate within each lesson and unit how a variety of activities can be adapted across the grades from kindergarten to 12th grade.

FIGURE 3.1 *Overview of Three Techniques and Grade Level Clusters*

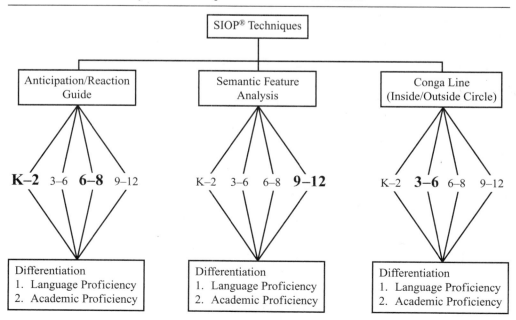

Activity #1: Anticipation/Reaction Guide (see Appendix E, #1)

The Anticipation/Reaction Guide (Ruddell, 2007; Vogt & Echevarria, 2008) is an effective SIOP® teaching technique that can be adapted to almost any grade level or level of language proficiency. Following are two lesson plans; one is written for a first grade reading/language arts class, and the second is written for a seventh grade English-language arts class. Remember, even if you don't teach at these grade levels, we recommend that you skim through each lesson plan to help you internalize varied elements of a SIOP® lesson plan.

Purpose of the Anticipation/Reaction Guide

- To activate students' background knowledge
- To introduce the main ideas of a concept or selection prior to learning/reading
- To engage and motivate students to read by determining whether the text will confirm or disconfirm their opinions or predictions
- To establish a purpose for learning/reading
- To illustrate the power of learning/reading to change opinions and viewpoints

Applications of the Anticipation/Reaction Guide

- Before and after lessons
- Text passage, novel or short story, nonprint media (television, video)

SIOP® Components Reinforced through the Anticipation/Reaction Guide

- Building Background
- Strategies
- Review & Assessment

Steps of the Anticipation/Reaction Guide

1. Choose an appropriate of topic of study.
2. Create the guide using short declarative statements about the major concepts.
3. Make sure the statements are thought-provoking and that they encourage students to anticipate and predict what the text content will reveal.
4. Prior to reading, direct students to write an "A" for agreement and a "D" for disagreement on the left side of the guide (Anticipation). Students should be prepared to support their positions.
5. Have students generate predictions about what they will be reading.
6. Ask students to read the selection in order to gather evidence that confirms or disconfirms their responses on the guide.
7. At the end of the lesson, ask students (individually or in groups) to revisit the statements and mark their responses on the right side of the guide (Reaction).
8. Ask students to share what they learned from their reading and to describe how and if their points of views may have changed.

The lessons that follow provide examples of how you could implement the Anticipation Reaction Guide in a SIOP® lesson for the grade bands K–2 and 6–8. Sample lessons for grade bands 3–6 and 9–12 are provided within the complete units in Chapters 5 and 7.

SIOP® Lesson Plan, Grade 1: Cluster K–2

This lesson was developed as a first grade lesson, but it could easily be adapted for a Kindergarten or second grade classroom as well. The first grade lesson is based on the book *Elvira* by Margaret Shannon. The story is about an eccentric young dragon who marches to the beat of her own drum. She is unlike other dragons because she likes to make daisy chains and refuses to eat princesses. The message of the book is that it is okay to be different.

SIOP® LESSON PLAN, *Grade 1, Day 3 (Part I):* *Making Predictions about Story Plot*

Part I—Before Reading

Key: SW = Students will; TW = Teacher will; SWBAT = Students will be able to . . . ;
HOTS = Higher Order Thinking Skills; SF = Student friendly

Unit: Character Analysis

SIOP® Lesson: Making Predictions about Story Plot
Grade: 1

Content Standards: 3.3 Make, confirm, and revise predictions.

Key Vocabulary:	*Supplementary Materials:*
Content Vocabulary: *courage (courageous), tease, creative*	Word-Definition-Picture chart (from Day 1—See unit in Chapter 4)
Academic Vocabulary: *opinion, belief, prediction*	Word Web with the word *Characteristics of a Dragon* in the middle. (from Day 1—See unit in Chapter 4)
HOTS: When is it okay to tease someone? Why does it take courage to be different? What makes you think that? Why do you feel that way?	*Elvira* by Margaret Shannon (1991), Tricknor & Fields
	Anticipation/Reaction Guide for each student plus overhead

Connections to Prior Knowledge/ Building Background Information:
Links to Students' Background Experiences—Ask students if they have ever been made fun of because of something they were wearing, or how their hair looked, or something they did, etc.
Links to Prior Learning—Remind students that they previously used a T-chart to make predictions about nontraditional dragons. Tell them that they are now going to make predictions about a character named Elvira who is a nontraditional dragon.

Objectives:	Meaningful Activities/Lesson Sequence:	Review/Assessment:
Content Objectives:		
1. SWBAT read statements and develop opinions and beliefs about the main ideas and concepts	• TW post and orally explain content and language objectives. • TW review key content and academic vocabulary.	

(continued)

SIOP® LESSON PLAN, *Grade 1, Day 3 (Part I):*
Making Predictions about Story Plot (continued)

Objectives:	Meaningful Activities/Lesson Sequence:	Review/Assessment:
of the book, *Elvira* by Margaret Shannon. **SF:** Your job today is to read and think about what it means to be different from other people. **2.** SWBAT make predictions about Elvira's character after viewing the cover of the book. **SF:** Your job today is to make predictions about the book *Elvira*. **Language Objectives:** **1.** SWBAT track words and read the Anticipation/Reaction Guide in a shared reading lesson. **SF:** Your job today is to read the Anticipation/Reaction Guide. **2.** SWBAT orally support opinions made about different statements on the Anticipation/Reaction Guide. **SF:** Your job today is to say the sentence frame: I feel _____ because _____. Or I believe that statement is true/false because _____.	● TW display and explain the Anticipation/Reaction Guide on the overhead. ● SW read the Anticipation/Reaction Guide along with the teacher ● TW ask students to think about the statements and decide if they agree or disagree with the statement. ● SW complete the first four boxes on the anticipation side of the Anticipation/Reaction Guide. ● TW show students the cover of the book *Elvira* by Margaret Shannon. SW describe the main character, Elvira, to a partner. ● SW complete the final four boxes on the anticipation side of the Anticipation/Reaction Guide. ● SW choose and share a statement from the final four boxes with a partner. They will use the frame, "I predict _____." ● TW use an overhead of the Anticipation/Reaction Guide to tally results of the prompts using Split Decision. In Split Decision, students will stand in the middle of the room with their Anticipation/Reaction guide in their hand. TW read a statement from the Anticipation/Reaction Guide. Students will move to opposite sides of the room (previously labeled Agree and Disagree) to demonstrate how they responded to the statement. TW select students to provide a rationale for their decisions. ● SW will orally share their opinions from their Anticipation/Reaction Guide during the Split Decision activity. Ex. "I feel it is okay to tease someone who is different than you because _____."	You can adjust your method of reading as needed based on the proficiency of readers in your class. Use a think-aloud demonstrating how to complete the Anticipation/Reaction Guide. After giving all directions, have students self-assess their understanding of the task with a finger response: 1—I need help. 2—I have a question. 3—I'm ready to start. 4—I could teach this. Once students begin independent work, focus on assisting those students that held up 1 or 2 fingers. When students complete the final four boxes of the guide, it is important to make clear that they are predicting characteristics about *Elvira* and what the story will be about. As you listen to partners share, you can challenge higher ability students with the frame, "I predict _____ because _____." Monitor students as they share with a partner. Make sure they are using complete sentences and they are referring to the t-chart adjectives as a resource. During the Split Decision, allow students to be persuaded to change their mind and move to the other side. Promote healthy discussion and debate on statements that appear heavily "split." This activity allows an excellent opportunity to observe students using academic language outside a sentence frame.

Wrap-up: SW say one sentence about the results of the Anticipation/Reaction Guide tally. Ex. "Most of the class thinks that it takes courage to be different."

Review content and language objectives with students.

Additional SIOP® Features

Preparation	Scaffolding	Group Options
■ Adaptation of content	■ Modeling	■ Whole class
■ Links to background	■ Guided practice	□ Small groups
■ Links to past learning	■ Independent practice	■ Partners
■ Strategies incorporated	■ Comprehensible input	■ Independent

Integration of Processes	Application	Assessment
■ Reading	□ Hands-on	■ Individual
□ Writing	■ Meaningful	■ Group
■ Speaking	■ Linked to objectives	■ Written
■ Listening	■ Promotes engagement	■ Oral

FIGURE 3.2 *Anticipation/Reaction Guide for* Elvira

Anticipation/Reaction Guide
for
***Elvira* by Margaret Shannon**

Directions: Next to each statement, write an "X" in the appropriate column. Be ready to discuss your opinion with the class.

Before Reading		Statements	After Reading	
Agree	Disagree		Agree	Disagree
☺	☹		☺	☹
		1. It is okay to tease someone who is different than you.		
		2. It takes courage to be different and be proud of it.		
		3. It is best to try to be like everyone else so people will like you.		
		4. It is okay to be afraid of someone who is different than you before you get to know him.		
		5. Elvira is a mean dragon.		
		6. Other dragons make fun of Elvira.		
		7. Elvira is going on a trip.		
		8. Elvira is proud.		

PLANNING POINTS

- The Split Decision activity, similar to Value Line (Vogt & Echevarria, 2008), is an effective way to engage students in learning while asking them to develop opinions about a topic. Again, this type of activity is an excellent vehicle for promoting higher-level thinking. More support and practice will be needed for grade K–2 students, and you may want to introduce the activity prior to this lesson using something more personally relevant. For instance, after reading a story to the students, ask them to stand in the middle of the room and say, "This was a very funny story." Have the students move to the "agree" or "disagree" side of the room. Ask students to explain their opinions using frames such as "The story was funny because _____ " or "The story was not funny because _____ ." Using a topic that is personally relevant to preteach an activity helps students become familiar with the procedures and routines of that activity. This way students are able to focus on the more academically challenging concepts of the activity without interference.

Part II: After Reading

Before the first grade students can complete Part II of the prediction lesson with the Anticipation/Reaction Guide, they will need to read the book or text that is being addressed. In this chapter, we are moving straight to Part II with no description of the interim reading lesson. However, in Chapter 4, we have provided complete lesson plans for each grade level band that include the reading lesson along with Parts I and II of the Anticipation/ Reaction Guide.

SIOP® LESSON PLAN, *Grade 1, Day 5 (Part II): Confirming Predictions about Character Traits*

Part II: After Reading (Grade 1 Lesson)

Key: SW = Students will; TW = Teacher will; SWBAT = Students will be able to . . . ; HOTS = Higher Order Thinking Skills; SF = Student friendly

Unit: Character Analysis

SIOP® Lesson: Confirming Predictions about Character Traits
Grade: 1

Content Standards: 3.3 Make, confirm, and revise predictions.

Key Vocabulary:	*Supplementary Materials:*
Content Vocabulary: *gobbling, princess, daisy chains, furious, normal, appreciated, mistaken, courage, tease*	Word-Definition-Picture chart (from Day 1—See unit in Chapter 4)
Academic Vocabulary: *opinion, belief, confirm, disconfirm*	Word-Definition-Picture chart (from Day 4—See unit in Chapter 4)
HOTS: Did you change your mind about any of the statements? If so, what made you change your mind?	Word Web with the word *Characteristics of a Dragon* in the middle (from Day 1— See unit in Chapter 4)
	Elvira by Margaret Shannon
	Anticipation/Reaction Guide for each student plus transparency

Connections to Prior Knowledge/ Building Background Information:
Links to Students' Background Experiences— NA
Links to Prior Learning— TW review the tallied Anticipation/Reaction Guide from Part I of this lesson. SW confirm or revise their statements on the Anticipation/Reaction Guide.

Objectives:	Meaningful Activities/Lesson Sequence:	Review/Assessment:

Content Objectives:

1. SWBAT confirm or revise their original opinions and beliefs about the main ideas and concepts of the book, *Elvira* by Margaret Shannon.

SF: Your job today is to read your opinions and either keep them or change them.

2. SWBAT confirm or disconfirm predictions about Elvira's character.

SF: Your job today is to read your predictions about Elvira and either keep them or change them.

Language Objectives:

1. SWBAT read the Anticipation/Reaction Guide in a shared reading lesson.

SF: Your job today is to read the Anticipation/Reaction Guide.

2. SWBAT tell if and how their original opinions have changed.

SF: Your job today is to read aloud the sentence frame: I used to feel _____ but now I feel _____ because _____.

3. SWBAT tell if and how their original predictions have changed.

SF: Your job today is to read aloud the sentence frame: I predicted _____. My prediction was confirmed/ was disconfirmed.

- TW post and orally explain content and language objectives.
- TW display and review the Anticipation/ Reaction Guide on the overhead and tell students that they will have a chance to change their answers from the anticipation side.
- SW read the Anticipation/Reaction Guide along with the teacher.
- SW complete all of the boxes on the reaction side of the Anticipation/ Reaction Guide, changing their opinion if they want to.
- SW will orally share with a partner if and how their opinions and/or predictions have changed using the sentence frames:

I used to feel _____ but now I feel _____ because _____.
and
I predicted _____. My prediction was confirmed/ was disconfirmed.

Again, use a think-aloud to demonstrate how to complete the Anticipation/Reaction Guide. After giving all directions, have students self-assess their understanding of the task with a finger response:
1—I need help.
2—I have a question.
3—I'm ready to start.
4—I could teach this.
Once students begin independent work, focus on assisting those students that held up 1 or 2 fingers.

Monitor students as they share with a partner. Make sure they are using complete sentences.

Wrap-up: Have students refer to the Outcome Sentences chart displayed in the room. Throw a rubber ball to individual students and have them orally complete the frames. (See Day 2 Lesson from Chapter 4 unit.)

Review content and language objectives with students.

Additional SIOP® Features

Preparation	Scaffolding	Group Options
☐ Adaptation of content	■ Modeling	■ Whole class
■ Links to background	■ Guided practice	☐ Small groups
■ Links to past learning	■ Independent practice	■ Partners
■ Strategies incorporated	■ Comprehensible input	■ Independent

Integration of Processes	Application	Assessment
■ Reading	☐ Hands-on	■ Individual
☐ Writing	■ Meaningful	■ Group
■ Speaking	■ Linked to objectives	■ Written
■ Listening	■ Promotes engagement	■ Oral

Adaptations for Language Proficiency

Although a first grade classroom may include students with various language proficiency levels, all students are still developing their foundational literacy skills and will benefit from SIOP® strategies. For this reason, scaffolded language support is embedded throughout the lesson to facilitate learning for students with different levels of proficiency as well as students with limited literacy skills. Still, EL students may need additional specialized differentiation depending on their language proficiency.

Beginning

Beginning students may benefit from L1 (primary or home language) clarification on the Anticipation/Reaction guide statements and key vocabulary from the teacher, aide, or peer. When they are asked to complete the Anticipation/Reaction Guide, beginning students may be paired with an Intermediate, Advanced, or English-only student for language support. Similarly, when the rest of the class is working independently, an aide or the teacher could pull out a small group of beginner students to provide additional language instruction. Finally, simplified sentence frames can be used to meet the needs of beginning students.

Intermediate and Advanced

As the lesson is already embedded with language support, most intermediate and advanced students should be able to participate in the activities as described. However, it is important to mention that ongoing assessment throughout the lesson is necessary to ensure your intermediate and advanced students are understanding the key concepts.

Adaptations for Academic Proficiency

Under-schooled or low-achieving EL learners can be supported with simplified sentence frames for use during the partner sharing activity, such as "It is okay to tease someone because _____ ," or "It takes courage to be different because _____ ." Additionally, the teacher or an aide could pull together a small group of low-achieving ELs and conduct a more individualized sharing activity while other students are working independently.

SIOP® Lesson Plan, Grade 7: Cluster 6–8

The following lesson plan was developed for grade 7, but it could easily be adapted for a sixth grade or eighth grade language arts classroom as well. This seventh grade lesson is based on two short stories that share a common theme of finding one's own identity and trying to fit in. The first story is *Seventh Grade* by Gary Soto. It is about an adolescent boy on his first day of seventh grade and the embarrassing lie he tells in order to impress a girl. The second short story is *The Special Powers of Blossom Culp* by Richard Peck. It is about an eccentric young girl who makes no excuses for who she is, but her quirkiness prevents her from fitting in at her new school until she earns the respect of the boys and her teacher by playing a trick on the rudest and most popular girl in the school.

SIOP® LESSON PLAN, *Grade 7:*
Making Predictions

Key: SW = Students will; TW = Teacher will; SWBAT = Students will be able to . . . ; HOTS = Higher Order Thinking Skills

Unit: Character Analysis

SIOP® Lesson: Making Predictions
Grade: 7

Content Standards: 2.72 Make and revise predictions based on evidence. 1.0 Students write and speak with a command of standard English conventions appropriate to the grade level.

Key Vocabulary:	*Supplementary Materials:*
Academic Vocabulary: *predict, confirm, justify*	Anticipation/Reaction Guide + Why (Buell, 2009)
HOTS: Why is it helpful to make predictions about the upcoming short stories BEFORE we read? What does it mean if your prediction is never confirmed?	Prediction T-Chart (Ongoing in student journal) Sentence Frames

Connections to Prior Knowledge/ Building Background Information:
Links to Students' Background Experiences— Students will rely on their own personal experiences and opinions to respond to the Anticipation statements and be able to justify why they feel strongly about their opinions.
Links to Prior Learning— Students will tap into their prior learning regarding other short stories and characters they've read about through the year in order to make predictions about the upcoming short stories.

Objectives:	*Meaningful Activities/Lesson Sequence:*	*Review/Assessment:*
Content Objectives: **1.** SWBAT read statements and develop opinions and beliefs about the main ideas of two stories. **2.** SWBAT make generalized predictions about the upcoming short stories.	• TW post and orally explain content and language objectives. • TW review meanings of previously taught academic language: *predict, confirm, justify* • SW turn to shoulder-partners to briefly practice saying the vocabulary words and definitions. • TW explain how students will predict and then confirm their predictions, and later they will have to justify their beliefs by agreeing or disagreeing with statements.	Anticipation section of the Anticipation/ Reaction Guide + Why TW walk around room monitoring students' understandings of academic language.

(continued)

SIOP® LESSON PLAN, *Grade 7:*
Making Predictions (continued)

Objectives:	Meaningful Activities/Lesson Sequence:	Review/Assessment:
Language Objectives: **1.** SWBAT write a justification as to why they agree or disagree with an Anticipation statement. **2.** SWBAT orally justify to the class why they believe their opinions are correct.	• TW introduce the Anticipation/Reaction guide and explain that students are going to agree or disagree with statements that relate to the themes and characters of the upcoming short stories they will read as a class. • TW guide students through the first three statements before they finish the rest independently. • SW write their predictions on the left-hand side of the T-Chart and leave space open on the right so they can confirm or disconfirm their statements as they begin reading the short stories. • SW add to their T-Chart throughout the course of the unit. Depending on their language proficiency levels, students might benefit from prediction Sentence Frames such as: "I predict we will read stories about..." "I predict we will read about characters who..." • Split Decision Activity: This activity is similar to the Anticipation/Reaction Guide, but it is done orally with the participation of the entire class. • Prior to the activity, the teacher will label one side of the room with a sign that reads "AGREE" and the other side with a sign that reads "DISAGREE." SW gather in front of the class. When the teacher reads one of the statements from the Anticipation/Reaction Guide, students will travel to the "Agree" or "Disagree" side depending on their opinion. Once on their chosen side, students should be ready and able to justify their position. After respectful discussion, students can switch sides if their minds are changed. • In order to support a respectful discussion, SW use the following sentence frames when addressing their classmates. "I justify my position _____ because I think _____." "I respectfully disagree with _____ because I think _____." "I changed my mind because _____."	Ongoing Prediction T-Chart Teacher observation of the Split Decision Activity Anticipation section of the Anticipation/Reaction Guide

Wrap-up: "Tickets-Out"
On a sticky note, SW write two of their predictions from their T-chart about what the upcoming short stories are going to be about. They will stick them to a poster entitled, "Short Story Predictions" on their way out the door. Examples might include:

I predict we will be reading about a character in an embarrassing situation.
I predict we will be studying different characters in the upcoming unit.
I predict we will be reading stories about characters trying to discover who they are.

Review content and language objectives with students.

Additional SIOP® Features

Preparation	*Scaffolding*	*Group Options*
☐ Adaptation of content	■ Modeling	■ Whole class
■ Links to background	■ Guided practice	■ Small groups
■ Links to past learning	■ Independent practice	■ Partners
■ Strategies incorporated	■ Comprehensible input	■ Independent

Integration of Processes	*Application*	*Assessment*
■ Reading	☐ Hands-on	■ Individual
■ Writing	■ Meaningful	■ Group
■ Speaking	■ Linked to objectives	■ Written
■ Listening	■ Promotes engagement	■ Oral

FIGURE 3.3 *Anticipation/Reaction Guide + Why*

Directions: Next to each statement, write an "X" in the appropriate column. Be ready to discuss your opinion with the class.

Before Reading		*Statements*	*After Reading*	
Agree	*Disagree*		*Agree*	*Disagree*
		1. It is important to try and be yourself even if others don't like you.		
Why?			Why?	
		2. It takes courage to be different and be proud of it.		
Why?			Why?	
		3. You should try to impress others to make new friends.		
Why?			Why?	
		4. Most people know exactly who they are and don't change much throughout their lives.		
Why?			Why?	
		5. It can be embarrassing when you are the center of attention.		
Why?			Why?	
		6. Most people care what others think about them.		
Why?			Why?	
		7. Teachers can relate to their students because they were kids once too.		
Why?			Why?	

PLANNING POINTS

You may notice that the Anticipation/Reaction Guide for the seventh grade lesson is slightly different than the one for the first grade lesson. The "Why" portion has been added to the lesson for older students because they should be able to state in writing *why* they agree or disagree with the statement. Also, since the students are also participating in the Split Decision activity where they have to verbally support their opinions, the Anticipation/Reaction Guide +Why helps to scaffold their responses and better prepare them to stand up for their opinions.

After Reading: Reaction Section of the Anticipation/Reaction Guide + Why

In the first grade lesson, the reaction portion of the Anticipation/Reaction guide required another whole day of instruction. In the seventh grade lesson, however, the reaction portion is completed as a wrap-up activity after both stories have been read. The teacher can decide how much instructional time is allotted to complete this portion of the activity. The lesson wrap-up for the description of the reaction portion of the guide is "Students will complete the right side of their Anticipation/Reaction Guide they started on Day 2 of the unit. After reading both stories, they will share one or two statements with a partner, describing how their opinion was changed and why."

Adaptations for Language Proficiency

It is possible to have many different levels of language proficiency in a middle school Language Arts class. For that reason, it may be necessary to differentiate some of your instruction to meet the needs of your linguistically diverse students. Scaffolding your instruction can be accomplished in a number of different ways. Following are some specific ideas to help you accommodate the different levels of language proficiency within your classroom.

Beginning

One of the biggest concerns with beginning students in a secondary classroom is the difficulty they may have with reading and comprehending grade-level texts. If it is available, the use of an L1 text can be empowering to beginning students because it enables them to participate in making meaning of the assigned text in their native language. Other options may be to allow beginning students to listen to the story on CD, have the text read aloud by the teacher, or partner less proficient students with more proficient peers who may also be able to clarify some content concepts in their native language.

Once the text is accessed, beginning students should be able to take part in the subsequent lesson activities as long as there is scaffolded support along the way. For instance, in the seventh grade prediction lesson with the Anticipation/Reaction Guide, beginning students would benefit from using sentence frames both for their prediction T-chart and as a verbal prompt for the "Split Decision" activity. Again, pairing beginning students with more proficient peers for the written portion of the Anticipation/Reaction Guide enables all students to participate in the higher level thinking that is necessary for the activity. It's important, however, that your more proficient English speakers have an opportunity to work with a variety of other students, not always with those who are less proficient speakers. Flexibly grouping students for varied activities works well for most lessons—with you providing additional support when necessary.

Intermediate

Although intermediate level students may still struggle with accessing grade-level texts, they should be able to comprehend content concepts with scaffolded support. A shared reading setting with teacher modeling and strategy think-alouds help clarify what strategies to use, precisely how to use them, and most importantly, why and when to use them. With guided instruction, intermediate students should be able to access the text and add to their inventory of comprehension strategies to practice and apply in the future.

Within the Anticipation/Reaction Guide lesson, some intermediate level students may need the support of sentence frames. Lessons that incorporate interaction such as the "Split Decision" promote English language development in all four language domains: reading, writing, listening, and speaking. These skills are essential for intermediate students to be able to advance to the next level of English proficiency.

Advanced

Students at the advanced level will continue to require some language support. Although they are at an advanced level of English proficiency, they still need opportunities to practice and apply academic language and content concepts in a more independent manner. Advanced students may still struggle with the readability of grade-level anthologies and other texts. Therefore, preteaching vocabulary and complex content concepts will provide them with the scaffolding they need. Review pages 34–38 of *Making Content Comprehensible for English Learners: The SIOP® Model* (Echevarria, Vogt, & Short, 2008) for additional ideas.

In the grade seven lesson plan, advanced English-proficient students should not need the support of the sentence frames; however, these students still require ongoing feedback as they progress through the lesson. Partner work, small group interactions, and teacher monitoring are all examples of ways to provide feedback while assessing your advanced students' understanding of the content concepts.

Adaptations for Academic Proficiency

A more individualized approach is essential when teaching under-schooled or low-achieving English learners. For example, you may have an intermediate student who is a struggling reader and who would benefit from listening to the text on tape, or an advanced student who would benefit from a shared reading experience. We know how difficult it can be to differentiate instruction for a group of diverse learners, but it is important to balance a student's EL proficiency level with his or her academic proficiency in order to determine what adaptations are necessary.

Activity #2: Semantic Feature Analysis (see Appendix E, #9)

The Semantic Feature Analysis (SFA) (Fisher & Frey, 2008; Pittelman et al., 1991) is another teaching technique that can be adapted to any grade level or level of language proficiency. It is especially appropriate for teaching within the SIOP® Model.

Purposes of Semantic Feature Analysis

- To provide a visual representation of key vocabulary and concepts in order to help strengthen the conceptual understandings of information presented
- To analyze relationships between a category of words and their features or characteristics
- To manage and organize ongoing vocabulary concepts throughout a unit of study

Applications of Semantic Feature Analysis

- Before the lesson to activate prior knowledge and build background
- During the lesson
- While reading a text passage, novel, or short story
- During a mini-lecture, or while watching nonprint media (television, video)
- After the lesson, for practice and application of key concepts

SIOP® Components Reinforced through Semantic Feature Analysis

- Building Background (vocabulary development)
- Strategies
- Practice & Application
- Review & Assessment

Steps for Semantic Feature Analysis

1. First, model this activity with your students using a familiar category such as sports, which is a topic that has a variety of features (e.g., sports with uniforms, sports with balls, sports that require running, etc.). This way, students will understand how to use SFA before moving on to a more complex topic.
2. Next, select the topic from grade-level appropriate themes or from a category of concepts to be analyzed in your current unit of instruction.
3. Start with more concrete examples, such as animals and their habitats or the different planets in the solar system, for younger students. For older, more experienced students, start with more abstract concepts, such as analysis of character traits or features of different literary genres.
4. Provide a list of words that are related to the category being studied. List these words on the left side of the semantic feature grid.
5. Next, have students identify traits or features of the categories and write them across the top of the grid. Most often, teachers generate the list of features; however, students can be effectively involved in the brainstorming process to come up with them.
6. Have students, either individually or in small groups, code each feature in terms of whether the related words typically possess that feature.
7. Students can mark a plus sign (+) if the word exhibits a particular feature, a minus sign (−) if the word does not exhibit that feature, or a question mark (?) if they are not sure.
8. As the lesson continues, have students update the semantic feature grid with more words and new, related features.

9. At the end of the lesson, examine the grid as a whole class or in small groups to discuss the similarities and differences between each word and the different features.

Using the visual semantic feature grid, students should be able to better differentiate the key vocabulary based on its positive or negative relationship to the specific features. Ultimately, this semantic feature grid provides students with an excellent visual summary of the content as well as an organized format for subsequent writing assignments.

The lesson that follows provides an example of how you could implement the Semantic Feature Analysis (SFA) in a tenth grade classroom. Sample lessons for the grade bands K–2, 4–6, and 6–8 are provided within the complete units in Chapters 4–7.

SIOP® Lesson Plan, Grade 10: Cluster 9–12

Although this SIOP® lesson was created for a tenth grade literature/language arts class, the techniques and activities are appropriate for any high school classroom, especially those that include English learners. The lesson was designed using the state-adopted literature anthology for tenth grade, which was created to meet state content standards in the English-language arts. As with most adopted reading and literature series, there are so many ideas and activities in the Teacher's Edition that it would be impossible (and most likely unwise) to include them all. Therefore, it is necessary to carefully plan SIOP® lessons, using what is appropriate for the students in a given class and determining what can be omitted while still covering the standards. We have included some of our favorite activities that help ELs (and other students) practice and apply key concepts and vocabulary so they can meet the lesson's content and language objectives. In addition, some selected activities came directly from the *Holt Literature & Language Arts* (2003) Teacher's Edition.

Throughout the planning of the grade 10 lessons and unit, we were continually aware of the needs of English learners, as well as native-English speaking students who are performing academically at or above grade level. At the high school level, the differences in individual students' language and literacy levels is greater than in any other grade-level cluster. Therefore, the need for differentiation of instructional materials, processes, and products is especially important.

The focus for the tenth grade lessons, as with the other lessons and units in this book, is on character analysis, a topic that is typically found in state content standards from Kindergarten through grade 12. Consequently, students who have been schooled in the United States have been learning how to think about fictional characters for many years. English learners who have been schooled elsewhere have undoubtedly been taught character analysis in literature in their primary language, so they will have some or a good amount of background. However, English learners with little or interrupted schooling may not have this background, and a tenth grade lesson about character analysis will need to be scaffolded carefully for them.

This SIOP® lesson plan illustrates that at the high school level, many lessons extend over a couple of days, especially if class periods are in the 45–55 minute range. We planned for this lesson to take two days, and our intent is that all 30 features of the SIOP® Model will be implemented during the two periods. On the day preceding this lesson, the teacher spends nearly the entire period building background and introducing the key content and academic language for the unit, "Character: Using Primary and Secondary Sources" (see Chapter 7 for the entire unit).

Please note: If your tenth (or ninth, eleventh, or twelfth) grade English-language arts curriculum is taught within block scheduling, additional instruction in the language arts (writing, grammar, spelling, vocabulary) will need to be included, and respective lessons also will need to include the SIOP® features if English learners are present.

SIOP® LESSON PLAN, *Grade 10, Day 2–3:* *"Everyday Use"*

Unit Character: Using Primary and Secondary Sources
SIOP® Lesson: "Everyday Use: For your Grandmama" by Alice Walker
Grade: 10

Content Standards: 3.4 Determine characters' traits by what the characters say about themselves in narration, dialogue, dramatic monologue, and soliloquy.

Key Vocabulary:	*Supplementary Materials:*
Content Vocabulary: *sidle, furtive, cowering, oppress, rifling; traits* **Academic Vocabulary:** *compare and contrast, infer, direct characterization, indirect characterization, dialogue* **HOTS:** • Statements from Anticipation/Reaction Guide + Why, such as: It is a parent's responsibility to provide for the emotional and physical needs of their children into adulthood: Agree or Disagree? Why? • How does Alice Walker use direct characterization when depicting Mama? • How does Alice Walker use indirect characterization to depict Maggie and Dee?	Students' homework paragraphs from their interviews in Day 1 lesson Students' vocabulary cards from Day 1 lesson Semantic Feature Analysis (Buehl, 2009; Fisher & Frey, 2008) handout for each student Transparency of blank Semantic Feature Analysis (SFA) Sticky notes

Connections to Prior Knowledge/ Building Background Information:
Links to students' background experiences— SW orally share their paragraph descriptions with their partners, focusing on the use of descriptive adjectives in the traits described.
Links to Prior Learning— SW review academic vocabulary and definitions from the previous day with the Mix-Mix-Trade activity.

Objectives:	*Meaningful Activities/Lesson Sequence:*	*Review/Assessment:*
Content Objectives: **1.** SWBAT compare and contrast direct and indirect characterization. **2.** SWBAT identify and match character traits to the characters in "Everyday Use." **Language Objectives:** **1.** SWBAT list in writing direct characterization traits through characters' words, thoughts, speech patterns, and actions.	• Review content and language objectives with students, clarifying any words as necessary. • Ask partners from previous day to reunite to share their character trait paragraphs. • Ask for 2–3 volunteers to orally share their paragraphs. Ask for examples of how the paragraph demonstrated a description of a round character (rather than flat or stock). SW turn in paragraphs to teacher. • TW distribute vocabulary cards from previous day. SW engage in a Mix-Mix-Trade, where they'll roam around until the teacher signals to stop. Facing a partner, one student will "test" the other by reading the definition on his or her card. The other	Circulate among partners, listening to paragraphs; note use of descriptive adjectives. TW monitor during the Mix-Mix-Trade to determine if students know the vocabulary, and reteach as needed.

2. SWBAT list in writing indirect characterization traits through the narrator's description.

3. SWBAT role play or identify from another student's role play the meanings of the story's content vocabulary: (*cowering, sidle, furtive, rifling, oppress*)

will try to identify the word defined, and will then do the same with his/her card. They trade cards and roam until the signal, where the process is repeated 5–6 times, as time allows.

- TW distribute the Anticipation/Reaction Guide + Why. TW read aloud the opening statement; for ELs (in a small group), TW also read about the statements, SW complete the guide (see p. 129 for the Anticipation/Reaction Guide + Why example.)

- SW return to their seats, open books to p. 83. TW introduce Alice Walker, author.

- TW introduce content vocabulary defined on p. 76. Students volunteer to role-play meanings while class tries to figure out the words. SW refer to definitions (*Holt Literature & Language Arts*, 2003, p. 76) while peers role play:

1. A cowering commoner who is trying to sidle up to a king
2. The actions of a furtive person rifling through your binder
3. A scene in which guards oppress a prisoner

- TW introduce "Everyday Use" on p. 77 of anthology. Explain that this is a story set in the 1960s with interesting characters who make up a family: Mama and her daughters Maggie and Dee.

- Problems arise when Maggie arrives from out of town, planning on taking her grandmother's quilt, a family heirloom.

- Ask students to note on sticky notes any character traits, both direct and indirect, as they are reading, some of which they may need to *infer*.

- Remind students to look carefully at the dialogue in the story. How does the dialogue give clues to character traits? Use sticky notes to mark dialogue passages that reveal traits.

- TW begin orally reading story to first break on p. 78.

- Distribute copies of the Semantic Feature Analysis.

- On the SFA transparency, TW model how students should list the character traits they have identified across the top of the SFA ("features").

- TW model how to add the characters' names down the side of SFA: Mama, Maggie, and Dee.

- Model how to determine if there is a match between a character and each of the traits. Mark a match with a "+" and in a box where there is no match, mark the box with "−". If there's a question, mark a "?".

- Proficient readers will continue reading silently, noting other character traits on their SFA charts.

- Less proficient readers can read in small groups or with the teacher, noting other character traits on their SFA charts.

- When students have completed the reading, have them complete the SFA, matching traits to the three characters.

Students are familiar with the Anticipation/Reaction Guide + Why, so a quick review is all that is necessary. ELs will receive small group assistance to help them get started. TW monitor for ELs' understandings.

Monitor and clarify as needed.

Ask for student volunteers to define and give an example of *inference*; clarify as needed.

Review meaning of *dialogue*. Have students identify examples of dialogue in the story.

Monitor by having students share traits and list them on a transparency of a SFA.

For ELs and less proficient readers, model how to find direct and indirect characterizations in the story; review how to find clue words and infer character traits from them.

Monitor ELs as they are writing and matching on the SFA. They may write words/phrases, but not understand them.

(continued)

SIOP® LESSON PLAN, *Grade 10, Day 2–3:*
"Everyday Use" (continued)

Meaningful Activities/Lesson Sequence:	Review/Assessment:
• With their table groups, have students compare their SFA charts with those of other students. If there are differences in opinions, have students return to the story and character descriptions to justify their decisions. • If some students finish early, they can begin their homework assignment: read the brief interview on page 89 of Alice Walker, who is also a quilter. Based on Ms. Walker's responses to the interviewer, what character traits describe this Pulitzer Prize-winning author? Add her name and the traits to the SFA chart, and look for matches across the chart's list of traits.	Intervene and help as needed. Some ELs may need to hear the interview selection read aloud prior to doing their homework assignment, or listen to tapes of the interview, if possible. More proficient readers who have completed their work could also tape the Alice Walker interview for ELs. Review, if necessary, how to determine which are the interviewer's words and which are Alice Walker's. Review meanings of key content and academic vocabulary; pull name sticks from a can for final review.

Wrap-up: SW complete the Reaction side of the Anticipation/Reaction + Why Guide, including new justifications based on "Everyday Use," if opinions have changed. Discuss.

Review content and language objectives with students.

Additional SIOP® Features

Preparation	Scaffolding	Group Options
☐ Adaptation of content*	■ Modeling	■ Whole class
■ Links to background	■ Guided practice	■ Small groups
■ Links to past learning	■ Independent practice	■ Partners
■ Strategies incorporated	■ Comprehensible input	■ Independent

Integration of Processes	Application	Assessment
■ Reading	■ Hands-on	■ Individual
■ Writing	■ Meaningful	■ Group
■ Speaking	■ Linked to objectives	■ Written
■ Listening	■ Promotes engagement	■ Oral

*If taped text is used, this would be an adaptation. Because the teacher will be reading with ELs and struggling readers, the grade-level text can be used.

FIGURE 3.4 *Semantic Feature Analysis (SFA) (Buehl, 2009; Fisher & Frey, 2008)*

Character Traits

	talented	tough	homely	inadequate	insecure	successful	confident	(etc.)
Mama	+	+	−	−	−	−	+	
Characters								
Maggie	−	−	+	+	+	−	−	
Dee	−	−	−	−	−	+	+	
Alice	+	−	−	−	−	+	+	
(etc.)								

Adaptations for Language Proficiency

Beginning

Homework from the previous day is to be shared at the beginning of this lesson. For beginning English speakers, the process of writing the assigned paragraph was scaffolded considerably, first with a Character Map completed with a partner, and then with a partially completed paragraph with sentence frames that the ELs could write in a small group with the teacher, with a partner, or, if appropriate, independently. Further, if the grade level text is read aloud or tape recorded so beginners can focus their concentration on listening, they are more likely to be successful. Again, notice that the goal is achievement of the objectives. Both the process and the product will differ to meet each student's language proficiency needs.

The lesson for days 2 and 3 includes several more accommodations:

1. Students will review the academic vocabulary and definitions from the previous day's lesson in a Mix-Mix-Trade activity.
2. The teacher will model how to complete a Semantic Feature Analysis chart on a transparency and overhead.
3. The teacher will begin reading the story "Everyday Use," and then beginning English speakers will read with the teacher.
4. The teacher will model for less-proficient English speakers (and struggling readers) how to find direct and indirect characterizations in a story by searching for clue words.
5. For homework (reading a short interview of Alice Walker), beginners will have access to a tape of the interview and a small, portable classroom tape recorder.

Intermediate

For English learners at the intermediate level of proficiency, the amount and types of scaffolding in this lesson should enable them to be successful. If necessary, they could also use the sentence frames in the partially completed paragraph for a guide. Whereas

SIOP® Lesson Plan, Grade 10: Cluster 9–12

beginners would be expected to fill in missing words and copy the paragraph to complete the homework assignment, intermediate students could use the structure of the paragraph model as an aid, and then be expected to write a simple paragraph mostly on their own. The role playing of vocabulary words (intermediate students could certainly participate) will be helpful, and the Mix-Mix-Trade activity will reinforce the meanings of the challenging academic vocabulary. Small group reading of the text will provide additional support. The Semantic Feature Analysis activity has a solid research background for helping students determine relationships, which helps to facilitate comprehension. Students are also expected to share their SFA charts with each other to gain more ideas and develop confidence. The use of sticky notes as another scaffold is intentional because they are temporary. ELs can write notes on them, place them in the story where they think they belong, and move them somewhere else if they find another place they think is better.

Advanced

Because of the amount of scaffolded support in this lesson, ELs at the advanced level of English proficiency should not have difficulty, except for the unusual content vocabulary (e.g., *sidle, furtive, cowering*) and the more abstract academic vocabulary. The teacher should be sensitive to a relatively proficient English speaker's difficulty with unknown English words and concepts, and be ready to assist as needed. Also, because the story ("Everyday Use") is written about the 1960s in the United States, additional background building about racial turmoil in the South during this time period may be helpful for both intermediate and advanced speakers. Beginning students will benefit also if additional supports such as period photographs are provided to make the information more comprehensible.

Adaptations for Academic Proficiency

If you have students who have learning and/or reading difficulties unrelated to their English language proficiency, the additional accommodations described for beginning English speakers may be necessary. For example, the taped text, recommended for the beginning speaker, might be essential for an intermediate or advanced English speaker with a severe reading problem, just as it would be for a native English speaker who has similar difficulty.

All too often, English learners at the secondary level are referred for special education services, regardless of whether they have a diagnosed learning disability. Therefore, it is critically important that mainstream content teachers provide the scaffolds needed, ideally through the SIOP® Model. If an English learner with intermediate or above English proficiency is still failing to achieve even with these scaffolds and consistent implementation of the SIOP® Model, certainly consultation with school and district learning specialists is warranted.

Activity #3: The Conga Line

The Conga Line (Vogt & Echevarria, 2008), adapted from Kagan's (1994) Inside/ Outside Circle, is an active and engaging technique that allows all learners to participate simultaneously. This activity provides the teacher with opportunities to assess understanding of content as well as observe language applications. It can be used at any level; in fact, we have used the Conga line with many levels from kindergartners to adults. That's not to say that K–2 students will not need more practice, but the benefits of this activity far outweigh the patience required by the teacher to "train" his or her students. Once your students have mastered the routines of the technique, you will find many ways to incorporate the Conga Line into your lessons in all curricular areas.

Purposes of the Conga Line

- To engage all students in previewing or reviewing topics in an active and motivating manner
- To assess prior knowledge or background knowledge before a lesson
- To practice content vocabulary and/or language structures
- To review content material during a lesson
- To assess learning after a lesson
- To develop students' language proficiency throughout the lesson as they clarify, repeat, ask and answer questions about what they are sharing with each other

Applications of the Conga Line

- Before, during, or after lessons
- Text passage, novel or short story, lecture, nonprint media (television, video, realia)

SIOP® Components Reinforced

- Building Background
- Comprehensible Input
- Interaction
- Review and Assessment

Steps for the Conga Line

1. Develop questions related to the content being studied. You will need one question for each student.
2. Write each question on a 3 × 5 card and write the answer on the back.
3. Have students line up in two equal lines (line A and line B) facing each other to make pairs.
4. Give each student a question card.

5. To begin the Conga Line, have a student from line A read the question on his card to his partner in line B.

6. The student in line B then gives an answer for the question.

7. Student A checks to see if the answer is correct and confirms it with Student B, or gives the correct answer.

8. Student B then asks his question of Student A.

9. At the signal of the teacher, students A and B trade cards and everyone in the A line moves one person to the right so they are now part of a new pair. The person at the end of the A line moves all the way to the beginning of that line (A). No one in the B line moves. Now all students have a new partner.

10. This process continues until students from line A have shared questions with several of the students from line B, as time permits.

As you can probably see, the trading of questions allows each student to have multiple exposures to each question, which reinforces the content and enables all students to have content and language practice.

Modified Versions

Instead of the teacher creating the questions, students can respond to a prompt or they can write their own questions on the cards. The answers can be factual or open-ended for the purpose of promoting conversation. In this version, you would have students keep their own cards throughout the Conga Line.

For students with limited English proficiency, provide pictures of content-related items on the cards. Students will then describe the picture to their partner using a frame such as, "This is a _____. It is used to _____."

Other Ideas for the Conga Line

- Provide pictures of people to be described.

- Provide questions that may be on an upcoming content assessment.

- Provide academic vocabulary, such as *predict, summarize, clarify, question,* and have students describe each process.

SIOP® Lesson Plan, Grade 4: Cluster 3–5

In Chapter 5 we provide a complete Semantic Feature Analysis activity that incorporates the Conga Line. Here, we have pulled out the Conga Line portion to show how it can be used to reinforce content and language. It's important to note that in the SFA lesson

FIGURE 3.5   *Semantic Feature Analysis Chart for* Crow Boy *and* The Rag Coat

	patient	proud	respectful	compassionate	generous	courageous	envious	regretful
Chibi	+	+	+	+	?	+	−	−
Mr. Isobe	+	?	+	+	+	?	−	−
Other students at Chibi's school	−	?	−	−	−	−	+	+
Minna	+	+	+	+	?	+	?	?
Quilting Mothers	+	+	+	+	+		?	?
Other students at Minna's school	−	?	−	−	?	−	+	+

prior to the Conga Line activity, students have completed the SFA for six characters from the books *Crow Boy* and *The Rag Coat* (see Figure 3.5). The purpose of the Conga Line in this lesson is to support the language objective: *Students will be able to orally give evidence supporting character classifications.*

The prompts to be used are:

1. Chibi is patient when he _____.
2. Chibi is proud when he _____.
3. Chibi is courageous when he _____.
4. Mr. Isobe is patient when he _____.
5. Mr. Isobe is compassionate when _____.
6. Chibi's schoolmates are envious when _____.
7. Chibi's schoolmates are regretful when _____.
8. Minna is patient when _____.
9. Minna is proud when _____.
10. Minna is respectful when _____.
11. Minna is courageous when _____.
12. Quilting mothers are patient when _____.
13. Quilting mothers are proud when _____.
14. Quilting mothers are respectful when _____.
15. Quilting mothers are compassionate when _____.
16. Quilting mothers are generous when _____.
17. Students at Minna's school are envious when _____.
18. Students at Minna's school are regretful when _____.

SIOP® LESSON PLAN, *Grade 4:*
Conga Line Activity (from Grade 4 Lesson, Day 6)

Objectives:	Meaningful Activities/Lesson Sequence	Review/Assessment:
Language Objectives: **1.** SWBAT orally give evidence supporting character classifications.	• In preparation for the Conga Line, TW write each prompt on a 3 × 5 card. • SW line up in two equal lines (line A and line B) facing each other to make pairs. • TW give each student a prompt card. Each student from line A will read the prompt and complete it for his partner in line B. • The partner in line B will evaluate his partner's response. • Student B will then read his prompt and finish the prompt. Student A will evaluate his response. • At the signal of the teacher, students A and B will trade cards and everyone in line A moves one person to the right so they are now part of a new pair. The person at the end of the line A moves all the way to the front of line A. Line B doesn't move. • This continues until students from line A have shared questions with the students from line B.	As you walk along the line monitoring students, make sure that you are allowing sufficient time for students to respond.

Adaptations for Language Proficiency

Many students in the upper elementary and middle school range falter once they reach the intermediate level. Although they continue to strive to achieve language proficiency, the academic environment becomes increasingly challenging. It is probably at these grade levels that many, if not all levels of proficiency are represented to some degree by the students in your class. For those reasons, differentiation and systematic scaffolding become essential to your instruction as you work to meet the needs of your linguistically diverse audience.

Beginning

Because this task is loaded with content but limited with visual clues, one way you can support your beginners is to pair them with proficient language students. The proficient student could model the responses and the beginner could repeat or echo. Another way to allow beginners to be more independent but continue to receive support is by limiting the number of sentence frames to which they need to respond. As the line moves, ELs can keep their cards and practice one frame several times before they trade with their partners.

Intermediate

Intermediate students may need some scaffolded practice. Before the Conga Line activity, the teacher can read aloud each frame that will be used on the cards. The students will have time to think about the frame and the evidence they will share. Allow students to share with a partner, and as they do, move around the class and listen to their responses. Provide clarification and use high-quality responses as models for the class. Continue through the list of prompts until the students feel comfortable with them. At this point, they will have some ideas for how they will respond in the Conga Line.

Advanced

Remember, advanced level students still need opportunities to practice and apply academic language and content concepts in a more independent manner. Although they might benefit from practicing the prompts with teacher support, usually this activity does not need to be modified for students at the advanced level of English proficiency.

Adaptations for Academic Proficiency

Reading through the lists of prompts allows students to practice their responses with a partner before moving into the Conga Line. This gives you a chance to monitor responses and provide clarification if needed. You might also model high-quality responses for the class. Spending time preparing for the Conga Line will ensure that all students are ready to share the prompts and responses independently.

Concluding Thoughts

Slowly but surely, Patricia Toledo, the teacher introduced in the opening of this chapter, has learned how to write SIOP® lesson plans for her language arts classes. Working with her grade-level colleagues, she has shared ideas, materials, and activities. Perhaps most important, the teachers have become "critical friends" and they frequently read over each other's lesson plans, including the content and language objectives. Patricia was happy to realize that many of the effective techniques and activities that she had used for years are very appropriate to her SIOP® lessons. She also understands that her objectives do not have to be perfectly written, and it's okay to struggle with trying to figure out how to distinguish between her language arts content that needs to be taught and the language objectives that need to be written. Sometimes the distinction just isn't very clear, and that's okay. Patricia is happy to report that her students are now in the routine of reading the objectives for each of their subjects at the beginning of class, and reviewing their progress toward meeting them at the end of each period. At present, as she continues to write lesson plans based on objectives (while including familiar and new activities and techniques), she finds the SIOP® lesson and unit planning process is getting easier and easier.

chapter 4

Sample SIOP® English-Language Arts Lessons and Units (Grades K–2)

By Lisa Mitchener and Karlin LaPorta

Introduction

Now that Patricia and her grade-level team are more comfortable writing SIOP® lesson plans, they are contemplating writing a complete SIOP® unit plan. Like all teachers, their planning is guided by a number of considerations. First, there are the state content standards that guide all curriculum development, as well as the adoption of instructional materials. Also, there may be a district English-language arts curriculum sequence that is based on the content standards. A district pacing chart, which is becoming more and more common—especially in the elementary grades, may dictate how much time is spent on particular standards. Ultimately, whatever the district policies, Patricia must ensure that the state ELA standards are addressed in her lessons, and she knows she is accountable for the degree to which these standards are met by her students, including the English learners.

Patricia and her ELA team generated the following questions as they began developing the SIOP® unit:

1. What must students learn in this unit?

2. Where do I need to start to make sure students meet the learning goals identified in the first question?

3. How will I assess students' learning of the unit's content concepts?

4. Is the time allotted sufficient to ensure that my students meet the content and language objectives?

5. How many lessons will it take to teach the concepts and lead students to mastery?

6. What materials and activities will I use to supplement the literature books and anthology?

7. What vocabulary must students know and what additional vocabulary must be taught, including academic language? How many vocabulary words should I select to teach, reinforce, and assess during each lesson?

8. How will I make the lessons meaningful so students are engaged and motivated to learn?

9. Given that this unit plan is for an English-language arts classroom, how will I make sure students have ample opportunity to practice the content concepts as well as read, write, listen, speak, and use academic language throughout the unit?

10. What additional ELA concepts should be taught to students who have had their education interrupted or who might lack the English proficiency required to comprehend the content and language objectives?

Using the SIOP® features as a guide for unit planning will naturally help to differentiate instruction for English learners as you address the multiple language and academic levels in your class or classes. As teachers, we also have the added challenge of needing to follow a specialized curriculum, and these curriculum requirements differ somewhat from district to district and state to state. Our goal for the following chapters is to illustrate how a SIOP® embedded language arts unit might look at the elementary, middle school, and high school levels, and at various stages of ELs' language proficiency. It is our hope that you can glean ideas from each of the units presented in this book and begin or continue the process of "SIOP®izing" your language arts units with your current curriculum.

Unit Planning Process

It is important to remember that your state English-Language Arts (ELA) and English Language Development (ELD) standards are your starting point and that they should drive your unit of instruction. The names and acronyms for your state's standards may differ, but they should be the basis for creating the content and language objectives you will be teaching throughout your unit. As we sat down to create these sample units, we had to constantly remind ourselves of this. As you read through the lesson plans, note the standards that guided our writing, as well as the content and language objectives that were derived from them. Also, observe the wide variety of techniques and activities that were selected to enable students to practice and apply the key content concepts and language identified in the objectives. The activities also provide us with multiple opportunities to assess students' progress in meeting the content and language objectives. Likewise, we encourage you to start with your standards, develop lesson objectives from them, and then select meaningful and appropriate activities, rather than simply incorporating an activity for activity's sake. To see how the activities in the four unit lesson plans in Chapters 4, 5, 6, and 7 map onto the components of the SIOP® Model, see the matrix in Appendix D. In addition, black-line masters for many of the activities in the units can be found in Appendix E. These are reproducibles for you to use for transparencies, student handouts, or PowerPoint slides.

It is important to note that two of the units (grades 7 and 10) were developed from the adopted middle school and high school literature anthologies, with some hints and ideas coming from the respective teacher's editions. The other two units (grades 1 and 4) were developed from grade-level appropriate trade literature, but not necessarily from an adopted reading series. Our purpose in taking this approach is twofold: (1) to demonstrate that effective SIOP® lessons and units, including content and language objectives, may be developed using adopted, mandated curricula that may or may not need to be adapted to meet the language and literacy needs of English learners; and (2) to demonstrate that effective SIOP® lessons may be developed with supplementary materials, in this case thematically related literature selections, using the SIOP® Model as the organizing structure for the lesson plan. We sometimes hear teachers complain that having an adopted reading series or anthology—often with a rather strict pacing guide—prohibits them from teaching SIOP® lessons. We maintain that effective SIOP® lessons can be developed and taught, regardless of the instructional materials, as long as they are standards-based. If the pacing guide is inappropriate for your English learners, it will be necessary for you to provide some differentiated instruction for these students. It may be helpful to refer back to Chapter 3 for some specific lesson adaptations for variances in students' academic and language proficiency.

Finally, as you read through the units, you will notice that there are Planning Points and teacher Think-Alouds throughout. The purpose of the Planning Points is to highlight the process of planning a SIOP® unit and to anticipate questions you may have about each specific lesson plan. The teacher Think-Alouds are questions we asked ourselves or issues that arose throughout the SIOP® unit planning process. We hope these will be helpful as a resource for your own planning.

Grade 1 Unit: Cluster K–2

Many children in grades K–2 come to school with limited practice in reading, writing, listening, and speaking. For English learners without preschool experiences, their opening day of kindergarten may be the first time they have heard conventional English throughout the day. Therefore, these children need many opportunities to practice in all four language domains. This is essential as they begin to tackle their grade-level standards. By the end of first grade, students are expected to be able to read simple decodable words as well

FIGURE 4.1 *Description of Grade 1 Unit and Content Standards*

Unit Focus:	Character Analysis
Standards:	2.0 Reading of grade-level appropriate text. 2.1 Acquire and use new vocabulary in relevant contexts. 2.2 Organize ideas using simple webs, maps, lists, or other graphic organizers. 3.2 Describe characters' traits within a literary selection, heard or read. 3.3 Make, confirm, and revise predictions. 3.4 Compare (and contrast) the characters in a literary selection.
Primary Source (TE, tradebook, etc.):	*A Practical Guide to Dragons* (Trumbauer, 2006) *Elvira* (Shannon, 1991)
Vocabulary:	Content Vocabulary: *dragon, mean, nice, fierce, scary, claws, scales, nostril, courage (courageous), tease, creative, gobbling, princess, daisy chains, furious, normal, appreciated, mistaken* Academic Vocabulary: *traditional, nontraditional, predict, prediction, opinion, belief, confirm, disconfirm, compare, contrast, but, however, on the other hand*
Supplementary Materials:	Primary sources listed above Word-Definition-Picture Chart Word Web with the phrase *Characteristics of a Dragon* in the middle. (See Appendix E, #11). Sentence strips Chart with the following sentence frames. The dragon is _____. The dragons are _____. The dragon looks _____. I think the dragon is _____. T-Chart on chart paper and a T-Chart for each student (see Appendix E, #10) Chart with the following sentence frames: A traditional dragon is _____, *but* I predict a nontraditional dragon is _____. A traditional dragon is _____; *however,* I predict a nontraditional dragon is _____. A traditional dragon is _____; *on the other hand,* I predict a nontraditional dragon is _____. Compare/Contrast Signal Words Chart (Vogt & Echevarria, 2008, pp. 36–39). Outcome Sentences chart (Echevarria, Vogt & Short, 2008, pp. 170–171). Anticipation/Reaction Guide for each student plus transparency (Vogt & Echevarria, 2008, pp. 82–83). (See Appendix E, #1) Chart with the following sentence frames: I predict _____ because _____. I think _____ because _____. I believe _____ because _____. Semantic Feature Analysis Chart (Fisher &Frey, 2008, pp. 78–80). Word-Definition-Chart: Displayed for student reference; a simple three-column chart (word, definition, picture) listing each vocabulary word with a student-friendly definition and a pictorial representation of the word; in the primary grades, the chart is developed by the teacher; similar to 4-Corners Vocabulary chart that students can make in the upper grades

as common irregular words (sight words) that do not fit the normal patterns of English. Students at this level allocate a great deal of mental energy toward decoding, which can limit their ability to comprehend. It is important that first graders become fluent decoders, but not at the expense of comprehension. This is the dilemma that K–2 teachers face when teaching reading. Add to that the various levels of children's language proficiency and the challenge is doubled.

Listening and speaking activities provide a vehicle for teaching comprehension at this early stage. Especially at the kindergarten and early first grade levels, children should be provided with listening opportunities that will enable them to practice answering comprehension questions orally. This lowers the demand on decoding and allows them to focus on meaning and vocabulary. As you will see in the grade 1 unit, we have provided many opportunities for students to practice comprehension through listening to a story read aloud by the teacher (see Figure 4.1).

Unit and Lesson Plans

Although this unit addresses several standards, there are three primary objectives: (1) to build academic vocabulary, including *predict, prediction, opinion, belief, confirm, disconfirm, compare,* and *contrast*; (2) to practice the skill of making and confirming predictions; and (3) to compare and contrast character traits, with a focus on the skill of comparing and contrasting using the vehicle of the story, *Elvira*. These three objectives support learning that will be used throughout the students' educational experience. Note that since this lesson is for first graders, it may be their initial introduction to these concepts.

PLANNING POINTS for SIOP® Lesson Plan, Grade 1, Day 1

- Note the HOTS (Higher Order Thinking Skills) box on the lesson plan. An important feature of the SIOP® model is Feature 15 in the Strategies Component: "A variety of questions or tasks that promote higher order thinking skills" (Echevarria, Vogt, & Short, 2008, Chapter 5). When teaching English-language arts in the primary grades, a good portion of instructional time and energy is dedicated to decoding and fluency. However, even at this early age, it is important to provide students with opportunities to engage in critical thinking. The questions provided in our lesson plans are intended to guide the teacher to initiate conversations that support student thinking at varied levels.

- Remember that the first two features of the SIOP® protocol state that content and language objectives are to be "clearly defined, displayed and reviewed with students" (Echevarria, Vogt, & Short, 2008, Chapter 2). As you develop SIOP® lessons, you know exactly what outcomes you are looking for because you have written content and language objectives. However, since your objectives come directly from your state content standards, they may be written in language that K–2 students or students with limited English proficiency may not understand—that is, "teacher talk." In order to guide the class toward the learning outcomes you expect, objectives may be written in student-friendly (SF) language so that they are more comprehensible and meaningful for children. Therefore, for the K–2 grade cluster we have provided you with a student-friendly version for each of the more formally written content and language objectives.

SIOP® LESSON PLAN, *Grade 1 Day 1:*
Building Content Vocabulary

Key: SW = Students will; TW = Teacher will; SWBAT = Students will be able to . . . ;
HOTS = Higher Order Thinking Skills; SF = Student friendly

Unit: Character Analysis

SIOP® Lesson: Building Content Vocabulary
Grade: 1

Content Standards: 2.1 Acquire and use new vocabulary in relevant contexts.

Key Vocabulary:	Supplementary Materials:
Content Vocabulary: *dragon, mean, fierce, scary, claws, scales, nostril* **Academic Vocabulary:** *traditional, nontraditional* **HOTS:** What are some differences between the dragons in the pictures? What would happen if a dragon landed on our playground? Why?	Word-Definition-Picture Chart (teacher-made) Word Web with the words *Characteristics of a Dragon* in the middle (see Appendix E, #11). Sentence strips *A Practical Guide to Dragons* (Trumbauer, 2006) Chart with the following sentence frames: The dragon is _____. The dragons are _____. The dragon looks _____. I think the dragon is _____.

Connections to Prior Knowledge/ Building Background Information:
Links to Students' Background Experiences—SW orally share information they know
about dragons.
Links to Prior Learning—Students are familiar with the format and have ample practice in use of both
the Word-Definition-Picture chart and the Word Web. Show students the Word-Definition-Picture chart.
Review and discuss all of the vocabulary words on the chart. Add these words to a Word Web with the
phrase *Characteristics of a Dragon* in the middle.

Objectives:	Meaningful Activities/Lesson Sequence:	Review/Assessment:
Content Objectives: **1.** SWBAT identify characteristics of a traditional dragon by looking at pictures of dragons. **SF:** Your job today is to look at pictures and describe a traditional dragon. **Language Objectives:** **1.** SWBAT orally describe characteristics of a traditional dragon to a partner in a complete sentence. **SF:** Your job today is to describe dragons to your partner in a complete sentence. **2.** SWBAT write a sentence describing the characteristics of a dragon.	• TW post and orally explain content and language objectives. • TW ask if students have ever seen pictures, read about, or seen a cartoon or movie about a dragon (e.g., Donkey's girlfriend in *Shrek*). • TW show pictures of traditional dragons and tell students that their job is to describe the dragons to their partner. TW add adjectives produced by students on *Characteristics of a Dragon* Word Web. • With a partner, SW orally complete the following sentence frames using the Word Web. The dragon is _____. The dragons are _____. The dragon looks _____. I think the dragon is _____.	Ask students to volunteer adjectives, but give opportunities to share with a partner before adding to the chart. Observe students as they share. Monitor students and promote discussion beyond the assigned statements for those who have the language ability. Allow students to read their partner's sentence to relieve anxiety and provide practice.

SF: Your job today is to write a complete sentence about a dragon.

- SW volunteer to read their descriptive sentence or their partner's descriptive sentence.

- SW write a description of their favorite dragon on a sentence strip using following frame:

My favorite dragon is because _____ .

Collect the sentence frames for evaluation and then place them in a pocket chart for further reading by the students.

Wrap-up: SW read their descriptive sentences to a partner. TW place sentence strips in pocket chart and revisit periodically.

Review content and language objectives with students.

Additional SIOP® Features

Preparation	*Scaffolding*	*Group Options*
◼ Adaptation of content	◼ Modeling	◼ Whole class
◼ Links to background	◼ Guided practice	☐ Small groups
◼ Links to past learning	◼ Independent practice	◼ Partners
◼ Strategies incorporated	◼ Comprehensible input	◼ Independent

Integration of Processes	*Application*	*Assessment*
◼ Reading	◼ Hands-on	◼ Individual
◼ Writing	◼ Meaningful	◼ Group
◼ Speaking	◼ Linked to objectives	◼ Written
◼ Listening	◼ Promotes engagement	◼ Oral

THINK-ALOUDS for SIOP® Lesson Plan, Grade 1, Day 1

- Consider partner match-ups. Will language proficiency levels affect partnerships? Can pairing limited English students with more proficient students help with language development? How can I insure that limited English students participate fully and are not dominated by a partner?

- How should I address academic vocabulary? Often academic vocabulary is not concrete and may not be easily depicted by a picture or another more simple word. How will I adapt and adjust? Should I preteach the vocabulary using examples that relate to students' prior knowledge or background? Or should I teach as I go, introducing and applying academic vocabulary to the content being taught?

SIOP® LESSON PLAN, *Grade 1, Day 2:*
Classifying Character Traits

Key: SW = Students will; TW = Teacher will; SWBAT = Students will be able to . . . ;
HOTS = Higher Order Thinking Skills; SF = Student friendly

Unit: Character Analysis

SIOP® Lesson: Classifying Character Traits
Grade: 1

Content Standards: 2.2 Organize ideas using simple webs, maps, lists, or other graphic organizers.

(continued)

SIOP® LESSON PLAN: *Grade 1, Day 2:*
Classifying Character Traits (continued)

Key Vocabulary:	Supplementary Materials:
Content Vocabulary: *dragon, mean, fierce, scary, claws, scales, nostrils*	T-Chart on chart paper and a T-Chart for each student (See sample in Figure 4.2.)
Academic Vocabulary: *traditional, nontraditional, predict*	Chart with the following sentence frames: A traditional dragon is _____, *but* I predict a nontraditional dragon is _____.
HOTS: Do you think traditional and nontraditional dragons are similar in some ways? How?	A traditional dragon is _____; *however*, I predict a nontraditional dragon is _____.
	A traditional dragon is _____; *on the other hand*, I predict a nontraditional dragon is _____.
	Writing paper for students
	Compare/Contrast Signal Words chart (Vogt & Echevarria, 2008, p. 36). (See sample in Figure 4.3.)
	Outcome Sentences Chart (Echevarria , Vogt & Short, 2008, p. 170). (See sample in Figure 4.4.)

Connections to Prior Knowledge/ Building Background Information:
Links to Students' Background Experiences—Review sentences from Day 1 (in pocket chart)
Links to Prior Learning—Review the Signal Words chart. Review the Word-Definition-Picture chart. Review the *Characteristics of a Dragon* Word Web. Tell students that they will be learning about a dragon that is *not* like normal/traditional dragons.

Objectives:	Meaningful Activities/Lesson Sequence:	Review/Assessment:
Content Objectives: **1.** SWBAT classify characteristics of a traditional dragon vs. a prediction of what a nontraditional dragon would be like. **SF:** Your job today is to make predictions about nontraditional dragons. **Language Objectives:** **1.** SWBAT write a comparison of a traditional and nontraditional dragon using sentence frames. **SF:** Your job today is to write a prediction about nontraditional dragons. **2.** SWBAT read a comparison of a traditional and nontraditional dragon using sentence frames. **SF:** Your job today is to read your prediction to other students.	● TW post and orally explain content and language objectives. ● Review key content and academic vocabulary. ● Review sentences from Day 1 in pocket chart. ● TW model how to use the T-chart to classify characteristics of a traditional dragon by completing the left column using words from the *Characteristics of a Dragon* Word Web. ● SW complete the left side along with the teacher. ● TW explain that a nontraditional dragon has characteristics that are different from or opposite to those of a traditional dragon. ● TW model, "If a traditional dragon is mean, what word can we use to describe a nontraditional dragon?" ● SW classify the difference in characteristics between a traditional dragon and a nontraditional dragon by writing opposite words on the right side of the T-chart.	Spot-check students' understanding of vocabulary. Use a think-aloud to model how to complete the T-chart. Continue to guide students through this lesson with modeling and think-alouds. When appropriate, release the task to the students to complete.

- With a partner, SW orally complete the following sentence frames using the Word Web.

A traditional dragon is _____, *but* I predict a nontraditional dragon is _____.

A traditional dragon is _____; *however,* I predict a nontraditional dragon is _____.

A traditional dragon is _____; *on the other hand*, I predict a nontraditional dragon is _____.

Ex. A traditional dragon is mean, but (however, on the other hand) I predict a nontraditional dragon is nice.

- SW choose one sentence frame and write a comparison sentence on a half sheet of paper.

- SW read their written work to other students in a Inside-Outside Circle (Conga Line).

- SW line up in two equal lines (line A and line B) facing each other to make pairs, holding their sentence.

- Students from line A will read their sentences to their partners in line B.

- Students from line B will then read their sentences.

- At the signal of the teacher, each student A moves one person to the right so each person has a new partner. The person at the end of line A moves all the way to the other end of line A. Line B doesn't move.

- This continues until all students from line A have shared sentences with all the students from line B.

Make sure to walk around and monitor the sentences that are being written. It is important that the sentences be meaningful and accurate, as they will be read to many partners in the next activity.

As you walk along the line monitoring students, make sure that you are allowing sufficient time for students to respond before you have students move.

Wrap-up: Have students refer to the Outcome Sentences (see Figure 4.4) displayed in the room. Throw a rubber ball to individual students and have them orally complete the frames.

Additional SIOP® Features

Preparation	Scaffolding	Group Options
■ Adaptation of content	■ Modeling	■ Whole class
□ Links to background	■ Guided practice	□ Small groups
■ Links to past learning	■ Independent practice	■ Partners
■ Strategies incorporated	■ Comprehensible input	■ Independent

Integration of Processes	Application	Assessment
■ Reading	■ Hands-on	■ Individual
■ Writing	■ Meaningful	■ Group
■ Speaking	■ Linked to objectives	■ Written
■ Listening	■ Promotes engagement	■ Oral

FIGURE 4.2 *Dragon T-Chart*

Dragon T-Chart

Traditional Dragon	*Nontraditional Dragon*
mean	
fierce	
fire-breathing	
dangerous	
scary	
nasty	
claws	
scales	
nostrils	
*_____	

*Add new words from the partner activity from Day 1.

FIGURE 4.3 *Compare and Contrast Signal Words Chart (Vogt & Echevarria, 2008, p. 36)*

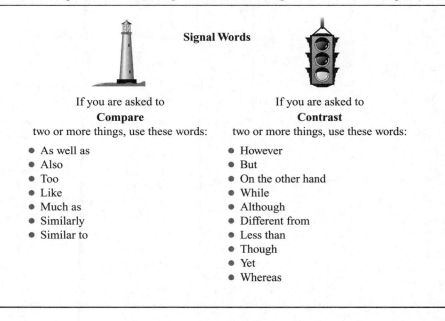

Signal Words

If you are asked to
Compare
two or more things, use these words:

- As well as
- Also
- Too
- Like
- Much as
- Similarly
- Similar to

If you are asked to
Contrast
two or more things, use these words:

- However
- But
- On the other hand
- While
- Although
- Different from
- Less than
- Though
- Yet
- Whereas

FIGURE 4.4 *Outcome Sentences (Echevarria, Vogt, & Short, 2008, p. 170)*

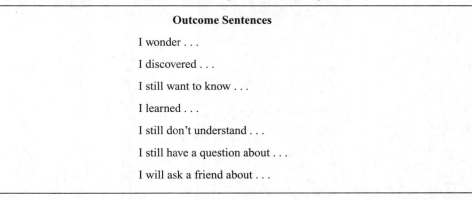

Outcome Sentences

I wonder . . .

I discovered . . .

I still want to know . . .

I learned . . .

I still don't understand . . .

I still have a question about . . .

I will ask a friend about . . .

PLANNING POINTS for SIOP® Lesson Plan, Grade 1, Day 2

- The T-chart portion of the lesson could be modified to reduce the amount of time spent with this activity. Since the writing task is essentially copying what the teacher writes, the teacher could choose to create one large T-chart for the whole class. This will still support the objectives, and will leave more time for student engagement later in the lesson.

- The students are both speaking and reading a lot of new vocabulary in this lesson: *traditional, nontraditional, predict, but, however, on the other hand*. What kind of practice should I give students so they are comfortable reading these words independently? How can I support those who struggle with reading during the Conga Line activity?

SIOP® LESSON PLAN, *Grade 1, Day 3:*
Making Predictions about Story Plot

Key: SW = Students will; TW = Teacher will; SWBAT = Students will be able to . . .;
HOTS = Higher Order Thinking Skills; SF = Student friendly

Unit: Character Analysis

SIOP® Lesson: Making Predictions about Story Plot
Grade: 1

Content Standards: 3.3 Make, confirm, and revise predictions.

Key Vocabulary:	Supplementary Materials:
Content Vocabulary: *courage (courageous), tease, creative*	Word-Definition-Picture chart (from Day 1)
Academic Vocabulary: *opinion, belief, prediction*	Word Web with the phrase *Characteristics of a Dragon* in the middle (from Day 1)
HOTS: When is it okay to tease someone? Why does it take courage to be different? What makes you think that? Why do you feel that way?	*Elvira* by Margaret Shannon
	Anticipation/Reaction Guide for each student plus overhead (see Appendix D, #1)

Connections to Prior Knowledge/ Building Background Information:
Links to Students' Background Experiences—Ask students if they have ever been made fun of because of something they were wearing, or how their hair looked, or something they did, etc.
Links to Prior Learning—Remind students that they made predictions about nontraditional dragons using the T-chart. Tell them that they are now going to make predictions about a character named Elvira who is a nontraditional dragon.

Objectives:	Meaningful Activities/Lesson Sequence:	Review/Assessment:
Content Objectives: 1. SWBAT read statements and develop opinions and beliefs about the main ideas and concepts of the book, *Elvira* by Margaret Shannon.	• TW post and orally explain content and language objectives. • TW display and explain the Anticipation/ Reaction Guide on the overhead.	

(continued)

SIOP® LESSON PLAN, *Grade 1, Day 3:*
Making Predictions about Story Plot (continued)

Objectives:	Meaningful Activities/Lesson Sequence:	Review/Assessment:
SF: Your job today is to read and think about what it means to be different from other people. **2.** SWBAT make predictions about Elvira's character after viewing the cover of the book. **SF:** Your job today is to make predictions about the book *Elvira*. **Language Objectives:** **1.** SWBAT track words and read the Anticipation/Reaction Guide in a shared reading lesson. **SF:** Your job today is to read the Anticipation/Reaction Guide. **2.** SWBAT orally support opinions made about different statements on the Anticipation/Reaction Guide. **SF:** Your job today is to say the sentence frame: I feel _____ because _____. Or, I believe that statement is true/false because _____.	• SW read the Anticipation/Reaction Guide along with the teacher. • TW ask students to think about the statements and decide if they agree or disagree with the statements. • SW complete the first four boxes on the anticipation side of the Anticipation/Reaction Guide. • TW show students the cover of the book *Elvira* by Margaret Shannon. SW describe the main character, Elvira, to a partner. • SW complete the final four boxes on the anticipation side of the Anticipation/Reaction Guide. So they now have eight responses. • SW express their opinions in a Split Decision activity. • During Split Decision, students will stand in the middle of the room with their Anticipation/Reaction guide in their hands. TW read a statement from the Anticipation/Reaction Guide. Students will move to opposite sides of the room (previously labeled Agree and Disagree) to demonstrate how they responded to the statement. TW select students to provide a rationale for their decisions. • SW will orally share their opinions from their Anticipation/Reaction Guide during the Split Decision activity. • Ex. "I feel it is okay to tease someone who is different than you because _____."	You can adjust your method of reading as needed based on the proficiency of readers in your class. Use a think-aloud demonstrating how to complete the Anticipation/Reaction Guide. After giving all directions, have students self-assess their understanding of the task with a finger response: 1—I need help. 2—I have a question. 3—I'm ready to start. 4—I could teach this. Once students begin independent work, focus on assisting those students that held up 1 or 2 fingers. Monitor students as they share with a partner. Make sure they are using complete sentences and they are referring to the T-chart adjectives as a resource. During the Split Decision activity allow students to be persuaded to change their mind and move to the other side. Promote healthy discussion and debate on statements that appear heavily "split." This activity provides an excellent opportunity to observe students using academic language outside a sentence frame.

Wrap-up: "Tickets-Out" SW share at least one opinion with a partner using a complete sentence.

Review content and language objectives with students.

Additional SIOP® Features

Preparation	Scaffolding	Group Options
■ Adaptation of content	■ Modeling	■ Whole class
■ Links to background	■ Guided practice	☐ Small groups
■ Links to past learning	■ Independent practice	■ Partners
■ Strategies incorporated	■ Comprehensible input	■ Independent

Integration of Processes	Application	Assessment
■ Reading	☐ Hands-on	■ Individual
☐ Writing	■ Meaningful	■ Group
■ Speaking	■ Linked to objectives	■ Written
■ Listening	■ Promotes engagement	■ Oral

FIGURE 4.5 *Anticipation/Reaction Guide*

**Anticipation/Reaction Guide
for
Elvira by Margaret Shannon**

Directions: Next to each statement, write an "X" in the appropriate column. Be ready to discuss your opinion with the class.

Before Reading		Statements	After Reading	
Agree	Disagree		Agree	Disagree
☺	☹		☺	☹
		1. It is okay to tease someone who is different than you.		
		2. It takes courage to be different and be proud of it.		
		3. It is best to try to be like everyone else so people will like you.		
		4. It is okay to be afraid of someone who is different than you before you get to know him.		
		5. Elvira is a mean dragon.		
		6. Other dragons make fun of Elvira.		
		7. Elvira is going on a trip.		
		8. Elvira is proud.		

THINK-ALOUDS for SIOP® Lesson Plan, Grade 1, Day 3

- How can I make adjustments to assist students who cannot complete the Anticipation/Reaction guide independently? Will all of my students need support and guidance through each question, or only a few? Could I work with a small group of struggling readers while the others work independently?

• How can I further promote healthy debate regarding the students' opinions and predictions? Are students able to provide specific evidence to support their opinions?

• The Split Decision activity doesn't always give an opportunity for every student to respond. In what ways can I assess each student's attempt at achieving the language objective?

PLANNING POINTS for SIOP® Lesson Plan, Grade 1, Day 3

• On the first day of this unit, we planned a background building activity with pictures of dragons. What would a teacher need to do on the following day(s) regarding building background if a new student or one who has been absent joins the class on Day 3 or 4 of this unit?

SIOP® LESSON PLAN, *Grade 1, Day 4: Shared Reading of the Book* Elvira

Key: SW = Students will; TW = Teacher will; SWBAT = Students will be able to . . . ;
HOTS = Higher Order Thinking Skills; SF = Student friendly

Unit: Character Analysis

SIOP® Lesson: Shared Reading of the Book *Elvira*
Grade: 1

Content Standards: 2.0 Reading of grade-level appropriate text.
3.3 Make, confirm, and revise predictions.

Key Vocabulary:	*Supplementary Materials:*
Content Vocabulary: *gobbling, princess, daisy chains, furious, normal, appreciated, mistaken*	Word-Definition-Picture chart (from Day 1)
Academic Vocabulary: *predict, think, believe*	Word-Definition-Picture chart for new vocabulary from text
HOTS: Did you change the way you feel about teasing? In what way? Did your predictions about *Elvira* come true? If your predictions were not confirmed, what happened instead? How would the story be different if Elvira had eaten the princesses?	Word Web with the phrase *Characteristics of a Dragon* in the middle (from Day 1)
	Elvira by Margaret Shannon
	Chart with the following sentence frames: I predict _____ because _____. I think _____ because _____. I believe _____ because _____.

Connections to Prior Knowledge/ Building Background Information:
Links to Students' Background Experiences—N/A
Links to Prior Learning—Show students the Word-Definition-Picture chart with words from the book, *Elvira*. Review all of the vocabulary words on the chart. SW read a story about a dragon named Elvira. Remind them that they have made predictions about Elvira during a previous lesson and to think about those predictions as they read.

Objectives:	Meaningful Activities/Lesson Sequence:	Review/Assessment:
Content Objectives: 1. SWBAT read the story *Elvira* and make predictions about the actions of the character Elvira and other characters in the story during a shared reading lesson. SF: Your job today is to read *Elvira* and make predictions. **Language Objectives:** 1. SWBAT use academic vocabulary when speaking: predict, think, and believe. SF: Your job today is to use the words *predict, think,* and *believe* when talking about the story.	• TW post and orally explain content and language objectives. • SW read the story *Elvira* with the teacher. • SW will stop at key points in the story and predict what will happen next. See Stop and Think (Vogt & Echevarria, p. 90). • SW share their predictions with a partner using the following sentence frames: I predict _____ because _____. I think _____ because _____. I believe _____ because _____. • TW continue reading, stopping to allow students to confirm, disconfirm, or modify their predictions.	Monitor students as they share their predictions. Make sure predictions are connected to the story. If predictions don't make sense, ask students to explain their predictions and guide them to a prediction connected to the text. Allow students to share with the class when a prediction is confirmed or disconfirmed. Use these opportunities to model the language used in the sentence frames.

Wrap-up: SW describe a character from the story using words from the vocabulary charts.

Review content and language objectives with students.

Additional SIOP® Features

Preparation	Scaffolding	Group Options
■ Adaptation of content	■ Modeling	■ Whole class
☐ Links to background	■ Guided practice	☐ Small groups
■ Links to past learning	■ Independent practice	■ Partners
■ Strategies incorporated	■ Comprehensible input	■ Independent

Integration of Processes	Application	Assessment
■ Reading	☐ Hands-on	☐ Individual
☐ Writing	■ Meaningful	■ Group
■ Speaking	■ Linked to objectives	☐ Written
■ Listening	■ Promotes engagement	■ Oral

THINK-ALOUD for SIOP® Lesson Plan, Grade 1, Day 4

• The content standard for this lesson is: "2.0. Reading of grade-level appropriate text." Although students are reading a grade-level text, they are doing so in a supported way through shared reading. This is needed because, as we know, not all students will be able to access grade-level text without support. However, what could I do to provide students with opportunities to read and practice this text independently after the initial shared reading?

SIOP® LESSON PLAN, *Grade 1, Day 5:*
Confirming Predictions about Character Traits

Key: SW = Students will; TW = Teacher will; SWBAT = Students will be able to . . .;
HOTS = Higher Order Thinking Skills; SF = Student friendly

Unit: Character Analysis

SIOP® Lesson: Confirming Predictions about Character Traits
Grade: 1

Content Standards: 3.3 Make, confirm, and revise predictions.

Key Vocabulary:	Supplementary Materials:
Content Vocabulary: *gobbling, princess, daisy chains, furious, normal, appreciated, mistaken, courage, tease* **Academic Vocabulary:** *opinion, belief, confirm, disconfirm* **HOTS:** Did you change your mind about any of the statements? If so, what made you change your mind?	Word-Definition-Picture chart (from Day 1) Word-Definition-Picture chart (from Day 4) Word Web with the phrase *Characteristics of a Dragon* in the middle (from Day 1) *Elvira* by Margaret Shannon Anticipation Reaction/Guide for each student plus transparency

Connections to Prior Knowledge/ Building Background Information:
Links to Students' Background Experiences—NA
Links to Prior Learning—TW review the tallied Anticipation/Reaction Guide from Day 3.
SW confirm or revise their statements on the Anticipation/Reaction Guide.

Objectives:	Meaningful Activities/ Lesson Sequence:	Review/Assessment:
Content Objectives: 1. SWBAT confirm or revise their original opinions and beliefs about the main ideas and concepts of the book, *Elvira* by Margaret Shannon. **SF:** Your job today is to read your opinions and either keep them or change them. 2. SWBAT confirm or disconfirm predictions about Elvira's character. **SF:** Your job today is to read your opinions about Elvira and either keep them or change them. **Language Objectives:** 1. SWBAT read the Anticipation/Reaction Guide in a shared reading lesson. **SF:** Your job today is to read the Anticipation/Reaction Guide. 2. SWBAT tell if and how their original opinions have changed. **SF:** Your job today is to read aloud the sentence frame: I used to feel _____ , but now I feel _____ because _____.	• TW post and orally explain content and language objectives. • TW display and review the Anticipation/Reaction Guide on the overhead and tell students that they will have a chance to change their answers from the left side. • SW read the Anticipation/Reaction Guide along with the teacher. • SW complete all of the boxes on the reaction side of the Anticipation/Reaction Guide, changing their opinions if they want to. • SW will orally share with a partner if and how their opinions have changed using the sentence frame: I used to feel _____, but now I feel _____ because _____.	Again, use a think-aloud to demonstrate how to complete the Anticipation/Reaction Guide. After giving all directions, have students self-assess their understanding of the task with a finger response: 1—I need help. 2—I have a question. 3—I'm ready to start. 4—I could teach this. Once students begin independent work, focus on assisting those students who held up 1 or 2 fingers. Monitor students as they share with a partner. Make sure they are using complete sentences.

. . . . ●

73

Wrap-up: Have students refer to the Outcome Sentences chart displayed in the room. Throw a rubber ball to individual students and have them orally complete the frames. (See Day 2 Lesson.)

Review content and language objectives with students.

Additional SIOP® Features

Preparation	*Scaffolding*	*Group Options*
☐ Adaptation of content	■ Modeling	■ Whole class
■ Links to background	■ Guided practice	☐ Small groups
■ Links to past learning	■ Independent practice	■ Partners
■ Strategies incorporated	■ Comprehensible input	■ Independent

Integration of Processes	*Application*	*Assessment*
■ Reading	☐ Hands-on	■ Individual
☐ Writing	■ Meaningful	■ Group
■ Speaking	■ Linked to objectives	■ Written
■ Listening	■ Promotes engagement	■ Oral

THINK-ALOUD for SIOP® Lesson Plan, Grade 1, Day 5

● As students complete the reaction side of the Anticipation/Reaction guide, their original beliefs may have changed. Students may feel as though they came up with the wrong answer if they change it later. How can I use this situation to teach students about opinions, beliefs, and persuasion? Does this provide a teachable moment to encourage student thinking at a higher level?

PLANNING POINT for SIOP® Lesson Plan, Grade 1, Day 5

● Many children's books provide opportunities for students to think about the author's purpose. Although determining the author's purpose is not an objective for this lesson, it is a common standard for literary analysis, and this particular book offers a perfect example of how the author uses a story to teach students about tolerance and courage.

SIOP® LESSON PLAN, *Grade 1, Day 6: Comparing and Contrasting Characters*

Key: SW = Students will; TW = Teacher will; SWBAT = Students will be able to . . . ; HOTS = Higher Order Thinking Skills; SF = Student friendly

Unit: Character Analysis

SIOP® Lesson: Comparing and Contrasting Characters
Grade: 1

Content Standards: 3.2 Describe character traits within a literary selection, heard or read. 3.4 Compare (and contrast) the characters in a literary selection.

Key Vocabulary:	*Supplementary Materials:*
Content Vocabulary: *fierce, mean, courageous, nice, creative, gobbling, princess, daisy chains, furious, normal, appreciated, mistaken*	Word-Definition-Picture (from Day 1) Word-Definition-Picture (from Day 4)

(continued)

SIOP® LESSON PLAN, *Grade 1, Day 6:*
Comparing and Contrasting Characters (continued)

Key Vocabulary:	Supplementary Materials:
Academic Vocabulary: *compare, contrast* **HOTS:** Think about all the characters. Why do you think the author wrote this book? Do you think she was trying to teach us something? If so, what?	Word Web with the phrase *Characteristics of Dragon* in the middle (from Day 1) *Elvira* by Margaret Shannon Semantic Feature Analysis Chart (see Figure 4.6) Compare/Contrast Signal Words Chart (see Figure 4.3)

Connections to Prior Knowledge/ Building Background Information:
Links to Students' Background Experiences—Review key vocabulary by linking it to characters the students are already familiar with. Ex. "The wolf from *The Three Little Pigs* is *fierce* because he is trying to eat the pigs. Can anyone think of another fierce character?"
Links to Prior Learning—SW compare and contrast the characters in the book *Elvira*.

Objectives:	Meaningful Activities/Lesson Sequence:	Review/Assessment:
Content Objectives: **1.** SWBAT classify character traits from three characters in the book, *Elvira*. **SF:** Your job is to match character traits to the character. **Language Objectives:** **1.** SWBAT orally compare and contrast characters using academic language from the Compare/Contrast Signal Words chart. **SF:** Your job today is to use signal words when comparing two characters.	• TW post and orally explain content and language objectives. • TW display the Semantic Feature Analysis Chart on the overhead and demonstrate how to complete the chart. • Students will determine if the character has the listed trait by coloring the box green. If the character does not have the trait, the student will color it red. • TW will guide the students to complete the Semantic Feature Analysis Chart one character at a time. • SW orally compare and contrast two characters from the Semantic Feature Analysis chart with a partner and give evidence that supports the characteristic. _____ and _____ are similar because _____. _____ and _____ are different because _____.	As the chart is completed, have students share with a partner their thoughts about each trait before determining as a class whether each character has a particular trait. Make sure they always provide evidence to support their opinions. Monitor students as they share.

Wrap-up: SW guess the character the teacher is describing based on his/her character traits. Ex. "This character is courageous and this character is not fierce. Who is the character?"
Review content and language objectives with students.

Additional SIOP® Features

Preparation	Scaffolding	Group Options
■ Adaptation of content	■ Modeling	■ Whole class
■ Links to background	■ Guided practice	☐ Small groups
■ Links to past learning	■ Independent practice	■ Partners
■ Strategies incorporated	■ Comprehensible input	■ Independent

Integration of Processes	Application	Assessment
■ Reading ■ Writing ■ Speaking ■ Listening	☐ Hands-on ■ Meaningful ■ Linked to objectives ■ Promotes engagement	■ Individual ■ Group ■ Written ■ Oral

FIGURE 4.6 *Semantic Feature Analysis Chart for* Elvira

	fierce (eats princesses, shoots fire out of his mouth)	**mean** (likes to fight, they tease her)	**creative** (makes daisy chains, makes clothes)	**courageous** (she left home)	**nice** (made dresses for the other dragons)
Elvira	Green	Red	Green	Green	Green
Other Dragons	Green	Green	Red	Red	Red
Princesses	Red	Red	Green	Green	Green

THINK-ALOUD for SIOP® Lesson Plan, Grade 1, Day 6

- Since this is the final lesson for this unit, I may consider adding a writing component as a final assessment. What support devices (charts, graphic organizers, etc.) have the students and I created throughout the unit that might assist in a writing task? Because they had many opportunities to practice the academic and content language using sentence frames, I wonder if they are prepared to respond to a writing prompt with little or no additional support. Would this type of assessment be a true reflection of what the students learned and can now apply independently? If not, what else might I need to use for additional assessment?

Concluding Thoughts

As we developed this unit, we again recognized the great challenges in developing a unit for emergent readers who may also be acquiring English. We decided that, for the purposes of this unit, we would focus more on vocabulary development, comprehension, and higher level thinking skills than on decoding grade-level text. Although students were provided opportunities to read grade-level text through shared reading experiences with the teacher, we chose to focus more on listening and speaking activities that would promote vocabulary and comprehension development. Is that okay? Of course. Emergent readers who are able to use tools such as predicting and comparing and contrasting will better comprehend text in other lessons that focus on decoding. What a perfect way to practice and apply learned skills.

Literature References

Rosenthal, A. K. (2006). *Cookies: Bite-size life lessons.* New York: HarperCollins.
Shannon, M. (1991). *Elvira.* New York: Ticknor & Fields.
Trumbauer, L. (2006). *A Practical Guide to Dragons.* Renton, WA: Mirrorstone.

chapter 5

Sample SIOP® English-Language Arts Lessons and Units (Grades 3–5)

By Lisa Mitchener and Karlin LaPorta

Introduction

It is sometimes said that children in kindergarten through third grade learn to read, whereas beginning at grade four, students engage in reading to learn. By the end of third grade, students are expected to have a strong grasp of decoding and word recognition skills, and they should be able to read grade-level texts independently with comprehension. With a reduction in focus on decoding comes an increased emphasis on vocabulary development and comprehension. Students begin to rely more on using metacognitive comprehension strategies such as clarifying new words, making predictions, connecting with personal experiences, and summarizing to make meaning of more complex texts.

Students in the upper grades will need much more practice in using specific learning strategies to support their comprehension development. Even though many students are now engaged more in "reading to learn," it is likely that we will have many students in our classes who are not yet solid decoders. The challenge becomes greater with English learners, who are still working toward competency in decoding, but now have to begin focusing cognitive energy on comprehension and making meaning of extended texts in a second language.

So how can upper elementary teachers juggle all of these priorities so that our EL students make progress in language proficiency while they are developing reading skills to make sense of more challenging texts and content? Upper grade English learners will benefit from many SIOP® techniques that support learning and language development. For example, to help ELs access content, reading instruction can be supported by adapting the text, or providing text at the students' independent or instructional reading level, depending on the amount of teacher support. Teaching students specific learning strategies, and planning lessons with these strategies embedded in them will scaffold learning until students become independent readers and can access the strategies independently (see Echevarria, Vogt, & Short, 2008, Chapter 5, for more information). In the following fourth grade unit, we provide many opportunities for students to practice reading, while focusing on developing comprehension through the use of learning strategies.

Unit and Lesson Plans

In this unit, it was important to us to demonstrate how a skill or strategy can be practiced and scaffolded to support initial learning, but then take it that important step further and provide students with the opportunity to show that they are able to apply those same skills independently and in a different context. You will also see that children at this level can be expected to develop opinions and support them with evidence in the text, when they are making and confirming predictions, and when they are comparing and contrasting character traits.

FIGURE 5.1 *Description of Grade 4 Unit and Content Standards*

Unit Focus:	*Character Analysis*
Standards:	1.1 Make, confirm, and revise predictions during reading. 1.4 Use resources to find and/or confirm meaning of unknown words encountered in text. 1.7 Expand vocabulary through listening. 2.0 Reading of grade-level appropriate text. 2.4 Connect information and events in text to life experiences and related sources. 2.6 Describe character's traits within a literary selection, heard or read. 2.8 Compare (and contrast) the characters in a story. 4.1 Participate in discussions to communicate statements that express an opinion. 4.4 Orally defend a position. 3.5 Describe a character's traits using evidence from the text.
Primary Source (TE, tradebook, etc.):	Taro Yashima. (1976) *Crow Boy*. Puffin Books. Lauren Bills. (1991) *The Rag Coat*. Little, Brown and Company. Amy Rosenthal. (2006) *Cookies: Bite-Sized Life Lessons*. Harper Collins Publishers.

(continued)

FIGURE 5.1 *Description of Grade 4 Unit and Content Standards (continued)*

Unit Focus:	*Character Analysis*
Vocabulary:	Content Vocabulary: *patient, proud, respect, compassionate, generous, courageous, envy, regret, afraid, curious, friendly, creative* Academic vocabulary: *predict, think, believe, confirm, disconfirm, compare, contrast*
Supplementary Materials:	Primary resources listed above. 4-Corners Vocabulary Poster (Vogt & Echevarria, 2008, p. 40); see Appendix E, #7 Thesaurus and dictionary for each student or group of students Anticipation/Reaction Guide (Vogt & Echevarria, 2008, p. 82); see Appendix E, #1 Outcome Sentences Chart (Echevarria, Vogt & Short, 2008, p. 170) Prediction T-Chart Chart with the following sentence frames: I predict _____ because _____. I think _____ because _____. I believe _____ because _____. I predicted _____ because _____. My prediction was confirmed when _____. Semantic Feature Analysis Chart (Fisher & Frey, 2008); see Appendix E, #9 Compare/Contrast Signal Words Chart (Vogt & Echevarria, 2008, p. 36)

SIOP® LESSON PLAN, *Grade 4, Day 1:*
Building Content Vocabulary

Key: SW = Students will; TW = Teacher will; SWBAT = Students will be able to . . . . ;
HOTS = Higher Order Thinking Skills,

Unit: Character Analysis

SIOP® Lesson: Building Content Vocabulary
Grade: 4

Content Standards: 1.4 Use resources to find and/or confirm meaning of unknown words encountered in text.
1.7 Expand vocabulary through listening.

Key Vocabulary:	*Supplementary Materials:*
Content Vocabulary: *patient, proud, respect, compassionate, generous, courageous, envy, regret*	*Cookies: Bite-Sized Life Lessons* by Amy Rosenthal (HarperCollins Publisher)
HOTS: Which of these traits describes you best? Why? When have you been courageous? How did you feel? Afraid? Brave?	4-Corners Vocabulary Poster (Vogt & Echevarria, 2008, pp. 40–41); see Figure 5.2 and Appendix E, #7
	Thesaurus and dictionary for each student or group of students

Connections to Prior Knowledge/ Building Background Information:
Links to Students' Background Experiences—How would you tell about yourself to someone else?
Links to Prior Learning—Ask students to name some character traits they have learned about in their character education program. Write them on the board. Tell them they are going to be defining and describing these traits and more using a 4-Corners Vocabulary Poster.

· ●

79

Objectives:	Meaningful Activities/Lesson Sequence:	Review/Assessment:
Content Objective: 1. SWBAT use multiple sources to define and describe character traits. **Language Objectives:** 1. As a group, SWBAT write a definition of a characteristic, which will include a picture and sentence. 2. SWBAT orally present their poster to the class.	• TW post and orally explain content and language objectives. • TW ask students to turn to a partner and describe ("tell about") themselves to each other. • TW read aloud *Cookies: Bite-Sized Life Lessons* by Amy Rosenthal, pausing to discuss each character trait. • TW assign a character trait to groups of students (four students per group) and tell students that they will be responsible for defining their assigned trait using a 4-Corners Vocabulary Poster. • TW reread *Cookies: Bite-Sized Life Lessons*, focusing on the eight characteristics selected. • SW take notes on their assigned characteristic. • TW assign jobs in order to complete the 4-Corners Vocabulary Poster. The jobs are reader, writer, drawer, presenter. • As a group, SW use the book, *Cookies: Bite-Sized Life Lessons*, a thesaurus, a dictionary, their notes, and their prior knowledge to complete the 4-Corners Vocabulary Poster. • As a group, SW present their poster to the class.	Monitor participation of students during discussion of characteristics. Have students share with a partner when a character trait applies to them. Pause after reading each characteristic and spot-check assigned groups to see what they are writing for notes. Give guidance as needed. Spot-check to make sure all partners are completing their assigned jobs. Guide students if necessary. Observe group presentations and tape posters on the wall for reference during future lessons.

Wrap-up:
- Choose one character trait and, on a sticky note, describe yourself using that trait. You can use the sentence frame, I am _____ when _____. Ex. I am proud when I get an A on my paper.
- Review key vocabulary from 4-Corners Vocabulary Posters.
- Review content and language objectives using thumbs up—I met this objective; thumbs in the middle (horizontal)—I need more practice; thumbs down—I need help.

Additional SIOP® Features

Preparation	*Scaffolding*	*Group Options*
■ Adaptation of content	■ Modeling	■ Whole class
■ Links to background	□ Guided practice	■ Small groups
■ Links to past learning	■ Independent practice	■ Partners
■ Strategies incorporated	■ Comprehensible input	■ Independent

Integration of Processes	*Application*	*Assessment*
■ Reading	■ Hands-on	■ Individual
■ Writing	■ Meaningful	■ Group
■ Speaking	■ Linked to objectives	■ Written
■ Listening	■ Promotes engagement	■ Oral

PLANNING POINTS for SIOP® Lesson Plan, Grade 4, Day 1

● As students reach the upper elementary grades, they become more familiar with the kind of academic language used in content and language objectives. There may not be a need to write your objectives in student-friendly language as we did for the first grade unit, but it is still imperative that the objectives be clearly defined and orally reviewed for the students prior to each lesson.

● The book used to begin this unit, *Cookies: Bite-Sized Life Lessons* (Rosenthal, 2006), is a picture book that teaches different human character traits through the example of baking cookies. The author introduces many related vocabulary words and defines them with a cookie baking example, such as, "*Cooperate* means: How about you add the chips while I stir?" Although there are many character traits in this book, we chose to emphasize the traits that correlate to the two books we are reading.

● Until English learners have had many opportunities to work in groups, they may be reluctant to participate fully. Some students may have come from more traditional classroom environments where talking among students was discouraged. With practice and encouragement, these students will become more involved in the group assignments, and as they do, the benefits of practicing the academic language and content will become apparent. Also, by assigning each member of the group an individual task, you can ensure that all students participate and stay engaged.

THINK-ALOUD for SIOP® Lesson Plan, Grade 4, Day 1

● According to SIOP® Feature 17, using a variety of grouping configurations facilitates learning. How might I group my students for different purposes and activities? How can I ensure flexibility in the groups, pairs, and triads, so that students benefit from many different perspectives over time?

FIGURE 5.2   *4-Corners Vocabulary Poster (Vogt & Echevarria, pp. 40–41)*

1. <u>Illustration</u>	3. <u>Sentence</u>
2. <u>Definition</u>	4. <u>Vocabulary Word</u>

SIOP® LESSON PLAN, *Grade 4, Day 2:*
Making Personal Connections with Character Traits

Key: SW = Students will; TW = Teacher will; SWBAT = Students will be able to . . . ;
HOTS = Higher Order Thinking Skills

Unit: Character Analysis

SIOP® Lesson: Making Personal Connections with Character Traits
Grade: 4

Content Standards: 2.4 Connect information and events in text to life experiences and related sources.
4.1 Participate in discussions to communicate statements that express an opinion.
4.4 Orally defend a position.

Key Vocabulary:	Supplementary Materials:
Content Vocabulary: *patient, proud, respect, compassionate, generous, courageous, envy, regret* **HOTS:** Why do you think people make fun of other people? Has anyone ever made fun of you? Have you ever made fun of anyone?	4-Corners Vocabulary Posters displayed in the classroom. *Cookies: Bite-Sized Life Lessons* by Amy Rosenthal Anticipation/Reaction Guide (Vogt & Echevarria, 2008, pp. 82–83); see Figure 5.3 and Appendix E, #1) Outcome Sentences Chart (Echevarria , Vogt & Short, 2008, pp. 170–171)

Connections to Prior Knowledge/ Building Background Information:
Links to Students' Background Experiences—Ask students if they have ever been made fun of or teased by other kids. Ask them how they felt when that happened, and what they did about it? Share with a partner.
Links to Prior Learning—Review the 4-Corners Vocabulary Posters.

Objectives:	Meaningful Activities/Lesson Sequence:	Review/Assessment:
Content Objective: 1. SWBAT read statements and develop opinions and beliefs about the main ideas and concepts of two books. **Language Objectives:** 1. SWBAT read the statements on the Anticipation/Reaction Guide. 2. SWBAT orally and in writing support opinions made.	• TW post and orally explain content and language objectives. • TW display the Anticipation/Reaction Guide on the overhead. (See Figure 5.3.) • TW model how to respond to the statements by reading and completing the first statement with the class. • SW read the remainder of the Anticipation/ Reaction Guide independently or with a partner. • SW either agree or disagree with the final four statements on the anticipation side of the Anticipation/Reaction Guide and write a statement to support their responses. • SW write a brief description about a time when they felt proud. • SW orally share their opinions from their Anticipation/Reaction Guide during the Split Decision activity. Ex. "I feel it is okay to tease someone that is different than you because _____." • Split Decision Activity. In Split Decision, SW stand in the middle of the room. TW	Use a think-aloud demonstrating how to complete the Anticipation/Reaction Guide. After giving all directions, have students self-assess their understanding of the task with a finger response: 1—I need help. 2—I have a question. 3—I'm ready to start. 4—I could teach this. Once students begin independent work, focus on assisting those students who held up 1 or 2 fingers.

(continued)

SIOP® LESSON PLAN, *Grade 4, Day 2:*
Making Personal Connections
with Character Traits (continued)

Content Objectives:	Meaningful Activities/Lesson Sequence:	Review/Assessment:
	read a statement from the Anticipation/ Reaction Guide. SW move to opposite sides of the room (previously labeled Agree and Disagree) to demonstrate how they responded to the statement. TW select students to provide a rationale for their decisions. Students can change sides if they are persuaded to do so.	

Wrap-up: Outcome Sentences (see Figure 5.4)
Have students refer to the Outcome Sentences Chart displayed in the room. Throw a rubber ball to individual students and have them orally complete the frames.
Review key vocabulary from 4-Corners Vocabulary Poster.
Review content and language objectives using thumbs up—I met this objective; thumbs in the middle—I need more practice; thumbs down—I need help.

Additional SIOP® Features

Preparation	Scaffolding	Group Options
■ Adaptation of content	■ Modeling	■ Whole class
■ Links to background	■ Guided practice	☐ Small groups
■ Links to past learning	■ Independent practice	■ Partners
■ Strategies incorporated	■ Comprehensible input	■ Independent

Integration of Processes	Application	Assessment
■ Reading	■ Hands-on	■ Individual
■ Writing	■ Meaningful	☐ Group
■ Speaking	■ Linked to objectives	■ Written
■ Listening	■ Promotes engagement	■ Oral

PLANNING POINT for SIOP® Lesson Plan, Grade 4, Day 2

● Notice that the Anticipation/Reaction Guide used at this grade level includes an additional step. Although students are still asked to agree or disagree with given statements, they are now asked to explain why. This component gets students thinking about the evidence that supports their beliefs and encourages higher levels of thought as they make their choices.

THINK-ALOUDS for SIOP® Lesson Plan, Grade 4, Day 2

● The Split Decision Activity provides an excellent forum for students to express their opinions and beliefs. This type of oral discussion may be new to students at this age.

How can I ensure that students will respectfully agree or disagree with other students in the class? Could I provide a sentence frame for this activity? For example, "I respectfully disagree with you because . . ."

- You will find that in many of our sample lessons, we have provided a review of key vocabulary in the wrap-up section. What are some other ways I could assess my students' understanding of key vocabulary during the lessons in this unit?

FIGURE 5.3 *Anticipation/Reaction Guide*

Anticipation/Reaction Guide
for
Crow Boy by Taro Yashima and *The Rag Coat* by Lauren Mills

Directions: Next to each statement, write an "X" in the appropriate column. Be ready to discuss your opinion with the class.

Before Reading		Statements	After Reading	
Agree	Disagree		Agree	Disagree
		1. It is okay to tease someone who is different than you.		
Why?			Why?	
		2. It takes courage to be different and be proud of it.		
Why?			Why?	
		3. It is best to try to be like every one else so people will like you.		
Why?			Why?	
		4. It is okay to be afraid of someone who is different than you before you get to know them.		
Why?			Why?	
		5. If you respect someone, he or she will respect you in return.		
Why?			Why?	

Write about a time when you felt very proud.

FIGURE 5.4 *Outcome Sentences (Echevarria, Vogt, & Short, 2008, p. 170)*

Outcome Sentences

I wonder . . .

I discovered . . .

I still want to know . . .

I learned . . .

I still don't understand . . .

I still have a question about . . .

I will ask a friend about . . .

SIOP® LESSON PLAN, *Grade 4, Day 3:*
Shared Reading of Crow Boy *by Taro Yashima*

Key: SW = Students will; TW = Teacher will; SWBAT = Students will be able to . . . ;
HOTS = Higher Order Thinking Skills

Unit: Character Analysis

SIOP Lesson: Shared Reading of *Crow Boy* by Taro Yashima
Grade: 4

Content Standards: 2.0 Reading of grade-level appropriate text.
1.1 Make, confirm, and revise predictions during reading.

Key Vocabulary:	*Supplementary Materials:*
New content vocabulary: *afraid, curious, friendly, creative*	4-Corners Vocabulary Posters displayed in the classroom.
Review content vocabulary from *Cookies:* *compassionate, patient, proud, respect, generous, courageous, envy, regret*	*Crow Boy* by Taro Yashima. Prediction T-Chart
Academic Vocabulary: *confirm, disconfirm*	Chart with the following sentence frames: I predict _____ because _____. I think _____ because _____. I believe _____ because _____.
HOTS: When is it okay to tease someone? Why does it take courage to be different? What makes you think that? Why do you feel that way? After reading, have you changed the way you feel about teasing? In what way?	I predicted _____ because _____. My prediction was confirmed when _____. I predicted _____ because _____. My prediction was disconfirmed when _____.

Connections to Prior Knowledge/ Building Background Information:
Links to Students' Background Experiences—Tell students to review their responses on the Anticipation/Reaction Guide and to be thinking about their own related experiences as they read.
Links to Prior Learning—Review the 4-Corners Vocabulary Posters. Tell students that they will be reading a story about a boy who displays some of those characteristics plus a few more. Review academic vocabulary.

Objectives:	*Meaningful Activities/Lesson Sequence:*	*Review/Assessment:*
Content Objective: **1.** SWBAT read the story *Crow Boy* and write predictions about the character actions of Chibi and other characters in the story.	• TW post and orally explain content and language objectives. • SW read the story *Crow Boy* with the teacher. • TW guide the pace of the reading, stopping at key points in the story.	Remind students as they read that this story will help them practice strategies that they will use independently when they read another story.
Language Objectives: **1.** SWBAT write predictions and read them to a partner. **2.** SWBAT use academic vocabulary when writing and speaking: predict, think, believe, confirm, disconfirm.	• TW model the task of predicting using the Stop and Think strategy (Vogt & Echevarria, 2008, p. 90). • SW use the Stop and Think strategy and write a prediction on their Prediction T-Chart. SW write their predictions on the left hand side of the T-Chart and leave space on the right side so they can confirm or disconfirm their predictions as they read. SW use the following sentence frames: I predict _____ because _____. I think _____ because _____. I believe _____ because _____.	Monitor students as they write and say their predictions. Make sure predictions are connected to the story. If predictions don't make sense, ask students to explain their predictions and guide them to a prediction connected to the text.

• SW share with a partner their predictions and explain how they developed them.	Observe students as they share.
• SW continue reading *Crow Boy* along with the teacher.	Allow students to share with the class when a pre-diction is confirmed or disconfirmed. Use these opportunities to model the language used later in the sentence frames.
• TW guide the pace, stopping periodically to allow opportunities for students to confirm, disconfirm, or revise their predictions.	
• On the right side of the T-Chart, SW confirm, disconfirm, or revise their predictions.	Collect T-Charts and assess for student understanding. Make adjustments to Lesson 5 if needed.

Wrap-up:
• SW work with a partner to discuss one of their predictions and the outcome of that prediction. SW use the frames below to assist their conversation:

I predicted _____ because _____. My prediction was confirmed when _____.

I predicted _____ because _____. My prediction was disconfirmed when _____.

Ex. I predicted <u>that all the kids would like Crow Boy by the end of the book</u> because <u>he seemed like a nice boy</u>. My prediction was confirmed when <u>the kids realized they had been wrong all those years</u>.

• Review content and language objectives using thumbs up—I met this objective; thumbs in the mid-dle—I need more practice; thumbs down—I need help.

Additional SIOP® Features

Preparation	*Scaffolding*	*Group Options*
■ Adaptation of content	■ Modeling	■ Whole class
■ Links to background	■ Guided practice	☐ Small groups
■ Links to past learning	■ Independent practice	■ Partners
■ Strategies incorporated	■ Comprehensible input	☐ Independent

Integration of Processes	*Application*	*Assessment*
■ Reading	☐ Hands-on	■ Individual
■ Writing	■ Meaningful	■ Group
■ Speaking	■ Linked to objectives	■ Written
■ Listening	■ Promotes engagement	■ Oral

 PLANNING POINTS for SIOP® Lesson Plan, Grade 4, Day 3

• The content standard for this lesson is "2.0. Reading of grade-level appropriate text." Like the first grade unit, the students are doing so in a supported way through shared reading. In the first grade unit, this was essential for student comprehension.

• The purpose of the shared reading in this unit is to give fourth grade students a chance to focus on the strategy of predicting and to provide evidence that supports the prediction. Later in this unit, students will read a second book in a more independent manner, and will have an opportunity to apply their knowledge to new material, but with less support.

• If you have had little practice with modeling strategy use for English learners, it can be a bit awkward at first. But, it's important for you to give it a try, especially for

ELs. Many students do not understand the processes our minds engage in when we comprehend text. The Stop and Think technique (Vogt & Echevarria, 2008, pp. 90–91) involves modeling for students the thinking processes involved in making predictions. For example, you might make an oral prediction about a character in a story: "Chibi is new at his school. I remember when I was in the fourth grade and I went to a new school and I didn't have any friends. I predict Chibi will have no friends at his new school." Later in the story, you can return to your prediction and explain how you either confirmed or disconfirmed it, depending on how the plot develops. What is important about predictions is not just that students can make them; they also need to see how predictions can help them comprehend better, and this is accomplished when their predictions are frequently revisited.

SIOP® LESSON PLAN, *Grade 4, Day 4:*
Compare and Contrast Characters from Two Texts

Key: SW = Students will; TW = Teacher will; SWBAT = Students will be able to . . . ; HOTS = Higher Order Thinking Skills

Unit: Character Analysis

SIOP® Lesson: Compare and Contrast Characters from Two Texts
Grade: 4

Content Standards: 2.6 Describe character traits within a literary selection, heard or read.
2.8 Compare (and contrast) the characters in a story.
4.4 Orally defend a position.

Key Vocabulary:	Supplementary Materials:
Content Vocabulary: *patient, proud, respect, compassionate, generous, courageous, envy, regret*	Semantic Feature Analysis Chart (Buehl, 2009; Fisher & Frey, 2008). See Figure 5.5 and Appendix E, #9
Academic Vocabulary: Words from Compare/ Contrast chart	*Crow Boy* by Taro Yashima
HOTS: Think about all the characters. Why do you think the author wrote this book? Do you think he was trying to teach us something? If so, what?	Compare/Contrast Signal Words Chart (Vogt & Echevarria, 2008, p. 90). (See Figure 5.6.)
	4-Corners Vocabulary Posters displayed in the classroom.

Connections to Prior Knowledge/ Building Background Information:
Links to Students' Background Experiences—NA
Links to Prior Learning—Review the 4-Corners Vocabulary Posters. Review the concepts of compare and contrast using the Compare/Contrast Signal Words chart. Tell students they will be comparing characters within the story, *Crow Boy.*

Objectives:	Meaningful Activities/ Lesson Sequence:	Review/Assessment:
Content Objective:		
1. SWBAT classify character traits of Chibi, Mr. Isobe, and the other students in the story.	• TW post and orally explain content and language objectives.	
	• TW display the Semantic Feature Analysis Chart on the overhead and demonstrate how to complete the chart.	Use a think-aloud demonstrating how to complete the Semantic Feature Analysis Chart. After giving all directions, have
Language Objectives:		
1. SWBAT orally compare and contrast characters using academic	• SW determine if each character has the listed trait by putting a "+" or a "−" in the box. If there is no	

vocabulary from the Compare/Contrast Signal Words Chart.

2. SWBAT orally give evidence to support comparisons of characters.

---

evidence that a trait is used, then SW write a "?".

- TW model for the students how to use the Semantic Feature Analysis Chart by completing the first character together.

- SW complete the remaining characters with partners.

- With a partner, SW orally compare and contrast two characters from the Semantic Feature Analysis Chart and give evidence that supports the comparison.

---

students self-assess their understanding of the task with a finger response:
1—I need help.
2—I have a question.
3—I'm ready to start.
4—I could teach this.

Once students begin independent work, focus on assisting those students who held up 1 or 2 fingers.

Monitor students and promote discussion between partners as they classify each character trait.

Have each partnership share one of their comparisons with the class. Use this time to ask questions about their supporting evidence and determine if there is a strong understanding of the task.

Wrap-up:

- SW guess the character the teacher is describing based on his/her character traits. Ex. "This character is patient and courageous. Who is the character?" Students can work in partners to guess the characters as well.

- Review content and language objectives using thumbs up—I met this objective; thumbs in the middle—I need more practice; thumbs down—I need help.

Additional SIOP® Features

Preparation	*Scaffolding*	*Group Options*
■ Adaptation of content	■ Modeling	■ Whole class
■ Links to background	■ Guided practice	☐ Small groups
■ Links to past learning	■ Independent practice	■ Partners
■ Strategies incorporated	■ Comprehensible input	■ Independent

Integration of Processes	*Application*	*Assessment*
■ Reading	☐ Hands-on	■ Individual
■ Writing	■ Meaningful	■ Group
■ Speaking	■ Linked to objectives	■ Written
■ Listening	■ Promotes engagement	■ Oral

FIGURE 5.5 *Semantic Feature Analysis Chart*

Crow Boy by Taro Yashima and *The Rag Coat* by Lauren Mills

Character Traits

		patient	proud	respectful	compassionate	generous	courageous	envious	regretful
Crow Boy	Chibi	+	+	+	+	?	+	−	−
	Mr. Isobe	+	?	+	+	+	?	−	−
	Other students at Chibi's school	−	?	−	−	−	−	+	+·
The Rag Coat	Minna								
	Quilting Mothers								
	Other students at Minna's school								

Characters

Key: + = Yes; − = No; ? = I don't know or I'm not sure

FIGURE 5.6 *Compare/Contrast Signal Words Chart*

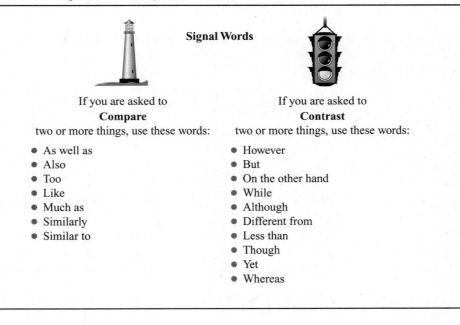

Signal Words

If you are asked to **Compare** two or more things, use these words:	If you are asked to **Contrast** two or more things, use these words:
• As well as	• However
• Also	• But
• Too	• On the other hand
• Like	• While
• Much as	• Although
• Similarly	• Different from
• Similar to	• Less than
	• Though
	• Yet
	• Whereas

THINK-ALOUDS for SIOP® Lesson Plan, Grade 4, Day 4

- How should I determine partners for this activity? Because the task is cognitively demanding, would it be best to pair an English-proficient student with a beginning or intermediate English speaker? How can I ensure that both partners are engaged?

Could I pull the beginners and early intermediate students into a small group and work with them as the others work independently? If so, how will I monitor the larger groups' progress of the task?

- Will beginning and early intermediate students be able to compare and contrast two characters without the assistance of a sentence frame or graphic support other than the Semantic Feature Analysis Chart? What else might I need to do to support these learners?

SIOP® LESSON PLAN, *Grade 4, Day 5:*
Making Personal Connections with Character Traits

Key: SW = Students will; TW = Teacher will; SWBAT = Students will be able to . . . ;
HOTS = Higher Order Thinking Skills

Unit: Character Analysis

SIOP Lesson: Making Personal Connections with Character Traits
Grade: 4

Content Standards: 2.0 Reading of grade-level appropriate text.
1.1 Make, confirm, and revise predictions during reading.
2.4 Connect information and events in text to life experiences and related sources.
4.1 Participate in discussions to communicate statements that express an opinion.
4.4 Orally defend a position.

Key Vocabulary:	*Supplementary Materials:*
Content Vocabulary: *patient, proud, respect, compassionate, generous, courageous, envy, regret* **Academic Vocabulary:** *predict, think, believe* **HOTS:** Did you change your mind about any of the statements? If so, what made you change your mind?	*The Rag Coat* by Lauren Mills Prediction T-Chart 4-Corners Vocabulary Posters displayed in the classroom. Anticipation/Reaction Guide from Day 2 lesson

Connections to Prior Knowledge/ Building Background Information:
Links to Students' Background Experiences—Remind students to continue thinking about their experiences with teasing and being teased.
Links to Prior Learning—SW review their statements on the Anticipation/Reaction Guide. Tell students that they will now read *The Rag Coat* with a partner or in small group with the teacher, making and confirming predictions as they read, just like they did with *Crow Boy.*

Objectives:	*Meaningful Activities/Lesson Sequence:*	*Review/Assessment:*
Content Objectives: **1.** SWBAT read the story *The Rag Coat* and write and confirm predictions about the character actions of Minna and others in the story. **2.** SWBAT reread statements and confirm or revise opinions and beliefs about the main ideas and concepts of two books.	• TW post and orally explain content and language objectives. • TW explain that students will now read the story *The Rag Coat* with a partner or in a small group with the teacher. • SW stop at key points in the story (page numbers provided by teacher) and write a prediction on their Prediction T-Chart using the following frames: I predict _____ because _____. I think _____ because _____. I believe _____ because _____.	Remind students to use the Stop and Think strategy. Monitor small group and model for them again if needed.

(continued)

SIOP® LESSON PLAN, *Grade 4, Day 5:*
Making Personal Connections with Character Traits (continued)

Objectives:	Meaningful Activities/Lesson Sequence:	Review/Assessment:
Language Objectives: **1.** SWBAT write predictions and read them to a partner. **2.** SWBAT use academic vocabulary when writing and speaking: *predict, think, believe, confirm, disconfirm.*	• SW share with their partner their predictions and explain how they developed them. • On the right side of the T-Chart, SW confirm, disconfirm, or revise their predictions as they continue reading. • After reading the book, SW work with their partner to discuss their predictions and the outcome of their predictions. SW use the frames below to assist their conversation: I predicted _____ because _____. My prediction was confirmed when _____. I predicted _____ because _____. My prediction was disconfirmed when _____.	Monitor students as they work in partners. Collect T-Charts for assessment purposes. (The purpose of the T-Chart is to help keep students engaged in the task.)

Wrap-up:
- SW complete the right side of the Anticipation/Reaction Guide. SW share one or two statements with a partner, describing how their opinion was changed and why.
- Review content and language objectives using thumbs up—I met this objective; thumbs in the middle—I need more practice; thumbs down—I need help.

Additional SIOP® Features

Preparation	Scaffolding	Group Options
■ Adaptation of content	☐ Modeling	☐ Whole class
■ Links to background	☐ Guided practice	☐ Small groups
■ Links to past learning	■ Independent practice	■ Partners
■ Strategies incorporated	■ Comprehensible input	■ Independent

Integration of Processes	Application	Assessment
■ Reading	☐ Hands-on	■ Individual
■ Writing	■ Meaningful	☐ Group
■ Speaking	■ Linked to objectives	■ Written
■ Listening	■ Promotes engagement	■ Oral

PLANNING POINT for SIOP® Lesson Plan, Grade 4, Day 5

- As you are planning how to provide scaffolding and support for ELs, it is important to be mindful of Feature 21 in the Practice & Application component: *Activities provided for students to apply content and language knowledge in the classroom.* In this unit, you may have noticed that the fifth lesson is similar to the third lesson, except that students will not engage in a shared reading with the teacher. This gives you the opportunity to assess your students' understanding of the material and their use of strategies taught previously in the third lesson. In the fifth lesson, students are given the opportunity to apply the learning strategies to new reading material. There may still be a need to provide some additional scaffolding for your less proficient ELs and/or readers, such as having them work in partners or small groups.

SIOP® LESSON PLAN, *Grade 4, Day 6:*
Give Evidence from the Text Supporting Character Traits

Key: SW = Students will; TW = Teacher will; SWBAT = Students will be able to . . . ;
HOTS = Higher Order Thinking Skills

Unit: Character Analysis

SIOP® Lesson: Give Evidence from the Text Supporting Character Traits
Grade: 4

Content Standards: 2.6 Describe character traits within a literary selection, heard or read.
2.8 Compare (and contrast) the characters in a story.
3.5 Describe a character's traits using evidence from the text.

Key Vocabulary:	Supplementary Materials:
Content Vocabulary: *patient, proud, respect, compassionate, generous, courageous, envy, regret* **HOTS:** Think about the characters in both books. Why do you think the books were so similar? What lesson were the authors trying to teach us? How could you change the ending to each book?	Semantic Feature Analysis Chart (See Figure 5.7.) *Crow Boy* by Taro Yashima. *The Rag Coat* by Lauren Bills. Compare/Contrast Signal Words Chart (Vogt & Echevarria, 2008, p. 36). (See Figure 5.6.) 4-Corners Vocabulary Posters displayed in the classroom.

Connections to Prior Knowledge/ Building Background Information:
Links to Students' Background Experiences—NA
Links to Prior Learning—Tell students that they will now complete the Semantic Feature Analysis Chart using the characters from *The Rag Coat.*

Objectives:	Meaningful Activities/Lesson Sequence:	Review/Assessment:
Content Objectives: **1.** SWBAT classify character traits from characters Minna, the Quilting Mothers, and the other students in the story. **2.** SWBAT use content vocabulary when describing character traits. **Language Objectives:** **1.** SWBAT orally give evidence supporting character classifications. **2.** SWBAT orally compare and contrast characters using academic language from the Compare/Contrast Signal Words chart.	• TW post and orally explain content and language objectives. • TW display the Semantic Feature Analysis Chart on the overhead and review how to complete the chart. • SW complete the Semantic Feature Analysis Chart for the three characters in *The Rag Coat*, determining if each character has the listed trait by putting a "+" or a "−" in the box. If there is no evidence that a trait is used, then SW write a "?". • TW read the following sentence frames aloud and SW orally complete the frames with a partner. Chibi is patient when he _____. Chibi is proud when he _____. Chibi is courageous when he _____. Mr. Isobe is patient when he _____. Mr. Isobe is compassionate when _____. Chibi's schoolmates are envious when _____. Chibi's schoolmates are regretful when _____. Minna is patient when _____.	Monitor students as they complete the chart. This is the time to confirm that they understand the meanings of the characteristics. Full understanding is expected at this point in the lesson. Provide support as needed. After reading each frame, give students time to think about their evidence. Move around the class listening to responses and providing clarification. Use high-quality responses as models for the class as you proceed through the list of prompts. It's important to spend some time with this activity to make sure they

(continued)

SIOP® LESSON PLAN, *Grade 4, Day 6:*
Give Evidence from the Text Supporting
Character Traits (continued)

Content Objectives:	Meaningful Activities/Lesson Sequence:	Review/Assessment:
	Minna is proud when _____.	are ready to attack these prompts independently in the Conga Line (Vogt & Echevarria, p. 110).
	Minna is respectful when _____.	
	Minna is courageous when _____.	
	Quilting mothers are patient when _____.	
	Quilting mothers are proud when _____.	
	Quilting mothers are respectful when _____.	
	Quilting mothers are compassionate when _____.	
	Quilting mothers are generous when _____.	
	Students at Minna's school are envious when _____.	
	Students at Minna's school are regretful when _____.	
	• SW practice and complete the sentence frames above through the use of a Conga Line.	As you walk along the line monitoring students, make sure that you are allowing sufficient time for students to respond.
	• In preparation, TW write each prompt on a 3 × 5 card.	
	• SW line up in two equal lines (line A and line B) facing each other to make pairs.	
	• TW give each student a prompt card. The student from line A will read the prompt on his card and complete the prompt to his partner in line B.	
	• The partner in line B will evaluate his partner's response.	
	• Student B will then read his prompt and finish the prompt. Student A will evaluate his response.	
	• At the signal of the teacher, students A and B will trade cards and everyone in line A will move one person to the right so they are now part of a new pair. The person at the end of line A moves all the way to the beginning of line A. Line B doesn't move.	
	• This continues until all the students from line A have shared questions with all the students from line B.	
	• Using sentence frames, SW orally compare and contrast two characters from the Semantic Feature Analysis Chart with a partner and give evidence that supports the comparison.	
	_____ and _____ are similar because _____.	
	_____ and _____ are different because _____.	

Wrap-up:
Review content and language objectives using thumbs up—I met this objective; thumbs in the middle—I need more practice; thumbs down—I need help.

Additional SIOP® Features

Preparation	Scaffolding	Group Options
■ Adaptation of content	■ Modeling	■ Whole class
■ Links to background	■ Guided practice	☐ Small groups
■ Links to past learning	■ Independent practice	■ Partners
■ Strategies incorporated	■ Comprehensible input	■ Independent

Integration of Processes	Application	Assessment
■ Reading	☐ Hands-on	■ Individual
■ Writing	■ Meaningful	■ Group
■ Speaking	■ Linked to objectives	■ Written
■ Listening	■ Promotes engagement	■ Oral

FIGURE 5.7 *Semantic Feature Analysis Chart*

Crow Boy by Taro Yashima and *The Rag Coat* by Lauren Mills

Character Traits

		patient	proud	respectful	compassionate	generous	courageous	envious	regretful
Crow Boy	Chibi	+	+	+	+	?	+	−	−
	Mr. Isobe	+	?	+	+	+	?	−	−
	Other students at Chibi's school	−	?	−	−	−	−	+	+
The Rag Coat	Minna	+	+	+	+	?	+	?	?
	Quilting Mothers	+	+	+	+	+	+	?	?
	Other students at Minna's school	−	?	−	−	?	−	+	+

Characters

Key: + = Yes; − = No; ? = I don't know or I'm not sure

THINK-ALOUD for SIOP® Lesson Plan, Grade 4, Day 6

● Reading each frame that will be used in the Conga Line provides students with supported practice before they read and complete the frames independently. What else can I do to help them practice? Would it benefit some of my students to have the frames displayed on a poster or overhead? Are some of the frames more challenging than others?

PLANNING POINT for SIOP® Lesson Plan, Grade 4, Day 6

• Remember that we want to make sure the students are able to read and complete the sentence frames during the Conga Line activity, but we must not lose sight of our content and language objectives. During the Conga Line, students should be able to use the content vocabulary and give evidence that supports the character classifications. While you are reading aloud the sentence frames and requiring oral participation from the class, carefully observe what your students are doing. Are they providing meaningful evidence for the frames? Does the evidence match the characteristic? Are all students participating? If not, what can you do to increase participation? Is there a need to stop and reteach, or are they ready to move on?

Concluding Thoughts

Every grade level has its own challenges. Upper elementary students are expected to comprehend more demanding texts with more challenging vocabulary. These students need to rely on comprehension strategies and will need much more practice using other learning strategies to support reading. This unit offers students scaffolded support as they read through the first text, *Crow Boy*. Activities are completed with varied support from the teacher, small groups, or partners to ensure student success.

However, at this level, students also need to practice and apply learned skills more independently in order for a true assessment of learning to take place. Allowing students to read *The Rag Coat* in various settings (independent, partner, with teacher), depending on the academic and language support needed, gives the opportunity to assess students' understanding of the material and strategies taught previously. Again, ultimately, we want to see how our students apply strategies and knowledge to new material.

Literature References

Mills, L. (1991). *The Rag Coat*. New York: Little, Brown Young Readers.
Rosenthal, A. (2006). *Cookies: Bite-Sized Life Lessons*. New York: Harper Collins.
Yashima, T. (1965). *Crow Boy*. New York: Puffin Books.

Sample SIOP® English-Language Arts Lessons and Units (Grades 6–8)

By Karlin LaPorta and Lisa Mitchener

Introduction

The challenges of succeeding academically increase as students move into middle school or junior high. Along with more rigorous academic standards, pre-adolescent and adolescent students often struggle with hormonal rollercoaster rides as they develop their own social identities and autonomy. Anyone who has taught this age group knows it is a unique time in a student's life (to say the least). For English learners, especially those who are new to American schools and culture during the adolescent years, these challenges are especially compounded.

If you are a middle school teacher, you know the routine at the beginning of the school year. The sixth graders (or seventh, depending on the middle school configuration) come into class during the first week, scared and quiet, unsure of what to do and where to go every time the bell rings. By the end of the first month, they emerge as confident (even cocky) middle schoolers; the honeymoon for teachers is over.

Contrast this scenario with English learners who enter middle school. Many lack the language proficiency to be able to interact with their peers and teachers, there may huge differences in their content knowledge compared to U.S. content standards, and little connection between their schooling experiences and that provided by their new schools (if they've been fortunate to have schooling experiences). For many older English learners, the gaps grow exponentially.

Teaching with the SIOP® Model is extremely important if these students are to make scholastic progress and develop academic language sufficient to prepare them for high school. This seventh grade English-language arts unit has been designed with these concerns in mind.

Unit and Lesson Plans

The primary focus of this Grade 7 character analysis unit is to teach the essential vocabulary and content concepts to enable students to differentiate the types of characters and characterization within narrative text (see Figure 6.1). While students are learning the new and rather abstract vocabulary, they are also expected to make predictions about the characters. In addition, they are expected to be able to compare and contrast the main characters as well as the stories themselves.

FIGURE 6.1 *Description of Grade 7 Unit and Content Standards*

Unit Focus:	*Character Analysis:*
Standards:	1.0 Use word analysis strategies and skills to comprehend new words encountered in text and to develop vocabulary.
	1.74 Comprehend, build, and expand vocabulary using context clues, pictures, and examples from the text.
	2.0 Students read and understand grade-level appropriate material.
	2.72 Make and revise predictions based on evidence.
	3.3 Analyze characterization as delineated through a character's thoughts, words, speech patterns, and actions; the narrator's description; and the thoughts, words, and actions of other characters.
	3.74 Describe internal and external conflict.
	4.0 Compare and contrast the characteristics and qualities of primary characters in literature.
	Written and Oral English Language Conventions
	1.0 Students write and speak with a command of standard English conventions appropriate to the grade level.
Primary Source (TE, tradebook, etc.):	Poem *Me* by Walter de la Mare (Prentice Hall Literature, 2005. Pg. 40 Bronze Level. Pearson Education Inc. New Jersey)
	Seventh Grade, short story by Gary Soto (Prentice Hall Literature, 2005. Pg. 116–121 Bronze Level. Pearson Education Inc. New Jersey)
	The Special Powers of Blossom Culp, short story by Richard Peck (In Richard Peck (2004) *Past, Perfect, Present Tense. New and Collected Stories. "The Special Powers of Blossom Culp."* Dial Books, New York.)
Vocabulary:	Content Vocabulary: *willow, elder, aspen, cypress, forlorn, primrose, individuality, unique*

FIGURE 6.1 *Description of Grade 7 Unit and Content Standards (continued)*

Unit Focus:	Character Analysis:
	Academic Vocabulary: *predict, confirm, justify, internal conflict, external conflict, direct characterization, indirect characterization, motive, semantic feature analysis, character traits, compare, contrast*
Supplementary Materials:	Primary sources listed above Student journal Character Traits Handout (Figure 6.3) Portrait Poem Template (see Figure 6.2 and Appendix E, #8) Anticipation/Reaction Guide + Why (see Figure 6.4 and Appendix E, #1) Prediction T-Chart (Ongoing in student journal) (see Appendix E, #10) Sentence Frames Characterization Vocabulary Chart Adapted 4-Corners Vocabulary Flip Book (see Figure 6.5 and Appendix E, #1) Textbook Glossary Dictionary Response Boards Prediction Sentence Frames Compare/Contrast Signal Words Chart (see Figure 6.7) Semantic Feature Analysis Chart (see Figure 6.6 and Appendix E, #9)

SIOP® LESSON PLAN, *Grade 7, Day 1:*
Building Background for a Thematic Unit on Character Analysis

Key: SW = Students will; TW = Teacher will; SWBAT = Students will be able to . . . ;
HOTS = Higher Order Thinking Skills

Unit: Character Analysis

SIOP® Lesson: Building Background for a Thematic Unit
Grade: 7

Content Standards: 2.0 Students read and understand grade-level appropriate material.
Written and Oral English Language Conventions: 1.0 Students write and speak with a command of standard English conventions appropriate to the grade level.

Key Vocabulary:	Supplementary Materials:
Content Vocabulary: *willow, elder, aspen, cypress, forlorn, primrose, individuality, unique, character traits* **HOTS:** Why do you think the poet used trees and flowers to represent the uniqueness of different individuals? Did this help or hinder your understanding of the poem?	Poem *Me* by Walter de la Mare Quickwrite prompt Student journal Character Traits Handout (See Figure 6.3.) Portrait Poem Template (See Figure 6.2 and Appendix E, #8)

Connections to Prior Knowledge/ Building Background Information:
Links to Students' Background Experiences:
* When students arrive, they will read the poem *Me* by Walter de la Mare together as a class.
* In preparation for students to respond to a Quickwrite prompt, students will discuss what they think the poem means and how they can apply its meaning to their own lives.
Quickwrite
  * What does the poem mean to you? What are some of the unique qualities you possess?
  * Have you ever tried to change who you are to impress someone else? What are some ways people try to impress others?
Links to Prior Learning—Remind students that a Quickwrite response encourages writing as a habit and it promotes critical thinking and focus for the upcoming unit. Students should know to write their response in their daily journal.

(continued)

SIOP® LESSON PLAN, *Grade 7, Day 1:*
Building Background for a Thematic Unit on Character Analysis (continued)

Objectives:	Meaningful Activities/Lesson Sequence:	Review/Assessment:
Content Objectives: **1.** SWBAT connect the meaning of a short poem to their own lives. **2.** SWBAT use descriptive adjectives to create a written portrait of themselves. **Language Objectives:** **1.** SWBAT read and analyze a poem and discuss its meaning with a partner. **2.** SWBAT write a Quickwrite response in their daily journal.	• TW post and orally explain content and language objectives. • TW briefly review the unfamiliar vocabulary within the poem, *Me*. This lesson's primary focus is on connecting the poem to the students' own experiences. • Quickwrite: What does the poem mean to you? What are some of the unique qualities you possess? Have you ever tried to change who you are to impress someone else? What are some ways people try to impress others? • SW respond to questions about their own unique qualities and whether they've ever tried to change who they are for someone else's benefit. • TW model how to create a portrait poem using a template. (See Figure 6.2.) SW use a character traits handout to assist their word choice in assigning unique character traits to themselves. (See Figure 6.3.) • SW discuss their interpretation of the poem with a partner. • SW respond to question prompts regarding their own unique qualities.	 Quickwrite Response: Differentiate, if needed, for levels of English proficiency by providing sentence frames for ELs who need them. Portrait Poem Teacher observation of partner discussions and whole class discussion Quickwrite Response

Wrap-up: Think about a character from one of the stories we've read who you really admire. What qualities does that character possess? Why did that one character stand out among all the rest? Turn and share your response with your neighbor. OR Think about what you learned about yourself today. Use as a Tickets-Out prompt or share with a neighbor.

Review content and language objectives with students.

Additional SIOP® Features

Preparation	Scaffolding	Group Options
☐ Adaptation of content	■ Modeling	■ Whole class
■ Links to background	■ Guided practice	☐ Small groups
■ Links to past learning	■ Independent practice	■ Partners
■ Strategies incorporated	■ Comprehensible input	■ Independent

Integration of Processes	Application	Assessment
■ Reading	☐ Hands-on	■ Individual
■ Writing	■ Meaningful	■ Group
■ Speaking	■ Linked to objectives	■ Written
■ Listening	■ Promotes engagement	■ Oral

FIGURE 6.2 *Portrait Poem Template*

Steps for a Portrait Poem	Example
The first line is "Who am I?"	Who Am I?
Then skip a line and write "I am . . ."	I am . . .
On the next five lines write down family relationships.	John's son Karen's brother Alice's grandson Barbara's nephew Nick's cousin
Then skip a line and write "I am . . ."	I am . . .
5. On the next four lines write down "job titles" that describe you.	a surfer a poet a reader a musician
6. Then skip a line and write "I am . . ."	I am . . .
7. On the next three lines write a word that physically describes you.	tall skinny handsome
8. Then skip a line and write "I am . . ."	I am . . .
9. On the next two lines write down a characteristic of yours.	ambitious imaginative
10. Then skip a line and write "I am . . ."	I am . . .
11. And finally the word "me."	me

PLANNING POINTS for SIOP® Lesson Plan, Grade 7, Day 1

- "Poetry deals with the emotions, just as music. An autobiographical poem is personal—it reveals something about the person writing the poem. It does not have to rhyme. Figure 6.2 provides a simple plan to write your own autobiographical poem. Just follow the steps and—before you know it—it's done" (Belliveau, 2008). This template for the "Who Am I?" poem was developed by Art Belliveau through the Sun Belt Writing Project.

- The Portrait Poem Template is just one example of a simple poem students can write about themselves. Middle school students tend to be more engaged in a lesson and more motivated to learn when they can write and talk about themselves and their interests. The purpose for including the Portrait Poem as the first lesson is to enable students to apply what they are going to be learning in the upcoming unit directly to their own lives. The Character Traits Handout provides scaffolding for students while they are completing the Portrait Poem, and it will be used by students again later in the units (see Figure 6.3).

THINK-ALOUDS for SIOP® Lesson Plan, Grade 7, Day 1

- Consider partner match-ups. Will language proficiency levels affect partnerships? Can pairing limited English students with more proficient students help with vocabulary development? How will I ensure that limited English students participate fully and are not dominated by partner?

- How can I motivate and engage my middle school students in their learning? What supplementary materials can I incorporate to increase student engagement?

FIGURE 6.3 *Sample Character Traits*

Sample Character Traits
(Read-Write-Think, 2004)

able	demanding	hopeless	restless
active	dependable	humorous	rich
adventurous	depressed	ignorant	rough
affectionate	determined	imaginative	rowdy
afraid	discouraged	impatient	rude
alert	dishonest	impolite	sad
ambitious	disrespectful	inconsiderate	safe
angry	doubtful	independent	satisfied
annoyed	dull	industrious	scared
anxious	dutiful	innocent	secretive
apologetic	eager	intelligent	selfish
arrogant	easygoing	jealous	serious
attentive	efficient	kindly	sharp
average	embarrassed	lazy	short
bad	encouraging	leader	shy
blue	energetic	lively	silly
bold	evil	lonely	skillful
bored	excited	loving	sly
bossy	expert	loyal	smart
brainy	fair	lucky	sneaky
brave	faithful	mature	sorry
bright	fearless	mean	spoiled
brilliant	fierce	messy	stingy
busy	foolish	miserable	strange
calm	fortunate	mysterious	strict
careful	foul	naughty	stubborn
careless	fresh	nervous	sweet
cautious	friendly	nice	talented
charming	frustrated	noisy	tall
cheerful	funny	obedient	thankful
childish	gentle	obnoxious	thoughtful
clever	giving	old	thoughtless
clumsy	glamorous	peaceful	tired
coarse	gloomy	picky	tolerant
concerned	good	pleasant	touchy
confident	graceful	polite	trusting
confused	grateful	poor	trustworthy
considerate	greedy	popular	unfriendly
cooperative	grouchy	positive	unhappy
courageous	grumpy	precise	upset
cowardly	guilty	proper	useful
cross	happy	proud	warm
cruel	harsh	quick	weak
curious	hateful	quiet	wicked
dangerous	healthy	rational	wise
daring	helpful	reliable	worried
dark	honest	religious	wrong
decisive	hopeful	responsible	young

SIOP® LESSON PLAN, *Grade 7, Day 2:*
Making Predictions

Key: SW = Students will; TW = Teacher will; SWBAT = Students will be able to . . . ;
HOTS = Higher Order Thinking Skills

Unit: Character Analysis

SIOP® Lesson: Making Predictions
Grade: 7

Content Standards: 2.72 Make and revise predictions based on evidence.
Written and Oral English Language Conventions: 1.0 Students write and speak
with a command of standard English conventions appropriate to the grade level.

Key Vocabulary:	*Supplementary Materials:*
Academic Vocabulary: *predict, confirm, justify* **HOTS:** Why is it helpful to make predictions about the upcoming short stories BEFORE we read? What does it mean if your prediction is never confirmed?	Anticipation/Reaction Guide + Why (Vogt & Echevarria, 2008, p. 82). (See Figure 6.4 and Appendix E, #1.) Prediction T-Chart (Ongoing in student journal) Sentence Frames

Connections to Prior Knowledge/ Building Background Information:
Links to students' background experiences—SW rely on their own personal experiences and
opinions to respond to the Anticipation statements and be able to justify why they feel strongly about
their opinions.
Links to Prior Learning—SW tap into their prior learning regarding other short stories and characters
they've read about through the year in order to make predictions about the upcoming short stories.

Objectives:	*Meaningful Activities/Lesson Sequence:*	*Review/Assessment:*
Content Objectives: 1. SWBAT read statements and develop opinions and beliefs about the main ideas of two stories. 2. SWBAT make generalized predictions about the upcoming short stories. **Language Objectives:** 1. SWBAT write a justification as to why they agree with an Anticipation statement. 2. SWBAT orally justify to the class why they believe their opinions are correct.	• TW post and orally explain content and language objectives. • TW introduce the Anticipation/Reaction Guide and explain that students are going to agree or disagree with statements that relate to the themes and characters of the upcoming short stories they will read as a class. • TW guide students through the first three statements before they finish the rest independently. • SW write their predictions on the left-hand side of the T-Chart and leave space open on the right side for them to confirm or disconfirm their statements as they begin reading the short stories. • SW add to their T-Chart throughout the course of the unit. Depending on their language proficiency levels, students might benefit from Prediction Sentence Frames such as I predict we will read stories about . . . I predict we will read about characters who . . . • Split Decision Activity: This activity is similar to the Anticipation/Reaction Guide, but it is done orally with the participation of the entire class.	• Anticipation section of the Anticipation/Reaction Guide + Why Ongoing Prediction T-Chart/ Ticket-Out Predictions Teacher Observation of the Split Decision Activity

(continued)

SIOP® LESSON PLAN, *Grade 7, Day 2:*
Making Predictions (continued)

Objectives:	Meaningful Activities/Lesson Sequence:	Review/Assessment:
	• Prior to the activity, the teacher will label one side of the room with a sign that reads "AGREE" and the other side with a sign that reads "DISAGREE." SW gather in front of the class. When the teacher reads one of the statements from the Anticipation/Reaction Guide, SW travel to the "Agree" or "Disagree" side depending on their opinion. Once on their chosen side, students should be ready and able to support their position. After respectful discussion, students can switch sides if their minds are changed. • In order to support a respectful discussion, SW use the following sentence frames when addressing their classmates. "I agree with _____ because I think _____." "I respectfully disagree with _____ because I think _____." "I changed my mind because _____."	Anticipation section of the Anticipation/ Reaction Guide

Wrap-up: "Tickets-Out"

On a sticky note, SW write two of their predictions from their T-Chart about what the upcoming short stories are going to be about. They will stick them to a poster entitled "Short Story Predictions" on their way out the door. Examples might include:

I predict we will be reading about a character in an embarrassing situation.

I predict we will be studying different characters in the upcoming unit.

I predict we will be reading stories about characters trying to discover who they are.

Additional SIOP® Features

Preparation	Scaffolding	Group Options
☐ Adaptation of content	■ Modeling	■ Whole class
■ Links to background	■ Guided practice	■ Small groups
■ Links to past learning	■ Independent practice	■ Partners
■ Strategies incorporated	■ Comprehensible input	■ Independent

Integration of Processes	Application	Assessment
■ Reading	☐ Hands-on	■ Individual
■ Writing	■ Meaningful	■ Group
■ Speaking	■ Linked to objectives	■ Written
■ Listening	■ Promotes engagement	■ Oral

FIGURE 6.4   *Anticipation/Reaction Guide + Why*

Directions: Next to each statement, write an "X" in the appropriate column. Be ready to discuss your opinion with the class.

Before Reading		Statements	After Reading	
Agree	Disagree		Agree	Disagree
		1. It is important to try and be yourself even if others don't like you.		
Why?			Why?	
		2. It takes courage to be different and be proud of it.		
Why?			Why?	
		3. You should try to impress others to make new friends.		
Why?			Why?	
		4. Most people know exactly who they are and don't change much throughout their lives.		
Why?			Why?	
		5. It can be embarrassing when you are the center of attention.		
Why?			Why?	
		6. Most people care what others think about them.		
Why?			Why?	
		7. Teachers can relate to their students because they were kids once too.		
Why?			Why?	

THINK-ALOUD for SIOP® Lesson Plan, Grade 7, Day 2

- Consider management issues. Having students move around in the class requires teacher tolerance and strong classroom management. How can I make certain that students are not goofing around? With different language proficiency levels, how can I ensure that the more fluent students won't dominate the discussion? Should I randomly select students to speak? Could I have them share in a small group then "Volunteer their Partner" and share their partner's idea?

PLANNING POINTS for SIOP® Lesson Plan, Grade 7, Day 2

- In many SIOP® classrooms, teachers use Sticks in a Can, a technique in which each student's name is written on a tongue depressor, and the sticks are placed in an empty soup can. Rather than indiscriminately calling someone's name to answer a question, the teacher randomly pulls a stick. With appropriate wait time after pulling the stick, all students must think of a response in case their stick is pulled. What are some other possible techniques to guarantee that all student voices are heard?

- Remember that your meaningful activities should always support your content and language objectives. Within this lesson, students are asked to write a justification as to why they support or don't support a statement. With this in mind, the Anticipation/Reaction Guide has been modified with the addition of a "Why" section for students to complete. Students are therefore able to write their justifications and prepare to orally share their responses as well.

- Notice that sentence frames have been included as part of the lesson to provide additional scaffolding for those students who may benefit from the extra language support. Depending on the language proficiency make-up of your class, you may or may not need to use the sentence frames.

SIOP® LESSON PLAN, *Grade 7, Day 3:* *Building Academic Vocabulary Related to Character Analysis*

Key: SW = Students will; TW = Teacher will; SWBAT = Students will be able to . . . ;
HOTS = Higher Order Thinking Skills

Unit: Character Analysis

SIOP® Lesson: Building Academic Vocabulary Related to Character Analysis
Grade: 7

Content Standards: 1.0 Use word analysis strategies and skills to comprehend new words encountered in text and to develop vocabulary.
1.74 Comprehend, build, and expand vocabulary using context clues, pictures, and examples from the text.

Key Vocabulary:	*Supplementary Materials:*
Academic Vocabulary: *internal conflict, external conflict, direct characterization, indirect characterization, motive* **HOTS:** When authors use indirect characterization, how is the reader able to create a picture of that character in his/her mind? How are the conflicts in a story tied to a character's motives?	Characterization Vocabulary Chart (teacher-made) Adapted 4-Corners Vocabulary Flip Book (Vogt & Echevarria, p. 40, p. 55) (See Figure 6.5 and Appendix E, #7) Textbook Glossary Dictionary Response Boards

Connections to Prior Knowledge/ Building Background Information:
Links to Students' Background Experiences—Think about a time when you haven't gotten along with another person. How did you resolve the situation? How did it make you feel?
Links to Prior Learning—Share examples from other stories and characters from previous texts to reinforce the new vocabulary. (Ex. When we read *Rikki Tikki Tavi*, the boa constrictor provided *external conflict* for the mongoose.) Add the examples to the characterization vocabulary chart to provide concrete examples throughout the unit.

Objectives:	*Meaningful Activities/Lesson Sequence:*	*Review/Assessment:*
Content Objectives: **1.** SWBAT differentiate between internal and external conflict, and direct and indirect characterization. **Language Objectives:** **1.** SWBAT define and illustrate the following key characterization	• TW post and orally explain content and language objectives. • TW introduce vocabulary and concepts using a Characterization Vocabulary Chart. • TW use examples from other books and popular movies to support students' understanding of the new terms. Examples will be added to the chart throughout the unit to enhance student understanding. • SW create a 4-Corners Vocabulary Flip Book using the key characterization vocabulary	Class discussion, Characterization Vocabulary Chart, Wrap-Up Activity 4-Corners Vocabulary Flip Book

terms: *internal conflict, external conflict, direct characterization, indirect characterization, motive.*	terms. TW model how to set up the book and how to complete the first three boxes for each word. (The fourth box will be completed after students have read the stories.)
	• SW use resource materials such as the glossary and dictionary to find the meaning of key vocabulary.	Wrap-up review

Wrap-up: Numbered Heads Vocabulary Review with Response Boards (Vogt & Echevarria, 2008, p. 183). SW get in groups of four and number off. TW read the definition of one of the characterization key vocabulary words introduced in today's lesson. Each small group will briefly discuss which term is correct. TW call a number from 1 to 4 and that person will hold up the response board with the correct vocabulary word written.

Review content and language objectives with students.

Additional SIOP® Features

Preparation	*Scaffolding*	*Group Options*
☐ Adaptation of content	■ Modeling	■ Whole class
■ Links to background	■ Guided practice	■ Small groups
■ Links to past learning	■ Independent practice	☐ Partners
■ Strategies incorporated	■ Comprehensible input	■ Independent

Integration of Processes	*Application*	*Assessment*
■ Reading	■ Hands-on	■ Individual
■ Writing	■ Meaningful	■ Group
■ Speaking	■ Linked to objectives	■ Written
■ Listening	■ Promotes engagement	☐ Oral

THINK-ALOUD for SIOP® Lesson Plan, Grade 7, Day 3

• The key vocabulary being introduced in today's lesson may be totally new and somewhat abstract for many students. Since the characterization vocabulary is the core of this unit, how will I continue to reinforce the concepts and make sure students are truly comprehending the new words? How should I assess my ELs' understandings of the key concepts and vocabulary along the way?

PLANNING POINTS for SIOP® Lesson Plan, Grade 7, Day 3

• By middle school, students should be familiar with using the textbook glossary and a dictionary. However, the reality is that many students may just copy a definition without truly understanding the meaning of the word. This is particularly true for English learners, who may not have acquired the necessary vocabulary to comprehend a complex dictionary definition. In the 4-Corners Vocabulary activity, students are encouraged to write the definitions in their own words and then link their illustrations to the focal concept in order to deepen their understanding of new vocabulary. Although students can share their definitions with one another, the illustrations should be more personal and meaningful to each individual student, so that the meaning can be gleaned by reviewing the flip book and illustrations throughout the unit. This activity is powerful because it contextualizes concepts and vocabulary. 4-Corners Vocabulary charts can be posted throughout the classroom, and changed as needed. Students can also design a personal dictionary using the 4-Corners idea.

FIGURE 6.5   *4-Corners Vocabulary*

1. <u>Vocabulary Term</u> EXTERNAL CONFLICT	3. <u>Illustration</u>
2. <u>Definition</u> *when a character struggles against some kind of outside force such as another character*	4. <u>Examples from *Seventh Grade*</u> Examples from *The Special Powers of Blossom Culp*

SIOP® LESSON PLAN, *Grade 7, Day 4:*
Analyzing Characters/Making and Confirming Predictions

Key: SW = Students will; TW = Teacher will; SWBAT = Students will be able to . . . ;
HOTS = Higher Order Thinking Skills

Unit: Character Analysis

SIOP® Lesson: Analyzing Characters/Making and Confirming Predictions
Grade: 7

Content Standards: 2.0 Students read and understand grade-level appropriate material.
2.72 Make and revise predictions based on evidence.
3.3 Analyze characterization as delineated through a character's thoughts, words, speech patterns, and actions; the narrator's description; and the thoughts, words, and actions of other characters.
3.74 Describe internal and external conflict.

Key Vocabulary:	*Supplementary Materials:*
Academic Vocabulary: *internal conflict, external conflict, direct characterization, indirect characterization, motive, illustrate* **HOTS:** Do you think it is more challenging for characters to deal with external conflict or internal conflict? Why?	*Seventh Grade,* short story by Gary Soto Characterization Vocabulary Chart Prediction T-Chart (introduced on Day 2—Ongoing in student journal) Prediction Sentence Frames 4-Corners Vocabulary Flip Book (Box #4 will be filled in with specific examples from the story)

Connections to Prior Knowledge/ Building Background Information:
Links to Students' Background Experiences—As a quick way to introduce the story, when the students have settled into their seats for the period, ask them to think about **their** first day of seventh grade. What were they most excited about? What were they most nervous about? Give them a few minutes to share their reflections with a partner.
Links to Prior Learning—Remind students that they will be continuing to fill in their 4-Corners Vocabulary Flip Book. The focus of today's lesson is to read the story and cite examples in the text that represent the different kinds of conflicts and types of characterization. As a class, review the Characterization Vocabulary Chart created in the previous lesson.

Objectives:	Meaningful Activities/Lesson Sequence:	Review/Assessment:
Content Objectives: **1.** SWBAT find evidence from the text to support their understanding of the academic vocabulary. **2.** SWBAT confirm and disconfirm predictions as they read. **Language Objectives:** **1.** In partners, SWBAT read a narrative story and make predictions in writing about a character's motives and consequent actions. **2.** SWBAT identify examples of *internal conflict, indirect characterization,* and *motive* within a narrative story and write the evidence in Box #4 of their 4-Corners Vocabulary Flip Book.	● TW post and orally explain content and language objectives. ● TW review the Characterization Vocabulary Chart and stress that the significance of the words *internal* and *external conflict, indirect* and *direct characterization,* and *motive* become much more clear when there are specific examples to illustrate their meanings. ● Before starting the story, SW add a few predictions to the ongoing prediction T-Chart they started in their student journal. TW set up the story and tell the students that the main character is a seventh grade boy who lies about being able to speak French. With a partner, the students can use a sentence frame to write one to two predictions as to his *motives* for lying. ● Depending on the language proficiency levels, students might benefit from prediction sentence frames such as: I predict the character lied because he . . . . I predict his *motive* for lying was . . . . ● In partners, SW read the short story, *Seventh Grade* by Gary Soto. Students will use a "Read Aloud/Think Aloud" approach where one student reads a paragraph aloud and then briefly summarizes what was read with his partner. Students take turns reading the short story in this format so both partners get the opportunity to read aloud and synthesize what's been read. During the "Think Aloud" portion of the partnership, either student can clarify what was read, ask questions, and confirm predictions. ● While students are reading the story, they should be attending to their original predictions about the story and characters as well as the predictions they made today regarding the *motive* for the main character's lie. ● With their "Read Aloud/Think Aloud" partners, SW confirm or disconfirm their predictions by using evidence from the text. If there is no evidence to support their prediction, they can write "No Evidence" on the right side of the T-Chart next to the unconfirmed prediction. If they find evidence to support their prediction, they will write the example from the story on the right side of the T-Chart. ● After completing their prediction T-Chart and reading of the story, TW model how to	Ongoing Prediction T-Chart Monitor to see if sentence frames are needed. Ongoing Prediction T-Chart 4-Corners Vocabulary Flip Book

(continued)

SIOP® LESSON PLAN, *Grade 7, Day 4:*
Analyzing Characters/Making and Confirming
Predictions (continued)

Meaningful Activities/Lesson Sequence:	Review/Assessment:
find examples to support the characterization terms to add to the fourth 4-Corners Flip Book box.	
• TW guide students to find examples of *internal conflict, indirect characterization,* and *motive* within the story. SW cite specific evidence to support each characterization term within the story and paraphrase the example in Box #4 of their 4-Corners Vocabulary Flip Book.	Monitor and adjust as necessary.
• Since there is no direct evidence in the story *Seventh Grade* to support the terms *direct characterization* and *external conflict,* SW write "No Evidence" under the heading "Examples from *Seventh Grade.*"	
• TW explain that SW find examples of the remaining characterization terms in the story they will be reading tomorrow.	

Wrap-up: SW use their response boards to differentiate between the key characterization vocabulary terms reviewed today. TW read aloud an example of one of the terms. SW write the key vocabulary word that matches that description on their response boards and everyone will hold their boards up when the teacher asks them to "Show Me."

(Ex. "I was a nervous wreck at school. I was so afraid that someone would discover my secret, my stomach actually ached." INTERNAL CONFLICT)

(Ex. "Tony walked through the halls with his head down low. He never made eye contact with any of the passing students. Even his clothes were gray and muted as if he didn't want to draw any attention to himself." INDIRECT CHARACTERIZATION)

Review content and language objectives. SW give a thumbs-up or thumbs-down to indicate if the objectives were met.

Additional SIOP® Features

Preparation	Scaffolding	Group Options
☐ Adaptation of content	■ Modeling	■ Whole class
■ Links to background	■ Guided practice	☐ Small groups
■ Links to past learning	■ Independent practice	■ Partners
■ Strategies incorporated	■ Comprehensible input	■ Independent

Integration of Processes	Application	Assessment
■ Reading	☐ Hands-on	■ Individual
■ Writing	■ Meaningful	■ Group
■ Speaking	■ Linked to objectives	■ Written
■ Listening	■ Promotes engagement	■ Oral

PLANNING POINTS for SIOP® Lesson Plan, Grade 7, Day 4

- Notice that we approached the building background section of the lesson as the <u>first</u> thing you would do in the lesson. For that reason, we didn't repeat it within the lesson sequence portion of the lesson plan. It would seem redundant otherwise.

- Depending on the language proficiency makeup of your ELA classes, you might consider pulling a small group of beginner or early intermediate students to read the story with you. Struggling readers would benefit from the extra teacher support and may feel less anxious than if they were trying to read aloud to a more proficient peer. Consider whom you would select for this group.

- Incorporating the Read Aloud/Think Aloud approach takes a fair amount of initial practice and teacher modeling before students are able to effectively and independently read aloud with partners. Students are used to reading a passage aloud and then zoning out while another student takes over. It is important for the students to understand that during the Read Aloud/Think Aloud approach, each student is accountable for what is being read regardless of who is reading. Both students in the partnership should be able to paraphrase and/or summarize what was read, and, more importantly, to glean the main idea behind the passage. This paraphrase/summarize step must be taught, modeled, and practiced by students before you let them do it alone. Once students have mastered the Read Aloud/Think Aloud format, you will notice they have a deeper understanding of the reading material and are actually more engaged in the lesson concepts.

SIOP® LESSON PLAN, *Grade 7, Day 5:*
Analyzing Characters/Making and Confirming Predictions

Key: SW = Students will; TW = Teacher will; SWBAT = Students will be able to . . . ;
HOTS = Higher Order Thinking Skills

Unit: Character Analysis

SIOP® Lesson: Analyzing Characters/Making and Confirming Predictions
Grade: 7

Content Standards: 2.72 Make and revise predictions based on evidence.
3.3 Analyze characterization as delineated through a character's thoughts, words, speech patterns, and actions; the narrator's description; and the thoughts, words, and actions of other characters.
3.74 Describe internal and external conflict.

Key Vocabulary:	Supplementary Materials:
Academic Vocabulary: *internal conflict, external conflict, direct characterization, indirect characterization, motive*	*The Special Powers of Blossom Culp,* short story by Richard Peck
	Characterization Vocabulary Chart
HOTS: How do characters' motives influence their behavior? Are there always underlying motives that drive characters to act a certain way?	Prediction T-Chart (introduced on Day 2—Ongoing in student journal)
	Prediction Sentence Frames
	4-Corners Vocabulary Flip Book (Box #4 will be filled in with specific examples from the story)
	Anticipation/Reaction Guide (introduced on Day 2)

(continued)

SIOP® LESSON PLAN, *Grade 7, Day 5: Analyzing Characters/Making and Confirming Predictions* (continued)

Connections to Prior Knowledge/ Building Background Information:
Links to Students' Background Experiences—Have you ever had to start out at a new school? What are some of the challenges with having to start over? If a new student arrives at your school, what could you do to make him/her feel welcome? Give students a few minutes to share their reflections with a partner.
Links to Prior Learning—Remind students that they will be continuing to fill in their 4-Corners Vocabulary Flip Book. The focus of today's lesson is to read the story and cite examples in the text that represent the different kinds of conflicts and types of characterization. As a class, review the 4-Corners Vocabulary Flip Chart that students worked on yesterday as well as the Characterization Vocabulary Chart created in a previous lesson.

Objectives:	Meaningful Activities/Lesson Sequence:	Review/Assessment:
Content Objectives: **1.** SWBAT find evidence from the text to support their understanding of the academic vocabulary. **2.** SWBAT confirm and disconfirm predictions as they read. **Language Objectives:** **1.** In partners, SWBAT read a narrative story and make predictions in writing about a character's motives and consequent actions. **2.** SWBAT identify examples of *external conflict, direct characterization, indirect characterization,* and *motive* within a narrative story and write the evidence in Box #4 of their 4-Corners Vocabulary Flip Book.	• TW post and orally explain content and language objectives. • TW read aloud the title of the new short story, *The Special Powers of Blossom Culp.* TW inform students that the story is about a new girl at school. With this information and the title of the short story, SW make predictions regarding the character's special powers and what they think might happen in the story. • SW add a few predictions to the ongoing prediction T-chart they started in their student journal. • In partners, SW read the short story, *The Special Powers of Blossom Culp* by Richard Peck using the "Read Aloud/Think Aloud" approach. • While students are reading the story, they should be attending to their predictions about the story and characters. • SW confirm or disconfirm their predictions by using evidence from the text. If there is no evidence to support their prediction, they can write "No Evidence" on the right side of the T-Chart next to the unconfirmed prediction. If they find evidence to support their prediction, they will write the example from the story on the right side of the T-Chart. • After completing their prediction T-Chart and the reading of the story, TW model how to find examples of *direct characterization* and *indirect characterization* within the story to add to the 4-Corners box. Since *direct characterization* and *indirect characterization* can be more difficult concepts to understand and distinguish, the teacher and students will complete these parts of the 4-Corners box together. • Since students had practice finding examples of the other characterization terms	 Ongoing Prediction T-Chart Monitor partners during Read Aloud/Think Aloud. Ongoing Prediction T-Chart 4-Corners Vocabulary Flip Book

yesterday, they will work in groups of three to find evidence to support the remaining terms today. Specifically, they will look for examples of *internal conflict, external conflict,* and *motive* within the story. SW cite specific evidence to support each characterization term within the story and paraphrase the example in Box #4 of their 4-Corners Vocabulary Flip Book.

Wrap-up: SW complete the right side of the Anticipation/Reaction Guide they started on Day 2 of the unit. After reading both stories, they will share one or two statements with a partner, describing how their opinion was changed and why.

Review content and language objectives. SW stand up or sit down to indicate if the objectives were met.

Additional SIOP® Features

Preparation	Scaffolding	Group Options
☐ Adaptation of content	☐ Modeling	■ Whole class
■ Links to background	■ Guided practice	☐ Small groups
■ Links to past learning	■ Independent practice	■ Partners
■ Strategies incorporated	■ Comprehensible input	■ Independent

Integration of Processes	Application	Assessment
■ Reading	☐ Hands-on	■ Individual
■ Writing	■ Meaningful	■ Group
■ Speaking	■ Linked to objectives	■ Written
■ Listening	■ Promotes engagement	■ Oral

PLANNING POINTS for SIOP® Lesson Plan, Grade 7, Day 5

- It is important to make the distinction that today's lesson, though seemingly redundant, is really an example of the different kinds of scaffolding that SIOP® teachers provide. For example, students were provided with prediction sentence frames on the fourth day of the lesson, but on the fifth day, they're writing predictions on their own. On Day 4, finding evidence of the different characterization terms was much more explicit and guided, but on Day 5, students will be more independent. Giving students the option to work in groups of three provides support for those who may still need it. Scaffolding is about *gradual release*, and some students may or may not be ready for complete independence in this task if they are still struggling with some of the concepts.

THINK-ALOUD for SIOP® Lesson Plan, Grade 7, Day 5

- The Day 5 lesson is a perfect example of providing students an opportunity to practice and apply content and language knowledge through interaction. While the partners are engaged with each other, I can assess how well they're explaining, paraphrasing, and summarizing the key content concepts during the Read Aloud/Think Aloud. But, what do I do if some partners are having difficulty?

SIOP® LESSON PLAN, *Grade 7, Day 6: Comparing and Contrasting Characters*

Unit: Character Analysis

SIOP® Lesson: Comparing and Contrasting Characters
Grade: 7

Content Standards: 3.3 Analyze characterization as delineated through a character's thoughts, words, speech patterns, and actions; the narrator's description; and the thoughts, words, and actions of other characters.
4.0 Compare and contrast the characteristics and qualities of primary characters in literature.

Key Vocabulary:	*Supplementary Materials:*
Content Vocabulary: *character traits*	Character Traits Handout
Academic Vocabulary: *semantic feature analysis, compare, contrast*	Compare/Contrast Chart (Vogt & Echevarria, p. 36) (See Figure 6.7.)
HOTS: Is there such a thing as situational character traits? For instance, do people always act the same in every situation? Is an outgoing person ALWAYS outgoing and a shy person ALWAYS shy? How do character traits relate to a character's behavior? How do character traits relate to a character's motive?	Semantic Feature Analysis Chart (See Figure 6.6 and Appendix E, #9)

Connections to Prior Knowledge/ Building Background Information:
Links to Students' Background Experiences—SW read a list of character traits and highlight five traits they attribute to themselves. SW confer with a partner and attempt to identify character traits of others. The class will have a brief discussion on the experience. Was your partner or small group able to correctly identify several of your highlighted traits? If not, what does that mean? If your highlighted traits differed greatly from your partner's identified traits, what does that say about you? (Ex. YOU highlighted outgoing, but your partner predicted you had selected shy.)
Links to Prior Learning—TW review concept of comparing and contrasting using the Compare/Contrast Signal Words Chart and remind students which words are appropriate when comparing and contrasting.

Objectives:	*Meaningful Activities/Lesson Sequence:*	*Review/Assessment:*
Content Objectives: 1. SWBAT analyze characters in a story by attributing character traits based on the characters' thoughts, actions, and the author's description. **Language Objectives:** 1. In small groups, SWBAT compare and contrast characters and their traits and will support their assertions by orally referencing evidence from the text. 2. SWBAT compare and contrast characters using academic language from the Compare/Contrast Signal Words Chart by	• TW post and orally explain content and language objectives. • After students have completed the Building Background activity, SW come back together as a class and discuss the term *character traits* and debrief the partner activity they just completed. TW ask students what they learned about their partner and the *character traits* their partner had highlighted. • Using the character traits handout, orally brainstorm as a class some of the character traits the main characters (Victor and Blossom) in the last two short stories possessed. As a character trait is attributed to either Victor or Blossom, the TW ask the students to think about evidence in the story to support their assertion. This whole group discussion provides additional support for students who may need more clarification on	Teacher observation Monitor brainstorming for accuracy Monitor discussion for accuracy

writing sentences and
displaying them in a
pocket chart.

the importance of character traits and the
effect they have on a story.

- Introduce the Semantic Feature Analysis
  chart on an overhead. TW explain that students will be analyzing different characters
  that they read about within the last two
  short stories in a more formal way.

- TW guide the students through
  analyzing the first character by writing a
  plus sign (+) if the character displays
  that characteristic, a minus sign (−) if
  the character does not display the
  characteristic, and "NE" if there is no
  evidence to support that characteristic.

- TW model by citing specific evidence
  from the text to support each characteristic
  by doing a think-aloud. (Ex. "Blossom
  Culp is eccentric because there are many
  occasions in the story when she acts
  different from the rest of the kids. One
  specific example is when she tells the
  whole class she has special powers and
  then goes on to predict what is in each
  gift before it is opened. This is strong
  evidence that Blossom is eccentric.")

- After discussing a few more characters as a
  whole class, students will complete the
  Semantic Feature Analysis (SFA) chart in
  small groups. While in their groups, they
  will orally provide specific evidence from
  the story that supports personality traits of
  characters in the story.

  Teacher observation during small group work

- Struggling students and EL learners can be
  placed in groups with strong, effective lead-
  ers so they have a positive model for supporting opinions.

- Once students have completed the
  SFA charts in their small groups, they
  will write sentences comparing two
  similar characters and contrasting two
  dissimilar characters on sentence strips.
  Students should use the Compare/Contrast
  Signal Words Chart as a guide when
  writing their sentences.

  Completed SFA Chart

  Sentence Strips

- At the end of the lesson, SW orally share
  their sentence strips and display them in a
  pocket chart for the class to see.

  Small group presentations

Wrap-up:

Review content and language objectives. SW give a thumbs up or a thumbs down to indicate if the
objectives were met.

Use HOTS questions as their "Ticket Out" for today. SW respond to the HOTS question on a notecard to
consolidate their learning from today and hand it to the teacher as they walk out the door.

(continued)

Additional SIOP® Features *(continued)*

Preparation	Scaffolding	Group Options
☐ Adaptation of content	■ Modeling	■ Whole class
■ Links to background	■ Guided practice	■ Small groups
■ Links to past learning	■ Independent practice	■ Partners
■ Strategies incorporated	■ Comprehensible input	■ Independent

Integration of Processes	Application	Assessment
■ Reading	■ Hands-on	■ Individual
■ Writing	■ Meaningful	■ Group
■ Speaking	■ Linked to objectives	■ Written
■ Listening	■ Promotes engagement	■ Oral

PLANNING POINTS for SIOP® Lesson Plan, Grade 7, Day 6

• It is important to mention that Semantic Feature Analysis (SFA) provides a visual representation of all the characters in the story. This helps to support English learners by making an abstract idea a bit more concrete. To promote higher level thinking with the completed graph, the teacher and students can make generalizations about the characters if they see a pattern. For example, "All the characters in *Seventh Grade* are compassionate. Do you think the author did this on purpose?" The SFA can also act as a springboard for a more formal writing assignment. One possible extension activity could be a Compare/Contrast Essay in which students use the SFA graph and the Compare/Contrast Signal Words Chart poster to choose two characters to compare and contrast. The focus of the essay could be on character traits and motivation.

FIGURE 6.6 *Example of Semantic Feature Analysis*

	confident	shy	eccentric	compassionate	easily embarrassed	cruel
Seventh Grade						
Victor	–	+	–	+	+	–
Teresa	+	–	–	+	NE	–
Michael	+	–	+	+	–	–
Mr. Bueller	+	–	–	+	–	–
The Special Powers of Blossom Culp						
Blossom	+	–	+	–	–	–
Blossom's Mama	+	–	+	–	–	–
Letty	+	–	–	–	NE	+
Miss Cartwright	+	NE	–	+	–	–

FIGURE 6.7 *Compare and Contrast Signal Words Chart (Vogt & Echevarria, 2008, p. 36)*

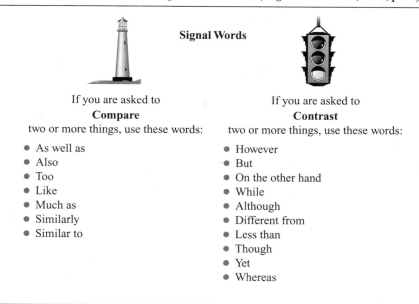

Signal Words

If you are asked to	If you are asked to
Compare	**Contrast**
two or more things, use these words:	two or more things, use these words:

Compare	Contrast
● As well as	● However
● Also	● But
● Too	● On the other hand
● Like	● While
● Much as	● Although
● Similarly	● Different from
● Similar to	● Less than
	● Though
	● Yet
	● Whereas

SIOP® LESSON PLAN, *Grade 7, Day 7:*
Review and Assessment of Characterization Unit

Key: SW = Students will; TW = Teacher will; SWBAT: Students will be able to . . . ;
HOTS = Higher Order Thinking Skills

Unit: Character Analysis

SIOP® Lesson: Review and Assessment of Characterization Unit
Grade: 7

Content Standards: 3.3 Analyze characterization as delineated through a character's thoughts, words, speech patterns, and actions; the narrator's description; and the thoughts, words, and actions of other characters.
Written and Oral English Language Conventions:
1.0 Students write and speak with a command of standard English conventions appropriate to the grade level.

Key Vocabulary:	Supplementary Materials:
Academic Vocabulary: *internal conflict, external conflict, direct characterization, indirect characterization, motive* **HOTS:** Why is character development so important to narrative writing? In general, what have you learned about characterization throughout the entire unit? How will this learning affect how you approach the next narrative story we read? What about the next narrative story you write?	Interactive Study Guide—Study guide questions and answers pasted on to the front and back of 3 × 5 cards to be used as prompts in a Conga Line activity

Connections to Prior Knowledge/Building Background Information:
Links to Prior Learning—Remind students that today's activities are all about reviewing the key concepts and key vocabulary they've learned over the course of the unit.

(continued)

SIOP® LESSON PLAN, *Grade 7, Day 7:*
Review and Assessment of Characterization Unit (continued)

Objectives:	Meaningful Activities/Lesson Sequence:	Review/Assessment:
Content Objectives: **1.** SWBAT identify the significance of character development in narrative writing. **Language Objectives:** **1.** SWBAT orally share their responses to the HOTS questions with a partner in a "Think, Pair, Share." **2.** SWBAT synthesize their learning by verbally asking and answering character-related questions in an Interactive Study Guide Conga Line.	• TW post and orally explain content and language objectives. • TW begin the class by posing the HOTS questions to the class for a brief whole class discussion on the importance of character development in narrative writing. • Students can do a quick "Think, Pair, Share" to solidify their ideas before sharing their thoughts with the whole class. • With the class, TW review the study guide for the summative unit assessment. The study guide includes specific multiple-choice and open-ended questions about characters from each story. (Ex. What was Victor's motive for saying he knew French? *He was trying to impress a girl.*) • The study guide also includes specific examples that students will have to match to their key vocabulary. (Ex. "I was a nervous wreck at school. I was so afraid that someone would discover my secret, my stomach actually ached." Internal Conflict) • After briefly reviewing the study guide together, each student will be given a 3 × 5 card with one of the study guide questions pasted to the front and the answer pasted on the back. • SW line up in two equal parallel lines (line A and line B) facing each other to make pairs. • The student from line A will read the question on his card to his partner in line B. • The partner in line B will answer the question in a complete sentence. The student from line A will evaluate his partner's response. • Student B will then read his question. Student A will answer in a complete sentence and Student B will evaluate his partner's response. • If one of the students does not know the correct answer, his partner can give hints and finally provide the correct answer if necessary. • At the signal of the teacher, students A and B will trade cards and everyone in line A moves one person to the right so they are now part of a new pair. The person at the end of the line A moves to the front of line A. Line B doesn't move. Model Activity.	Teacher observation of "Think, Pair, Share" / whole class discussion Conga Line Activity

• This continues until all students from line A have shared questions with all the students from line B.	
• By the end of the Conga Line activity, all students will have asked and answered all the questions on the study guide, preparing them for the formal unit assessment.	Formal unit assessment

Wrap-up:

Review content and language objectives. SW give a thumbs up or a thumbs down to indicate if the objectives were met.

Outcome Sentences: SW refer to the Outcome Sentence prompts on the board, and when their name is called, they will respond to one of the sentence starters regarding the character analysis unit.

Outcome Sentences (Echevarria, Vogt, & Short, 2008, p. 170)
- I wonder . . . .
- I discovered . . .
- I still want to know . . .
- I learned . . .
- I still don't understand . . .
- I still have a question about . . .

Additional SIOP® Features

Preparation	*Scaffolding*	*Group Options*
☐ Adaptation of content	■ Modeling	■ Whole class
☐ Links to background	■ Guided practice	☐ Small groups
■ Links to past learning	■ Independent practice	■ Partners
■ Strategies incorporated	■ Comprehensible input	■ Independent

Integration of Processes	*Application*	*Assessment*
■ Reading	■ Hands-on	■ Individual
■ Writing	■ Meaningful	■ Group
■ Speaking	■ Linked to objectives	■ Written
■ Listening	■ Promotes engagement	■ Oral

 PLANNING POINT for SIOP® Lesson Plan, Grade 7, Day 7

• The Conga Line activity is a fun and engaging way to assess your students' comprehension of content concepts. Initially, it does take some practice and time, but once students understand the expectations of the activity, the process becomes routine and much easier to manage. For best results, you need to model and practice it more than once before the students do it on their own.

 THINK-ALOUD for SIOP® Lesson Plan, Grade 7, Day 7

• How could I modify this activity if I have English learners who are newcomers or at the beginning stages of English proficiency? How might they still participate, yet not be overwhelmed by the activity?

Concluding Thoughts

As students move into the middle school grades, the reading material and academic language that goes with it become more challenging for our English learners. The primary focus of this unit was to teach students how to differentiate among characters in narrative text through characterization. Students learned both content and academic vocabulary and were expected to make predictions and compare and contrast the main characters and the various stories.

On paper, these academic tasks may seem above and beyond what English learners may be able to accomplish, but the unit is also filled with sufficient scaffolding and differentiated instruction to meet the needs of the wide spectrum of ELs in a middle school English classroom. Context-embedded activities, such as the 4-Corners Flip Book and Semantic Feature Analysis, provided a visual component to help make the concept of characterization more concrete. In addition, the Anticipation/Reaction +Why Guide and Conga Line activity allowed students an opportunity to actually practice and apply what they learned throughout the unit. Although being able to analyze characters and understand the nuances of characterization is just one area within the English-Language Arts standards, our hope is that through this unit, you can see how you may be able to adapt some of your own standards-based lessons to fit the SIOP® Model. At the same time, you will be meeting the needs of the English learners in your classroom.

Literature References

de la Mare, W. (2005). Me. *Prentice Hall Literature, Bronze Level*. Upper Saddle River, NJ: Pearson Education, Inc., 40.

Peck, R. (2004). The special powers of Blossom Culp. *In past, perfect, present tense: New and collected stories*. New York: Dial Books, 50–59.

Soto, G. (2005). Seventh grade. *Prentice Hall Literature, Bronze Level*. Upper Saddle River, NJ: Pearson Education, Inc., 116-121. Original source: Soto, G. (1990). Seventh grade. *In Baseball in April and other stories*. Orlando, FL: Harcourt Publishing Company, 52–59.

Sample SIOP® English-Language Arts Lessons and Units (Grades 9–12)

By Karlin LaPorta, Lisa Mitchener, and Mary Ellen Vogt

Introduction

English learners at the high school level are often at a distinct disadvantage compared to their more English-proficient peers. The academic success rate of many high school English learners is dismal because of their higher drop-out rates, difficulties with passing high-stakes exit exams (despite passing all other graduation requirements), and reading levels that fall far below what is required to be successful in content classes. In addition, many native-born students who are classified as limited English proficient, despite years of schooling in the United States, still score far below their peers on national assessments (Biancarosa & Snow, 2004; National

Center for Education Statistics, 2002; Parish, Merikel, Perez, Linquanti, Socias, & Spain, 2006).

Add to these difficulties the challenges of moving through the adolescent years, perhaps in a different culture with new rules about how to be a teenager, and we end up with many high school English learners who are frustrated and confused, and who are reluctant to speak English or read aloud in front of others. Many of these same ELs are also eager to learn English *and* be successful in school.

A critical issue for many of these students is that the end of their public K–12 education is looming. In order to graduate from high school, their content and language learning must be accelerated if they are to finish in a timely manner and be proficient in English. Therefore, especially for these English learners, their content teachers must be well-trained in the SIOP® Model, and able to implement the components and features consistently and systematically in every lesson.

Unit and Lesson Plans

To demonstrate that it is possible to use your adopted curriculum materials and incorporate the SIOP® Model's components and features, the following tenth grade lesson plans were developed from an extended unit on characterization in the anthology, *Holt Literature & Language Arts* (2003). In this particular anthology, there are ten chapters (or units), and the chapter used for developing this unit is second in the book, ostensibly falling in the first semester of the school year. Like the other units in this book, the focus of the unit and lesson plans is on character analysis and development, and both primary and secondary sources will be used.

A timeline for completing the unit in the Holt literature program would probably be about a month if all the lessons, including vocabulary, spelling, and grammar, were taught. For the purposes of this book, we're including an abbreviated unit for approximately 6 to 8 days for class periods of about fifty-five minutes, with the understanding that things happen in classrooms to disrupt the flow, so one day's lesson may well move into the next day, if needed. The lessons are designed for a heterogeneous group of tenth graders, including English learners at various levels of English proficiency.

FIGURE 7.1 *Description of Grade 10 Unit and Content Standards*

Unit Focus:	*Character: Using Primary and Secondary Sources*
Standards:	Reading Comprehension 2.5 Extend ideas presented in primary or secondary sources through original analysis, evaluation, and elaboration. Literary Response and Analysis 3.3 Analyze interactions between main and subordinate characters in a literary text (e.g., internal and external conflicts, motivations, relationships, influences) and explain the way those interactions affect the plot. 3.4 Determine characters' traits by what the characters say about themselves in narration, dialogue, dramatic monologue, and soliloquy. 3.10 Identify and describe the function of dialogue, scene designs, soliloquies, asides, and character foils in dramatic literature. Writing Applications 2.1 Write biographical or autobiographical narratives or short stories.

(continued)

· ●

121

Unit Focus:	Character: Using Primary and Secondary Sources
	a. Locate scenes and incidents in specific places.
	b. Describe with concrete sensory details the sights, sounds, and smells of a scene and the specific actions, movements, gestures, and feelings of the characters; use interior monologue to depict the character's feelings.
Primary Source (TE, tradebook, etc.):	Chapter 2: Character: Using Primary and Secondary Sources. In *Holt Literature & Language Arts* (Fourth Course: Grade 10). Austin, TX: Holt, Rinehart and Winston, 73–145.
	Freeman, R. L. (2003). Interview with Alice Walker. In *Holt Literature & Language Arts* (Fourth Course: Grade 10). Austin, TX: Holt, Rinehart and Winston, 89–90.
	Leggett, J. (2003). Characters: The Actors in a Story. In *Holt Literature & Language Arts* (Fourth Course: Grade 10). Austin, TX: Holt, Rinehart and Winston, 74–75.
	Leggett, J. (2003). Character Interactions: Relationships and Conflicts. In *Holt Literature & Language Arts* (Fourth Course: Grade 10). Austin, TX: Holt, Rinehart and Winston, 96–97.
	Masters, E. L. (2003). Lucinda Matlock. In *Holt Literature & Language Arts* (Fourth Course: Grade 10). Austin, TX: Holt, Rinehart and Winston, 85.
	Tan, A. (2003). Two Kinds. In *Holt Literature & Language Arts* (Fourth Course: Grade 10). Austin, TX: Holt, Rinehart and Winston, 99–107.
	Walker, A. (2003). Everyday Use. In *Holt Literature & Language Arts* (Fourth Course: Grade 10). Austin, TX: Holt, Rinehart and Winston, 77–83
Unit Vocabulary:	Content vocabulary: *sidle, furtive, cowering, character traits; flat, round, stock and dynamic characters, protagonist, conflict, biographical narrative, sensory details*
	Academic vocabulary: *narrator, dialogue, interview, primary source, direct and indirect characterization, compare/contrast, defend a position, sequence of events, anecdotes*
Supplementary Materials:	Semantic Feature Analysis (Buehl, 2009; Fisher & Frey, 2008) (see Figure 7.6 and Appendix E, #9) Character Map (Macon, Bewell, & Vogt, 1991, p. 19) (see Figure 7.2 and Appendix E, #4) Word Web (see Figure 7.7 and Appendix E, #11) Students' Personal Academic Glossary Bio Pyramid (adapted from Story Pyramid; Macon, Bewell, & Vogt, 1991, p. 24) (see Figure 7.9 and Appendix E, #3) Dinner Party (Vogt & Echevarria, 2008, pp. 105–106)

SIOP® LESSON PLAN, *Grade 10, Day 1:* *Introduction to Character Analysis and Content Vocabulary*

Key: SW = Students will; TW = Teacher will; SWBAT = Students will be able to . . . ; HOTS = Higher Order Thinking Skills

Unit: Character: Using Primary and Secondary Sources

SIOP® Lesson: Introduction to Character Analysis and Content Vocabulary
Grade: 10

Content Standards: 3.4 Determine characters' traits by what the characters say about themselves in narration, dialogue, dramatic monologue, and soliloquy.

(continued)

SIOP® LESSON PLAN, *Grade 10, Day 1:*
Introduction to Character Analysis and
Content Vocabulary (continued)

Key Vocabulary:	Supplementary Materials:
Content Vocabulary: *flat character, round character, stock character*	Handout with interview questions (See Figure 7.3.)
Academic Vocabulary: *interview, primary source*	Character Map handout (Macon, Bewell, & Vogt, 1991, p. 19) for each student (See Figure 7.2 and Appendix E, #4)
(Note: As the unit progresses, some of the "content vocabulary" will evolve into "academic vocabulary" with continued practice.)	Handout with partially completed paragraph for the written description (See Figure 7.4.)
HOTS:	
Based on an interview of your partner, how would you describe him or her in order to create a "round character"?	

Connections to Prior Knowledge/ Building Background Information:
Links to Students' Background Experiences—In pairs, SW interview each other about: (1) interests, (2) favorite sports, and (3) goals for the future.
Links to Prior Learning—Review the definition of descriptive adjectives and brainstorm some examples. List on the board. Review the process for the Jigsaw activity.

Objectives:	Meaningful Activities: Lesson Sequence:	Review/Assessment:
Content Objectives: **1.** SWBAT determine the interests, favorite sports, goals for the future, and three character traits of a partner. **2.** SWBAT distinguish among flat characters, round characters, and stock characters. **Language Objectives:** **1.** SWBAT interview a peer about his or her interests, favorite sports, goals for the future, and describe them in writing on a Character Map. **2.** SWBAT use descriptive adjectives to describe three character traits of the fellow students they interviewed. **3.** SWBAT read in a Jigsaw Activity information about how authors write about characters.	• TW orally review the content and language objectives posted on a pocket chart, reviewing academic vocabulary as objectives are discussed. • TW review the definition of descriptive adjectives and brainstorm with students some adjectives that could be used to describe people. • TW count off students so everyone has a partner (or is in a triad). • TW go over the interview directions written on the board (use simple drawings, if necessary, for newcomers or beginning English speakers): 1. Interview your partner (for 5 minutes). 2. Ask about his or her interests, favorite sports, and goals for the future, and ask for several specific examples. 3. Switch roles for 5 more minutes (interviewer and interviewee). 4. Return to your seats. 5. On your Character Map, write your partner's name in the center box. 6. On the top three ovals, write Interests, Favorite Sports, Goals. 7. Fill in as many circles as you can with specific examples you learned from your interview. 8. Write the word "traits" in the fourth oval. 9. Based on your interview, write three character traits of the person you interviewed. Use descriptive adjectives!	Check for understanding of objectives. Explain that the new vocabulary will be defined during the lesson. Monitor students' understanding of the directions. Provide a half-sheet with the interview questions to those who may need them. Monitor and assist as needed. Remind ELs to look at the descriptive adjective examples on the board.

10. After you have completed the Character Map, meet with your partner to check for accuracy.
11. Make changes as needed.

- TW explain that an interview represents a primary source for authors and that they will be reading a primary source interview later in the unit.
- TW review steps for the Jigsaw activity for reading texts (Echevarria, Vogt, & Short, 2008, p. 159)
- TW direct students to pp. 74–75 in their anthologies.
- In groups of four or five, SW Jigsaw read the section "Characters" (by J. Leggett). The brief sections are:

  1. What they tell us
  2. Creating characters: How do they do it?
  3. Dramatic Monologue and Soliloquy
  4. Flat, round, and stock characters.

- Each student will read and be responsible for one section. He or she is responsible for sharing the information with the others in the group.
- On an index card, SW write one content vocabulary word from his or her section of the text read. On the other side of the card, SW write a brief definition of the word. SW will turn cards in at the end of the period.
- Homework: Write a brief paragraph (7–10 sentences or so) about your partner, using your completed Character Map as a guide. Describe your partner as a round character, not flat or stock.

Partner less-proficient ELs (in terms of English proficiency) with another student for the reading, sharing, and summarizing steps of Jigsaw.

If needed, form a small group of ELs and struggling readers and work with them on reading each section.

TW check definitions for accuracy and save them for the next lesson.

TW review the meaning of traits ("special qualities") to make sure everyone understands the meaning.

For ELs with little English proficiency, provide a partially completed paragraph so students can fill in the missing information (see Figure 7.4).

Review the meaning of "round character," with examples of why descriptive adjectives are necessary when writing a description of a "round character."

Wrap-up: TW read some of the definitions to spot-check for students' ability to identify the content vocabulary.

Review content and language objectives. SW respond with fingers in front of their chests so only the teacher can see: (1) Yes, I got it, (2) I'm a bit confused still, (3) I'm lost.

Additional SIOP® Features

Preparation	*Scaffolding*	*Group Options*
■ Adaptation of content	■ Modeling	☐ Whole class
■ Links to background	■ Guided practice	■ Small groups
■ Links to past learning	■ Independent practice	■ Partners
■ Strategies incorporated	■ Comprehensible input	■ Independent

Integration of Processes	*Application*	*Assessment*
■ Reading	■ Hands-on	■ Individual
■ Writing	■ Meaningful	■ Group
■ Speaking	■ Linked to objectives	■ Written
■ Listening	■ Promotes engagement	■ Oral

PLANNING POINTS for SIOP® Lesson Plan, Grade 10, Day 1

- It's difficult to identify one component of the SIOP® Model as being more important than another. However, Building Background may be one of the most critical components for English learners' success when embarking on a unit of study. If ELs in your class have little prior knowledge or experience with the content concepts you are teaching, even a carefully planned lesson will fail if you have not provided adequate background building. When designing the first lesson for this unit, we were mindful that although most high school students watch television and movies and know what "characters" are in these media, they may have little background in recognizing how authors (or screenwriters) create fully developed characters, especially in varied genres of literature. Therefore, we decided to spend an entire period building background for this unit about the role of character in literary analysis. Note how the lesson is differentiated for students' varying reading, writing, and English language proficiencies, and yet there is an expectation that all students will meet the content and language objectives. How they get there (process) and what they submit for the homework assignment (product) differ somewhat.

THINK-ALOUDS for SIOP® Lesson Plan, Grade 10, Day 1

- Whenever high school students are partnered for in-class activities, there's always an issue about whether the teacher should form the partnerships or whether students should be allowed to work with whomever they wish. I wonder for this particular activity (the interview), if it would be better to let students select someone they want to interview. If I allow choices, will students take the activity as seriously as they would if they're numbered off? I want students to do the interviews not only to develop the Character Map and paragraph but also because we'll be reading an interview in a few days as part of the genre study and conducting a formal interview later on in the unit.

  Another issue is what if I number them off, and two students are partnered and neither is strong academically nor English proficient? Is there another technique I could use to decide who will interview whom?

- One way I could differentiate this lesson is by giving higher achieving students the option of asking their own interview questions, and providing the interview questions only for those who need additional scaffolding. Since my objective is to have them determine their interviewee's traits, would it be better to just let students come up with their own questions? If I do that, this activity will take longer than I want. I'm planning on only about ten minutes for the interview (five for each interview), and five to seven minutes for the Character Map. My objective is less about the actual interviewing process than it is about the information the interview will yield, so students can understand that character traits in a "round character" come from knowing the three-dimensional qualities of real-life people. So, I think it will be better to just provide the interview questions to move the activity more quickly while students are interacting with each other in a meaningful way.

PLANNING POINTS for SIOP® Lesson Plan, Grade 10, Days 2–3

- As you certainly know, a lesson like this—with a lengthy grade-level piece of text that must be read by students, including English learners—is always a big challenge. Too often, teachers just assign the reading, assuming that students who can't read it won't read

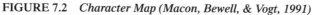
FIGURE 7.2 *Character Map (Macon, Bewell, & Vogt, 1991)*

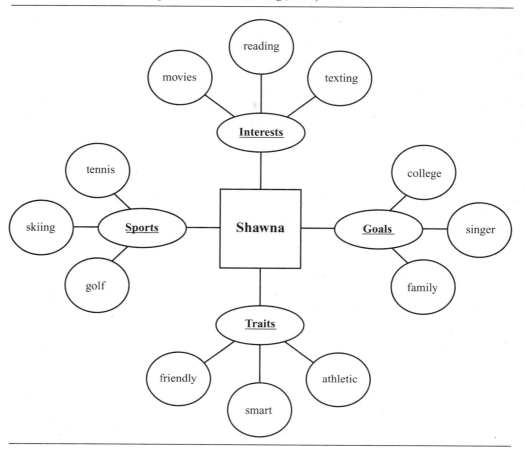

FIGURE 7.3 *Interview Questions for Partners*

1. What are three things you are interested in?
2. What are three sports you enjoy?
3. What are three goals you have for the future?

it, or they decide to read the entire piece aloud to the class, thinking it's the only way that students will be exposed to the text. For a variety of ways to involve students in reading grade-level texts, see Alternatives for Text Reading in Chapter 2, pp. 25–28.

FIGURE 7.4 *Paragraph Frame for Beginning English Speakers*

    The person I interviewed is named _____. She is interested in many things, including _____, _____, and _____. I also learned that _____ (name) _____ enjoys several sports, including _____, _____, and _____. After talking with <u>him or her</u>, I think <u>he or she</u> is _____ (descriptive adjectives) _____, _____, and _____.

(Note: The information for the blanks comes from the completed Character Map. An English learner is expected to copy the completed paragraph frame into a written paragraph. English learners who have intermediate or advanced English fluency should be able to write a paragraph on their own, without the paragraph frame.)

SIOP® LESSON PLAN, *Grade 10, Days 2–3:*
Examining Characters in "Everyday Use"

Key: SW = Students will; TW = Teacher will; SWBAT = Students will be able to . . . ;
HOTS = Higher Order Thinking Skills

Unit: Character: Using Primary and Secondary Sources

SIOP® Lesson: Examining Characters in "Everyday Use: For your Grandmama" by Alice Walker
Grade: 10

Content Standards: 3.4 Determine characters' traits by what the characters say about themselves in narration, dialogue, dramatic monologue, and soliloquy.

Key Vocabulary:	*Supplementary Materials:*
Content Vocabulary: *sidle, furtive, cowering, traits*	Students' homework paragraphs from their interviews in Day 1 lesson
Academic Vocabulary: *compare and contrast, infer, direct characterization, indirect characterization, dialogue*	Students' vocabulary cards from Day 1 lesson
HOTS:	Semantic Feature Analysis (Buehl, 2009; Fisher & Frey, 2008) handout for each student (See Figure 7.6.)
● Statements from Anticipation/Reaction Guide + Why, such as: It is a parent's responsibility to provide for the emotional and physical needs of their children into their adulthood: Agree or Disagree? Why?	Transparency of blank Semantic Feature Analysis (SFA) (See Figure 7.6 and Appendix E, #9)
● How does Alice Walker use direct characterization when depicting Mama?	Anticipation/Reaction Guide + Why (Buehl, 2009) (See Figure 7.5 and Appendix E, #2)
● How does Alice Walker use indirect characterization to depict Maggie and Dee?	Sticky notes
	"Everyday Use" by Alice Walker (short story)

Connections to Prior Knowledge/ Building Background Information:
Links to Students' Background Experiences—SW orally share their paragraph descriptions with their partners, focusing on the use of descriptive adjectives in the traits described.
Links to Prior Learning—SW review academic vocabulary and definitions from the previous day with a Mix-Mix-Trade activity.

Objectives:	*Meaningful Activities/Lesson Sequence:*	*Review/Assessment:*
Content Objectives: 1. SWBAT take a stand, with justification, on a controversial issue. 2. SWBAT compare and contrast direct and indirect characterization. 3. SWBAT identify and match character traits to the characters in "Everyday Use."	● TW review content and language objectives with students, clarifying any words as necessary. ● TW ask partners from the previous day to reunite to share their character trait paragraphs. ● TW ask for 2–3 volunteers to orally share their paragraphs. Ask for examples of how the paragraph demonstrated a description of a round character (rather than flat or stock). SW turn in paragraphs to teacher.	Circulate among partners, listening to paragraphs; note use of descriptive adjectives.
Language Objectives: 1. SWBAT list in writing direct characterization traits through characters' words,	● TW distribute vocabulary cards from the previous day. SW engage in a Mix-Mix-Trade (an adapted Conga Line), during which they roam until the teacher signals them to stop. Facing a partner, one student reads the definition on his or her card.	TW monitor the Mix-Mix-Trade to determine if students know the vocabulary, and reteach as needed.

thoughts, speech patterns, and actions.

2. SWBAT list in writing indirect characterization traits through the narrator's description.

3. SWBAT role play or identify from another student's role play the meanings of the story's content vocabulary: (*cowering, sidle, furtive, cowering, rifling, oppress, traits*)

The other student will try to identify the word defined, and will then do the same with his/her card. They trade cards and roam until the signal; the process is repeated 5–6 times, until all words are reviewed.

- TW distribute the Anticipation/Reaction Guide + Why Guide. TW read aloud the opening statement; for ELs (in a small group), TW also read aloud the statements. SW complete the guide.

- SW return to their seats, open books to p. 83. TW introduce Alice Walker, author.

- TW introduce content vocabulary defined on p. 76. Students volunteer to role-play meanings while the class tries to figure out the words. SW refer to definitions (Holt *Literature & Language Arts,* 2003, p. 76) while peers role play:

1. A *cowering* commoner who is trying to *sidle* up to a king;
2. The actions of a *furtive* person *rifling* through your binder.
3. A scene in which guards *oppress* a prisoner.

- TW introduce "Everyday Use" on p. 77 of the anthology. TW explain that this is a story set in the 1960s with interesting characters who make up a family: Mama and her daughters Maggie and Dee.

- Problems arise when Maggie arrives from out of town, planning on taking her grandmother's quilt, a family heirloom.

- Ask students to note on sticky notes any character traits, both direct and indirect, as they are reading, some of which they may need to *infer.*

- Remind students to look carefully at the dialogue in the story. How does the dialogue give clues to character traits? Use sticky notes to mark dialogue passages that reveal traits.

- TW begin orally reading the story to first break on p. 78.

- Distribute copies of the Semantic Feature Analysis.

- On the SFA transparency, TW model how students should list the character traits they have identified across the top of the SFA ("features").

- TW model how to add the characters' names down the side of the SFA: Mama, Maggie, and Dee.

English learners, especially at early stages of learning the language, might benefit from having a partner with whom he or roams, rather than having to do the Mix-Mix-Trade all alone.

Students are familiar with the Anticipation/Reaction Guide + Why, so a quick review is all that is necessary. ELs will receive small group assistance to help them get started. TW monitor for ELs' understandings.

Monitor and clarify as needed.

Ask for a student volunteer to define and give an example of *inference*; clarify as needed.

Review meaning of *dialogue*. Have students identify examples of dialogue in the story.

Monitor by having students share traits and list them on a transparency of a SFA.

For ELs and less proficient readers, model how to find direct and indirect characterizations in the story; review how to find clue words and infer character traits from them.

(continued)

SIOP® LESSON PLAN, *Grade 10, Days 2–3:*
Examining Characters in "Everyday Use" (continued)

Meaningful Activities/Lesson Sequence:	Review/Assessment:
• TW model how to determine if there is a match between a character and each of the traits. Mark a match with a "+" and in a box where there is no match, mark the box with "−". If there's a question, mark a "?". • Proficient readers will continue reading silently, noting other character traits on their SFA charts. • Less proficient readers can read in small groups or with the teacher, noting other character traits on their SFA charts. • When students have completed the reading, have them complete the SFA, matching traits to the three characters. • With their table groups, have students compare their SFA charts with each other. If there are differences in opinion, have students return to the story and character descriptions to justify their decisions. • If some students finish early, they can begin their homework assignment: Read the brief interview on p. 89 of Alice Walker, who is also a quilter. Based on Ms. Walker's responses to the interviewer, what character traits describe this Pulitzer Prize-winning author? Add her name and the traits to the SFA chart, and look for matches across the chart's list of traits.	Monitor ELs as they are writing and matching on the SFA. They may write words/phrases, but not understand them. Intervene and help as needed. Some ELs may need to hear the interview selection read aloud prior to doing their homework assignment; if possible, have tapes of the interview available for them to use. More proficient readers, who have completed their work, could also tape the Alice Walker interview for ELs. Review, if necessary, how to determine in an interview which are the interviewer's words and which are Alice Walker's. Review meanings of key content and academic vocabulary; pull name sticks from a can for final review.

Wrap-up: SW complete the Reaction side of the Anticipation/Reaction + Why Guide, including new justifications based on "Everyday Use," if opinions have changed. Discuss.

Review content and language objectives with students.

Additional SIOP® Features

Preparation	Scaffolding	Group Options
☐ Adaptation of content*	■ Modeling	■ Whole class
■ Links to background	■ Guided practice	■ Small groups
■ Links to past learning	■ Independent practice	■ Partners
■ Strategies incorporated	■ Comprehensible input	■ Independent

Integration of Processes	Application	Assessment
■ Reading	■ Hands-on	■ Individual
■ Writing	■ Meaningful	■ Group
■ Speaking	■ Linked to objectives	■ Written
■ Listening	■ Promotes engagement	■ Oral

*If taped text is used, this would be an adaptation. Because the teacher will be reading with ELs and struggling readers, the grade-level text can be used.

FIGURE 7.5   *Anticipation/Reaction Guide + Why*

Anticipation Guide + Why

(Buehl, 2009)

Directions: Next to each statement, write an "X" in the appropriate column.
Be ready to discuss your opinion with the class.

Before Reading		*Statements*	*After Reading*	
Agree	*Disagree*		*Agree*	*Disagree*
		It is a parent's responsibility to provide for the emotional and physical needs of their children into their adulthood.		
Why?		Why?		
		Family heirlooms and/or treasures should always be divided equally among the children in a family.		
Why?		Why?		
		When adult children leave home, it is inevitable that everything they left will seem old-fashioned and out-of touch.		
Why?		Why?		
		Compared to the 1960s, *everything* is different now.		
Why?		Why?		

FIGURE 7.6   *Semantic Feature Analysis (SFA) (Buehl, 2009; Fisher & Frey, 2008)*

Character Traits

	talented	tough	homely	inadequate	insecure	successful	confident
Mama	+	+	−	−	−	−	+
Maggie	−	−	+	+	+	−	−
Dee	−	−	−	−	−	+	+
Alice	+	−	−	−	−	+	+
(etc.)							

Characters

SIOP® LESSON PLAN, *Grade 10, Days 4–5:*
Analyzing Character Interactions

Key: SW = Students will; TW = Teacher will; SWBAT = Students will be able to . . . ;
HOTS: Higher Order Thinking Skills

Unit: Character: Using Primary and Secondary Sources

SIOP® Lesson: Analyzing Character Interactions
Grade: 10

(continued)

SIOP® LESSON PLAN, *Grade 10, Days 4–5:*
Analyzing Character Interactions (continued)

Content Standards: 2.5 Extend ideas presented in primary or secondary sources through original analysis, evaluation, and elaboration.

3.3 Analyze interactions between main and subordinate characters in a literary text (e.g., internal and external conflicts, motivations, relationships, influences), and explain the way those interactions affect the plot.

3.4 Determine characters' traits by what the characters say about themselves in narration, dialogue, dramatic monologue, and soliloquy.

3.10 Identify and describe the function of dialogue, scene designs, soliloquies, asides, and character foils in dramatic literature.

Key Vocabulary:	Supplementary Materials:
Content Vocabulary: *protagonist, dynamic character, conflict* **Academic Vocabulary:** *narrator, defend a position* **HOTS:** After reading "Two Kinds," engage in an informal debate arguing for either Jing-mei's or her mother's position, using evidence from the text and the character's traits to support your opinion. Debate question: Should parents pressure their children so they'll achieve great things?	Students' Semantic Feature Analysis (SFA) charts from Days 2–3 Videocassette: "Chinese Americans: Culture and Contributions" (segment two); from *Holt Literature & Language Arts* Discussion Web (Buehl, 2009): one per student Discussion Web transparency (See Figure 7.8. and Appendix E, #6) Word Web Word Web transparency (see Figure 7.7 and Appendix E, #11) Chart paper for debate rules "Two Kinds" by Amy Tan (short story) "Lucinda Matlock" by Edgar Lee Masters (poem)

Connections to Prior Knowledge/ Building Background Information:
Links to Students' Background Experiences—Video: "Chinese Americans: Culture and Contributions" with discussion.
Links to Prior Learning—Review of characters and traits identified on SFA; reading of "Lucinda Matlock" (Edgar Lee Masters). Review of previously taught academic vocabulary with modeling of Word Web.

Objectives:	Meaningful Activities/Lesson Sequence:	Review/Assessment:
Content Objectives: **1.** SWBAT identify character traits in two pieces of literature, a poem and a short story. **2.** SWBAT identify the protagonist and conflict in "Two Kinds" (by Amy Tan). **3.** SWBAT determine the differing motivations of the protagonists Jing-mei and her mother. **Language Objectives:** **1.** SWBAT define in writing the literary terms *protagonist, conflict,*	• TW review content and language objectives with students. • To review character traits, SW read with partners the short poem, "Lucinda Matlock," by Edgar Lee Masters. • SW identify Lucinda's character traits and add any new ones to the Semantic Feature Analysis charts they began the previous day. • TW direct students to pp. 96–97 of their anthology: "Character Interactions: Relationships and Conflicts" • TW distribute copies of the Word Web handout and will model how to use it (on the overhead) with a review of the previous days' academic vocabulary.	Monitor and assist as needed. Review students' Word Webs (through teacher observation) for accuracy.

dynamic characters, static characters, motivation

2. SWBAT orally defend the positions and actions of Jing-mei and her mother in an informal debate.

- In groups of 3 to 4, SW read together the expository text (pp. 96–97) using the Equal Portions reading alternative.

- After each section is read, SW complete one "branch" on the Word Web, until all four sections are completed.

- TW introduce the short story, "Two Kinds," by showing a video about Chinese Americans and their culture and contributions, followed by a brief discussion.

- With the whole class, TW read and explain the brief "Before You Read" sections on Conflict and Motivation (p. 98).

- TW distribute copies of the Discussion Web and will model its use on the overhead with a Discussion Web that provides two sides of the conflict between Maggie and her mother (from "Everyday Use").

- In groups, students will read "Two Kinds" using the Page or Paragraph alternative. As conflicts between Jing-mei and her mother are noted in the story, students will jot them on the Discussion Web.

- When students have finished reading the story, they will work with a partner to complete the Discussion Web by deciding on the motivations and character traits of Jing-mei and her mother for the conflicts students noted during the reading.

- TW explain the "rules" of an informal debate that are written on chart paper:

  1. Students must use evidence from the story to argue their position.
  2. Students must stick to the debate topic (see question on the Discussion Web).
  3. Students must use character traits of Jing-mei and her mother in their arguments.
  4. Students must disagree with each other respectfully.
  5. Students who use the academic language of character analysis will receive an extra credit point each time a vocabulary word is used during the debate.

- TW number off the groups. Students in the groups with even numbers (2, 4, 6), must prepare to argue for Jing-mei's positions as delineated on the Discussion Web. Students in the uneven groups (1, 3, 5), must argue for Mother's positions.

- Provide enough time for students to prepare for the informal debate.

Monitor as needed. If there are beginning English speakers (or advanced beginners) and there are peers who are more proficient in the same language, group them together so the more proficient speaker can clarify and assist in the L1. The majority of their work together, however, should be in English.

Because these words may be very challenging for English learners, again, clarification in the L1 may be warranted (if possible). If not, the teacher may wish to work on this task in a small group with ELs who need extra support and assistance.

Check for students' understanding of how to use a Discussion Web.

For the reading activity, students can stay in the same groups, or the groups can be shuffled to ensure more heterogeneity in reading ability. The groups should be no more than five students.

Beginning English speakers might benefit from listening to the story on an audiotape. However, if there's a possibility of clarification in the student's L1, the audiotape may not be as helpful as the clarification.

While reading, students can note areas of confusion with sticky notes. Monitor and respond with assistance if students' texts are marked with sticky notes.

Note: At the end of Day 4, a homework assignment could be given to work on the SFA to add more character traits, along with

(continued)

SIOP® LESSON PLAN, *Grade 10, Days 4–5:*
Analyzing Character Interactions (continued)

Meaningful Activities/Lesson Sequence:	Review/Assessment:
• Depending on time, have the debate or carry it over to the next day. • Homework: Complete SFA for Jing-mei and her mother.	conflicts between Jing-mei and her mother. TW will meet with various table groups throughout this step to ensure that everyone is understanding what to do and how to do it. Check EL's work and assist with creating some sentences or sentence frames they could use in the informal debate. Review Key Content Concepts and Vocabulary.

Wrap-up: In pairs, SW do a spot-check with each other on the content and academic vocabulary words. One says a word, and then the other tries to give a quick definition. SW then trade roles.

Review content and language objectives. SW respond showing fingers (1–3): 1 = I could teach this; 2 = I'm getting there; 3 = I'm confused.

Additional SIOP® Features

Preparation	*Scaffolding*	*Group Options*
■ Adaptation of content	■ Modeling	■ Whole class
■ Links to background	■ Guided practice	■ Small groups
■ Links to past learning	■ Independent practice	■ Partners
■ Strategies incorporated	■ Comprehensible input	☐ Independent

Integration of Processes	*Application*	*Assessment*
■ Reading	☐ Hands-on	■ Individual
■ Writing	■ Meaningful	■ Group
■ Speaking	■ Linked to objectives	■ Written
■ Listening	■ Promotes engagement	■ Oral

THINK-ALOUD for SIOP® Lesson Plan, Grade 10, Days 4–5

• If I have beginning English learners who have little or no English proficiency, this lesson might still be difficult for them even with the scaffolding, group work, taped story, and teacher support. I'm wondering what else I could do for these students, especially if there are no peers who speak their language to help clarify concepts and vocabulary. I could partially fill in the Word Web with headings and I could work with a small group of beginners or advanced beginners to help prepare them for the debate. Also, I could include sentence frames for them to use during the debate to reduce their anxiety and enable them to participate.

However, this still may not be enough for beginning speakers. If my school (or district) has no intensive ESL (English as a Second Language) or ELD (English Language Development) program in place, I need to be an advocate for ELs in the beginning stages of English proficiency. Although the SIOP® Model will certainly assist English learners in being able to access grade-level content and is a must for them, it probably isn't sufficient for students who are in the beginning stages of learning English. These students also must have intensive English instruction with an ESL or ELD teacher, especially at the secondary level, because their learning of English must be greatly accelerated if they are going to be able to graduate from high school.

FIGURE 7.7 *Word Web for Academic Vocabulary*

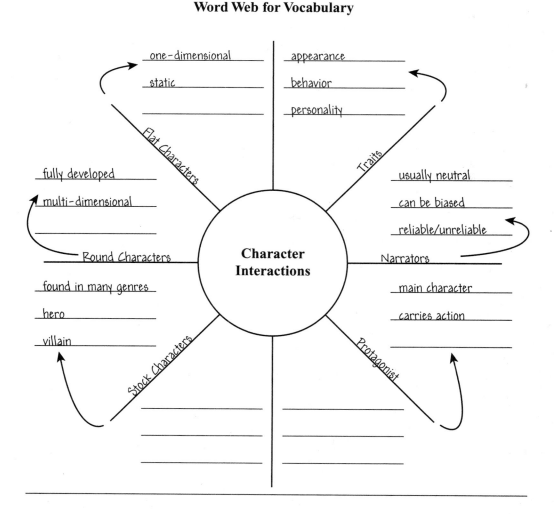

Word Web for Vocabulary

FIGURE 7.8 *Example of Discussion Web*

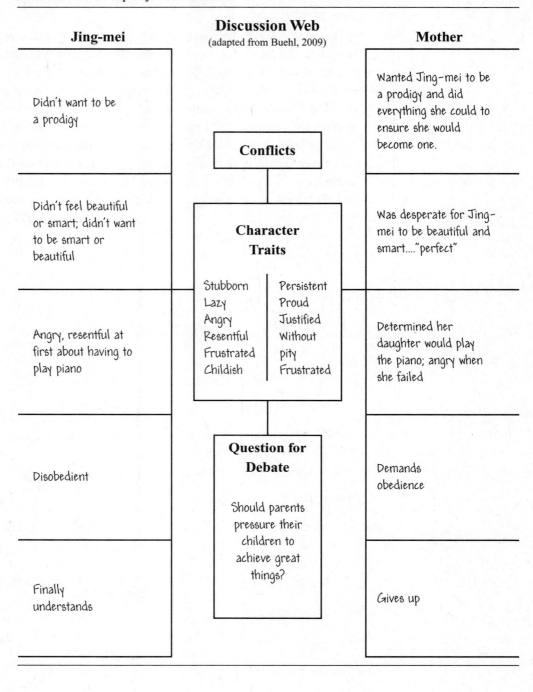

Discussion Web
(adapted from Buehl, 2009)

Jing-mei

Didn't want to be a prodigy

Didn't feel beautiful or smart; didn't want to be smart or beautiful

Angry, resentful at first about having to play piano

Disobedient

Finally understands

Conflicts

Character Traits

Stubborn	Persistent
Lazy	Proud
Angry	Justified
Resentful	Without
Frustrated	pity
Childish	Frustrated

Question for Debate

Should parents pressure their children to achieve great things?

Mother

Wanted Jing-mei to be a prodigy and did everything she could to ensure she would become one.

Was desperate for Jing-mei to be beautiful and smart...."perfect"

Determined her daughter would play the piano; angry when she failed

Demands obedience

Gives up

SIOP® LESSON PLAN, *Grade 10, Days 6–8:*
Writing a Biographical Narrative

Note: It is intended that this lesson will begin on a Friday so that students have the weekend to conduct the required interview with a parent, caregiver, or other adult relative.

Key: SW = Students will; TW = Teacher will; SWBAT = Students will be able to . . . ;
HOTS = Higher Order Thinking Skills

. . . . ●

135

Unit: Character: Using Primary and Secondary Sources

SIOP® Lesson: Writing a Biographical Narrative
Grade: 10

Content Standards: 3.4 Determine characters' traits by what the characters say about themselves in narration, dialogue, dramatic monologue, and soliloquy
2.1 Write biographical or autobiographical narratives or short stories.

   a. Locate scenes and incidents in specific places.
   b. Describe with concrete sensory details the sights, sounds, and smells of a scene and the specific actions, movements, gestures, and feelings of the characters; use interior monologue to depict the character's feelings.

Key Vocabulary:	*Supplementary Materials:*
Content Vocabulary: *biographical narrative, interior monologue, sensory details*	Semantic Feature Analysis (from previous lessons)
Academic Vocabulary: *sequence of events, anecdotes*	Bio-Pyramid (Macon, Bewell, & Vogt, 1991); one per student (See Figure 7.9 and Appendix E, #3.)
HOTS: What do you think is meant by the quote, "One cannot 'make' characters. They are found"? (Elizabeth Bowman) Do you agree or disagree? why?	Sentence Frames for Narrative (See Figure 7.12.)
	Sequence Signal Word Chart (See Figure 7.11.)
	Description Signal Word Chart (See Figure 7.10.)

Connections to Prior Knowledge/ Building Background Information:
Links to Students' Background Experiences—TW ask students about a photo they've seen that captures the person perfectly. How does the photo do this? SW reflect on and discuss Van Gogh's portrait in the anthology (p. 71) regarding his character traits. SW interview a parent, caregiver, or other adult relative for the biographical narrative. SW participate in a Face-in-a-Crowd activity to "picture" the subject for the narrative.
Links to Prior Learning—SW finish the debate, if needed, from the previous lesson. SW use Semantic Feature Analysis (SFA) character traits to assist with describing a person for their Biographical Narrative. SW review Description and Sequence Signal Words Charts. SW use previous short stories to find examples of interior monologue, sensory detail, dialogue, and anecdotes.

Objectives:	*Meaningful Activities/Lesson Sequence:*	*Review/Assessment:*
Content Objective: **1.** SWBAT select important anecdotes, events, and/or accomplishments in a person's life after conducting an interview. **Language Objectives:** **1.** SWBAT write interview questions and conduct an oral interview with a parent, caregiver, or other adult relative. **2.** SWBAT write a biographical narrative as an interior monologue about the subject interviewed, including relevant character traits, anecdotes, sensory details, and anecdotes.	• TW review posted content and language objectives with students. • TW ask students to think of a favorite photo of a family member or friend. Did you think when you saw the photo, "This is a great picture! It captures him (or her) perfectly!"? Why does this happen? What specific character traits did the photographer capture? • TW ask students to turn to the opening page of this unit in the anthology, p. 72 (the portrait of Vincent van Gogh, painted by Dr. Paul Gachet, Van Gogh's psychiatrist). • What does this painting tell you about Van Gogh? Does it tell you anything about Dr. Gachet? • SW take out SFA charts from the past week. What techniques did the authors use in their writing to create characters you can remember? • TW have students turn to p. 122 in the anthology and introduce writing a Biographical Narrative.	TW check for understanding of objectives, clarifying as needed. Depending on responses and if needed, TW go back to pieces of literature and review how authors wrote the direct and indirect characterizations.

(continued)

SIOP® LESSON PLAN, *Grade 10, Days 6–8:*
Writing a Biographical Narrative (continued)

Meaningful Activities/Lesson Sequence:	Review/Assessment:
• TW lead class through the Prewriting section, pp. 112–123, on choosing a subject, creating a controlling impression, and gathering details.	
• SW silently read model about Kelly and Aunt Thelma and Anecdote 1 on p. 124.	
• Based on this information, what elements should be in a biographical narrative?	Monitor responses as they're written on board.
• Model (or ask students to) an example of an interior dialogue.	
• Refer back to "Everyday Use" for examples of interior monologue in Mama's narration.	
• With a partner, SW refer back to "Everyday Use," "Two Kinds," and "Lucinda Matlock" to find examples of sensory detail, dialogue, and the use of anecdotes. Mark examples with sticky notes.	Review academic vocabulary and monitor how well students can find examples in previous readings. Spot-check where sticky notes are placed in books.
• TW explain the interview assignment; the steps of the process are written on chart paper:	
1. Select someone to interview who will become the subject of your biographical narrative.	Supply written directions to ELs and other students who would benefit from having them.
2. Your subject should be a parent, caregiver, or other adult relative.	
3. With a partner, write interview questions so that you learn about your subject's childhood, problems overcome, and accomplishments.	
4. Take notes and tape record the interview, if possible.	
• In pairs, SW write ten interview questions; share them with group members; revise as needed.	Check for understanding to ensure everyone understands the interview directions.
• For homework: SW conduct interview, following guidelines.	Spot-check interview questions for all students.
(Depending on the time, the lesson could break at this point for the weekend. If so, TW go over content and language objectives with students at the end of the period. On the following day, TW again review objectives and academic vocabulary with students, and check students' interview notes.)	Depending on language proficiency, English learners may need to complete an abbreviated and adapted Bio-Pyramid, with fewer words to produce, and one or two accomplishments. A word could be included on each line, as an example.
• Introduce the Bio-Pyramid with the example of Uncle Bob.	
• Based on interview notes, SW work with partners. Each will complete a Bio-Pyramid as a pre-writing activity (either as homework or in class).	
• SW share their Bio-Pyramids with other small group members.	Beginning English speakers may need to work in a small group with the teacher. The students will require some assistance
• SW turn to pp. 124–125, and together will read (Paragraph or Pass alternative) the	

section on Plan Organization and Pacing, the Writer's Model, and Framework. On p. 127, SW read "Guidelines: Writing a Biographical Narrative."

- TW refer students to the Description and Sequence Signal Words Charts posted on the bulletin board. TW remind students to use these words and phrases in their narratives, as needed.
- SW write a first draft of the biographical narrative. TW encourage students to use their Semantic Feature Analysis charts to remind them of character traits and sensory details. TW remind students to refer back to the literature they have read for other examples of sensory details.
- In their groups, SW read pp. 127–128 on Revising: Evaluate and Revise Your Narrative. SW use the section "Revision Techniques" to complete a second draft.
- SW share their writing with a partner, editing each other's work prior to creating the final draft. SW use sticky notes to indicate areas on their partner's paper needing editing or revision.
- SW write the final drafts of their biographical narratives.
- Prior to submitting the narrative, SW reflect on the following questions (p. 129 in Holt anthology), and will jot brief answers to be attached to the narrative:

1. What is your favorite line or passage in your narrative? Why?
2. Did your view of your subject change as you worked on your narrative? If so, why do you think so?
3. If someone wrote a biographical narrative about you, what controlling impression might it offer? Why do you think so?

with the Bio-Pyramid, even if it is adapted.

Depending on English learners' proficiency levels, TW read these sections with ELs in a small group.

All of the Signal Words charts (Compare/Contrast; Cause/Effect or Problem/Solution; Sequence or Order; and Description or List) remain on the bulletin throughout the year. While primarily intended for ELs and struggling readers and writers, all students refer to them when they're readily available. (For other lists, see Vogt & Echevarria, 2008.)

TW supply English learners at lower levels of language proficiency with the Sentences Starters that are based on the Signal Words.

TW read text with small group of ELs who need the extra support. Of course, struggling readers or writers can be part of this small group, too.

SW submit their narratives to the teacher.

Review Key Vocabulary.

Wrap-up: SW turn to p. 73 in anthology. What do you think is meant by the quote: "One cannot 'make' characters . . . They are found." (Elizabeth Bowman). Do you agree or disagree? Why? Share with your table group for two minutes. Be ready to share with the class.

Review content and language objectives with students.

Additional SIOP® Features

Preparation	Scaffolding	Group Options
■ Adaptation of content	■ Modeling	■ Whole class
■ Links to background	■ Guided practice	■ Small groups
■ Links to past learning	■ Independent practice	■ Partners
■ Strategies incorporated	■ Comprehensible input	■ Independent

Integration of Processes	Application	Assessment
■ Reading	■ Hands-on	■ Individual
■ Writing	■ Meaningful	■ Group
■ Speaking	■ Linked to objectives	■ Written
■ Listening	■ Promotes engagement	■ Oral

FIGURE 7.9   *Bio-Pyramid*

Bio-Pyramid
(Macon, Bewell, & Vogt, 1991)

Uncle Bob
Name of the person.

smart   interesting
Two words describing the person.

Iowa   involved   talented
Three words describing childhood.

alcoholism   brave   AA   sponsor
Four words indicating problem overcome.

trombone   musical   jazz   expert   teacher
Five words stating one accomplishment.

obstetrician   babies   mothers   students   health   professor
Six words stating a second accomplishment.

loving   father   grandfather   uncle   brother   friend   mentor
Seven words stating a third accomplishment.

He   has   been   an   inspiration   to   our   family
Eight words stating how people benefited from accomplishments.

FIGURE 7.10   *Description Signal Words Chart (Vogt & Echevarria, 2008, p. 39)*

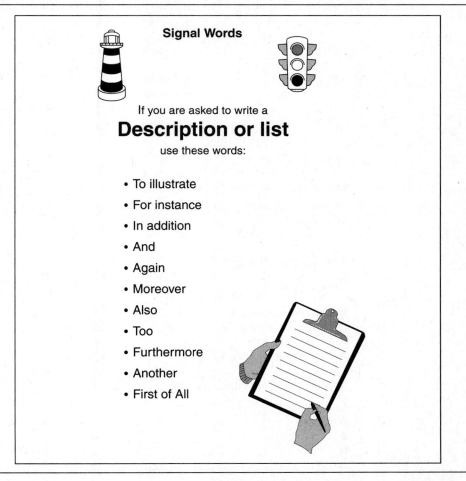

Signal Words

If you are asked to write a
Description or list
use these words:

- To illustrate
- For instance
- In addition
- And
- Again
- Moreover
- Also
- Too
- Furthermore
- Another
- First of All

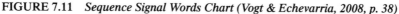

FIGURE 7.11   *Sequence Signal Words Chart (Vogt & Echevarria, 2008, p. 38)*

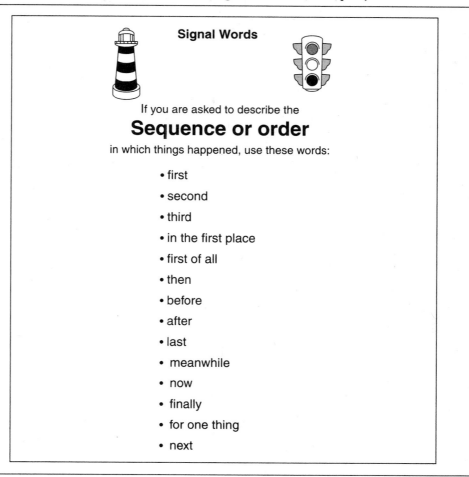

Signal Words

If you are asked to describe the
Sequence or order
in which things happened, use these words:

- first
- second
- third
- in the first place
- first of all
- then
- before
- after
- last
- meanwhile
- now
- finally
- for one thing
- next

PLANNING POINTS for SIOP® Lesson Plan, Grade 10, Days 6–8

- If you have skimmed or read the other lesson plans and units in this book, you will have noticed that most are planned for one day or class period. In this unit, as you have probably noted, the lessons are planned for multiple days. Prescribing these lesson plans for one or two days is somewhat arbitrary. The two-day lessons could easily turn into three-day lessons given the makeup of your classes. With advanced English speakers and accelerated learners, some of the modifications and adaptations could be eliminated. However, if your classes include English learners at various levels of proficiency, including beginning or advanced beginning students, then these modifications and adaptations should be included.

  Sometimes high school teachers (and parents) worry that if they implement the SIOP® Model, their on-level and above-level students will be penalized by instruction that is watered down, slowed down, or inappropriate. With the lessons in this unit, we hope you will see that this is not a valid concern, *if* grade-level content, standards, and reading materials and activities are used consistently. Look again carefully at the sequence for this lesson. *All* students are writing a biographical narrative; *all* students are using their ongoing Semantic Feature Analysis to trigger the use of descriptive adjectives in their narrative; *all* students are expected to include anecdotes, sensory details, and chronological order in their writing. What differs are the supports that are put in

FIGURE 7.12 *Sentence Frames Using Signal Words*

1. To illustrate how _____ my _____ is, here is a story I was told. One day, he (or she) _____
   _____ . . .

2. Then, _____ . . .

3. Before he (or she) knew it, _____ . . .

4. Meanwhile, _____ . . .

5. In addition, he (or she) _____
   _____ . . .

6. Another example is _____ . . .

7. Furthermore, _____ . . .

8. For instance, _____ . . .

9. Finally, _____ . . .

place, such as the Bio-Pyramid (although this is not an easy activity—try it yourself before you introduce it to students), sentence starters, and the Sequence and Description Signal Words Charts. These adaptations will not slow down or water down instruction for your native-English speaking students who are performing satisfactorily academically. What they will do is provide access for all the rest of your students so they also have a chance of being successful.

- The lessons that are included in this unit are planned for six to eight days. The unit could be extended to further meet the Grade 10 ELA content standards. There are additional pieces of literature in the anthology, as well as additional grammar and vocabulary lessons. Here, we have included the key concepts and academic vocabulary for character analysis. We did not include in the lesson plans for this unit anything about what needs to be submitted for a percentage or letter grade. Most of the activities could be graded, if necessary, but they're also appropriate for practice and application of the key concepts and vocabulary. It's certainly your call as to what would need to be graded.

- An idea for concluding the unit that is also a great assessment opportunity is the Dinner Party (Vogt & Echevarria, 2008, pp. 105–106). The purpose of Dinner Party is for students to assume the persona of characters in novels or short stories, or authors, historical figures, and so forth. The Dinner Party could be a written assignment, but it is also great fun to have students act it out. Although scripts can be written (probably a good idea for English learners at lower levels of English proficiency), improvisation is also appropriate. What follows are prompts for either an author or character study. The Dinner Party prompts work for either a written essay or a role play.

Author Study Suppose you could have a dinner party for six or eight of the authors or poets we have studied in this unit. Whom would you invite? Why would you select them? What would be the seating order of the guests at your table, and why would you place them in that order? What do you think the guests would talk about during dinner? Include specific references to the authors' lives and works in your response.

Character Study Suppose you could have a dinner party for six or eight of the characters we have read about in this unit. Whom would you invite? Why would you select them? What would be the seating order of the guests at your table, and why would you place them in that order? What do you think the guests would talk about during dinner? Include specific references to the characters' traits and lives in your response.

- Just like you do, we have struggled in the English-language arts as we tried to determine what our content and academic vocabulary was for each lesson in this unit. The words seem so intertwined. Look back at the overview for the Unit (see Figure 7.1) and you'll notice that some content vocabulary words are from the literature in this unit. Other academic vocabulary words are those taught and practiced throughout the unit to learn about characterization and literary analysis, also very necessary and important content for the unit.

As you read through the lessons, you may have noticed some that were classified in individual lessons as content vocabulary rather than as academic vocabulary. What we're coming to understand is that in ELA, with the overlap between content and academic language, when the words and concepts are initially taught, they're taught as content vocabulary. As students come to understand the words and concepts in the study of literature, they become the necessary academic language that students need to apply in subsequent lessons. The temptation might be to just to lump everything together, but there's a danger in that. Students, especially English learners, need to realize that although each ELA lesson will have new vocabulary to learn, there is also a core of vocabulary within the discipline that must be mastered for ongoing learning. Therefore, even though there is confusion sometimes (just as there is when writing content and language objectives for ELA), we strongly recommend that you separate the content and academic vocabulary (and content and language objectives) as best you can.

Concluding Thoughts

If you have read this far, you're probably thinking, "SIOP® lesson planning must take hours to accomplish!" In the beginning stages of learning the SIOP® Model, it might; but as we've mentioned several times in this book, once you understand the model well, the time spent planning is significantly reduced. And, of course, your own lesson plans need not be as detailed as the ones presented here. We needed to include a great deal of detail so you could follow the lesson plans, but you'll be using your own cryptic notes, codes, and abbreviations for whatever SIOP® lesson plan format you choose. Recall how you felt when you learned to ride a bike. You undoubtedly fell off several times before you could sit, hold on, and pedal at the same time. The more you practiced, the better bike rider you became. The same goes with SIOP® lesson and unit planning in the English-language arts. Just remember that your high school English learners will be all the better for the efforts you extend on their behalf.

Literature References

Freeman, R. L. (2003). Interview with Alice Walker. In *Holt Literature & Language Arts* (Fourth Course: Grade 10). Austin, TX: Holt, Rinehart and Winston, 89–90.

Edgar Lee Masters (2003). Lucinda Matlock. In *Holt Literature & Language Arts* (Fourth Course: Grade 10). Austin, TX: Holt, Rinehart and Winston, 85.

Tan, A. (2003). Two Kinds. In *Holt Literature & Language Arts* (Fourth Course: Grade 10). Austin, TX: Holt, Rinehart and Winston, 99–107.

Walker, A. (2003). Everyday Use. In *Holt Literature & Language Arts* (Fourth Course: Grade 10). Austin, TX: Holt, Rinehart and Winston, 77–83.

Pulling It All Together

As we planned this final chapter, we decided it might be helpful if we shared some of the things we have learned in the process of writing this book, related to our collaborations with our content contributors and our understandings of lesson planning and teaching using the SIOP® Model. We also asked our contributors to share what they have learned, and we have included their thoughts and insights.

What We Have Learned

One important finding for all of us is the confirmation that becoming an effective SIOP® teacher is a process that takes time, reflectivity, practice, and commitment. Unlike many of the educational initiatives that we have all been involved in during our careers, the SIOP® Model is not about tweaking our teaching a little here and adding a little

something there, while expecting immediate results in our students' academic achievement. Instead, the SIOP® Model is about purposeful planning, consistent attention to teaching the academic language and content of your discipline, and maintaining the belief that all students, including English learners, can reach high academic standards while developing their English proficiency. We know from our SIOP® research studies that if teachers are high implementers of the model, their students' academic performance increases significantly (Center for Applied Linguistics, 2007; Echevarria, Richards, & Canges, in press).

We also have become even more aware that good teaching is about attention to detail. For example, as we were reading the lesson and unit plans created by our contributors, occasionally we had to call or email and ask questions about the purpose of a particular handout, the steps to a process, or the name of an activity. This made us realize how important it is to use precise language with English learners, both in our speech and in the materials we prepare for them. Consistent labeling for classroom routines, procedures, and activities reduces ambiguity and confusion, and serves as additional scaffolding for ELs.

Another similar insight concerns the role of teachers as content experts. As such, you know where you're going, and what needs to be taught, learned, and assessed. Students, including English learners, don't have this insider information, and sometimes they're academically lost because they don't know what is expected of them. Obviously, this is a primary function of content and language objectives: to point the way and assist students in knowing what to expect. But, when we make assumptions about what students know and can do, we may be basing those assumptions on what *we* know and what *we* can do. Once again, being precise in your use of terms, and carefully explaining and modeling processes and procedures related to the content you're teaching will assist your English learners in becoming more successful in learning your content.

We also sharpened our skills in designing SIOP® lessons and units, and we became even more aware of how challenging it is to write detailed SIOP® lesson and unit plans. Teachers new to the SIOP® Model often balk at the time and work it will take to plan lessons, yet as we have mentioned previously, with practice, the amount of time and effort is diminished. The end goal needs to be kept in sight: the academic and language proficiency benefits for the English learners who will be productive members of our society in the future.

Finally, we have learned from our contributors that experienced, knowledgeable, successful teachers who are well-versed in the SIOP® Model continue to grow and learn through the process of carefully planning and teaching effective and appropriate lessons for English learners. In the section that follows, you will hear their voices about what they learned during the process of working together to help write this book.

What Our English-Language Arts Contributors Have Learned

Karlin LaPorta and Lisa Mitchener

Even as teachers who know the SIOP® Model really well, we learned through contributing to this book that lesson planning and especially longer term unit planning is *much* easier when collaborating with colleagues. We would strongly encourage teachers to find a partner or small group of like-minded teachers at their school site who want to work together. To do this, use a similar prep time, occasional sub release time, PLC (Professional Learning Communities) planning time, and/or curriculum mapping time. Focused time and energy needs to be applied when creating high-quality SIOP® lessons and units, and it's so important to be able to then come back together and reflect.

Differentiation continues to be one of the most challenging tasks, especially when teachers may have very diverse levels of language proficiency within their classrooms. As we developed the lessons, we noticed that it takes prior planning to differentiate for the varied learners . . . it can't and it won't just happen as you teach. Forethought is necessary when creating sentence frames to scaffold instruction, and when creating appropriate grouping configurations to support different levels of language proficiency.

As well, HOTS (higher order thinking skills) take forethought and preplanning in order to ensure that we are incorporating them into lessons. It is much easier to think of a literal question on the fly than a high-quality inferential question. If HOTS are not integrated into the lesson plan format, you most likely will not focus on them when it's time to teach the lesson.

As we were planning the units, we had to continually remind ourselves that the focus was the content and language objectives. It is easy to get excited about an activity and forget the purpose behind it. As teachers, we need to make sure that incorporating an activity helps *support* the objectives, not lead us away from them.

We learned through the lesson planning/unit planning process the importance of continual reflection on review and assessment. The question should always be: Were the objectives achieved by all students? If not, what needs to be done? Does the concept need to be taught in a different way for some students? The reality of unit planning is that adjustments and changes must be made as the unit is taught. A flexible approach to teaching is necessary to ensure students are truly achieving the objectives.

As we sat down and began thinking about how this book might help teachers begin to implement the SIOP® Model in their classrooms, we thought about the frustrations and roadblocks during our own SIOP® implementation. In the beginning, we felt like novice teachers again, overwhelmed by the amount of planning time and the discomforts of refining and modifying our teaching style to fit the SIOP® Model. Looking back, the process of our own SIOP® implementation was similar to having to learn that nine-step lesson plan when we were beginning teachers and thinking: How am I going to do this for *every* lesson? As we gained more experience and more practice using the SIOP® Model, however, it just became an internalized part of our natural teaching style. We're not denying that it was hard work and we experienced successes as well as failures along the way, but we realized that, like anything in life, once you begin to reap the benefits of a challenging task, the challenges don't seem so immense.

The benefits of the SIOP® Model to student language and academic development were well worth any extra effort we put toward our lesson planning and lesson delivery. With practice, it became easier, and we found that the task of "SIOP®ing" a lesson became so engrained in our teaching style that even the students were beginning to internalize our teaching methods. Students began to hold themselves more accountable for their ability to achieve the content and language objectives. They knew when they needed more practice, and they knew when they were ready to apply knowledge to new information. They began to ask questions to clarify the task at hand and realized they could not complete a task if they didn't understand it. Movement to different grouping configurations became automatic and interaction within groups became meaningful and engaging.

Once students became comfortable in our SIOP® classrooms, engagement and motivation increased while management issues decreased. We were able to assess understanding of tasks and content in many different ways and were able to differentiate when needed. The idea of differentiating instruction sounds so simple, but it is one of the trickiest things to do with a diverse class. It is important to acknowledge though, that by implementing all the features of the SIOP® Model, differentiation becomes more natural.

We understand that teachers can feel overwhelmed by the normal daily rigors of teaching the state standards in a diverse classroom. We promised you that the SIOP® Model is different. We hope that the lessons and units found in this book have provided you with a planning resource to help you succeed in implementing consistent and systematic English-language arts sheltered instruction for all of your students at different levels of academic and language proficiency. Finally, we would like to remind you, as you endeavor to implement SIOP®, that the SIOP® Model is *not* about changing everything you do . . . the SIOP® Model is about *refining* your current teaching practices to meet the needs of your EL students. This is our mantra and we hope it becomes yours.

Final Thoughts

As you read the thoughts and insights of our contributors, you may have noticed they mentioned the importance of collaboration. We couldn't agree more. For over fifteen years, we have collaborated about the SIOP® Model, with each other and with educators throughout the country (and now throughout the world). We are convinced that these collaborations have resulted in a comprehensive model of instruction for English learners that is not only empirically validated, but is appropriate, essential, and *doable* for teachers, despite the time and effort it takes to create, write, and then teach SIOP® lessons.

We hope this book, and the other SIOP® books in the series, help you pull it all together as you create your SIOP® English-language arts lesson plans and units. We also hope that as you become a successful SIOP® teacher, you will find rewards in your students' academic and language growth, and confidence in how to effectively teach the English-language arts to your English learners.

appendix a: A Review of the Eight Components of the SIOP® Model

(Echevarria, Vogt, & Short, 2000; 2004; 2008)

The SIOP® Model was designed to help teachers systematically, consistently, and concurrently teach grade-level academic content and academic language to English learners (ELs). Teachers have found it effective with both ELs and native-English speaking students who are still developing academic literacy. The model consists of eight components and 30 features. (See Appendix B for the complete SIOP® protocol.) The following brief overview is offered to remind you of the preparation and actions teachers should undertake in order to deliver effective SIOP® instruction.

1. Lesson Preparation

The focus for each SIOP® English-language arts lesson is the content and language objectives. We suggest that the objectives be linked to curriculum standards and the academic language students need for success in English-language arts. Your goal is to help students gain important experience with key grade-level content and skills as they progress toward fluency in English. Hopefully, you now post and discuss the objectives with students each day, even if one period continues a lesson from a previous day, so that students know what they are expected to learn and/or be able to do by the end of that lesson. When you provide a road map at the start of each lesson, students focus on what is important and take an active part in their learning process.

The Lesson Preparation component also advocates for supplementary materials (e.g., visuals, multimedia, adapted or bilingual texts, publisher-supplied summaries of literature selections, study guides) because grade-level reading series and/or anthologies are often difficult for many English learners to comprehend. You may also adapt the literature for comprehensibility by providing supportive handouts, grouping students for reading activities (mixed groups, not just the highs with the lows), and having audiotaped selections available (these often come with reading series and anthologies for students of varying reading and English proficiency levels). Graphics or illustrations may be used before reading a selection, for example, to teach key points. You may differentiate a graphic organizer, depending on students' needs, with some parts partially completed with headings or subheadings, or notes for less English-proficient students. When you include accessible reading material that is appropriate to the students' interests and then adapt content as needed, you are on your way to making the activities meaningful—the final feature of this component. It is important to remember that meaningful activities provide access to the key concepts in your English-language arts lessons; this is much more important than just providing "fun" activities that students readily enjoy. Certainly, "fun" is good, but "meaningful" and "effective" are better. You will also want to plan tasks and projects for students so they have structured opportunities for oral interaction throughout your lessons.

2. Building Background

In SIOP® lessons, you are expected to connect new concepts with students' personal experiences and past learning. As you prepare ELs for reading, writing, and oral language tasks, you may at times have to build background knowledge because many English learners either have not been studying in U.S. schools or are unfamiliar with American culture. At other times, you may need to activate your students' prior knowledge in order to find out what they already know, to identify misinformation, or to discover when you need to fill in gaps. However, you will likely find that your ELs also have funds of knowledge different from those of native English speakers and you can tap them as resources, perhaps in lessons related to short story characters or plots, poetry, native-language nursery rhymes, songs they have learned previously, universal themes in literature, and so forth. As you prepare lessons, examine the anthologies, novels, and other texts you are using for cultural biases or idiomatic speech so you can anticipate problems and pre-teach potentially confusing concepts. Granted, you already teach idiomatic expressions as part of your curriculum, but for your English learners, you need to be especially sensitive to figurative language that may pop up in conversations, literature, and informational texts.

The SIOP® Model places great significance on building a broad vocabulary base for students. We need to increase vocabulary instruction across the curriculum so our students will become effective readers, writers, speakers, and listeners. As an English-language arts teacher, you already explicitly teach key vocabulary and word structures, word families, and word relationships. Go even further for your ELs by helping them develop word learning strategies beyond decoding. Share strategies such as using context clues, word parts (e.g., affixes), visual aids (e.g., illustrations), and cognates (a word related in meaning and form to a word in another language). Then be sure to design lesson activities that give students multiple opportunities to use new vocabulary both orally and in writing, such as those found in this book and in *99 Ideas and Activities for Teaching with the SIOP® Model* (Vogt & Echevarria, 2008). In order to move words from receptive knowledge to expressive use, vocabulary needs reinforcement through different learning modes.

3. Comprehensible Input

If you present information in a way that students cannot understand, such as an explanation that is spoken too rapidly, or literature selections that are far above students' reading levels with no visuals or graphic organizers to assist them, many students—including English learners—will be unable to learn the necessary content. Instead, modify "traditional" instruction with a variety of ESL methods and SIOP® techniques so your students can comprehend the lesson's key concepts. These techniques include, among others:

- Teacher talk appropriate to student proficiency levels (e.g., simple sentences, slower speech, instruction about how to recognize and understand idioms, and familiar vocabulary terms for beginning level students)
- Demonstrations and modeling (e.g., modeling how to complete a task or participate in a debate, write a friendly letter, or use the language of literary critique)
- Gestures, pantomime, and movement
- Role-plays, improvisation, and simulations
- Visuals, such as pictures, real objects, illustrations, charts, and graphic organizers
- Restatement, paraphrasing, repetition, and written records of key points on the board, transparencies, or chart paper
- Previews and reviews of important information (perhaps in the native language, if possible and as appropriate)

- Hands-on, experiential, and discovery activities (e.g., writing and performing skits or plays, poetry readings, readers' theatre performances, and author's chair)

Remember, too, that academic tasks must be explained clearly, both orally and in writing for students. You cannot assume English learners know how to do an assignment because it is a regular routine for the rest of your students. Talk through the procedures and use models and examples of good products and appropriate participation, so students know the steps they should take and can envision the desired result.

When you are dealing with complicated and abstract concepts, it can be particularly difficult to convey information to less proficient students. You can boost the comprehensibility of what you're teaching through native language support, if possible. Supplementary materials (e.g., adapted texts, audiotapes, or CDs) in a student's primary language may be used to introduce a new topic, and native language tutoring (if available) can help students check their understanding.

4. Strategies

This component addresses student learning strategies, teacher-scaffolded instruction, and higher-order thinking skills. By explicitly teaching cognitive and metacognitive learning strategies, you help equip students for academic learning both inside and outside the SIOP® classroom. You should capitalize on the cognitive and metacognitive strategies students already use in their first language because those will transfer to the new language.

As a SIOP® teacher, you must frequently scaffold instruction so students can be successful with their academic tasks. You want to support their efforts at their current performance level, but also move them to a higher level of understanding and accomplishment. When students master a skill or task, you remove the supports you provided and add new ones for the next level. Your goal, of course, is for English learners to be able to work independently. They often achieve this independence one step at a time.

You need to ask your ELs a range of questions, some of which should require critical thinking. It is easy to ask simple, factual questions, and sometimes we fall into that trap with beginning English speakers. We must go beyond questions that can be answered with a one- or two-word response, and instead, ask questions and create projects or tasks that require students to think more critically and apply their language skills in a more extended way. Remember this important adage: "Just because ELs don't speak English proficiently doesn't mean they can't *think*."

5. Interaction

We know that students learn through interaction with one another and with their teachers. They need oral language practice to help develop and deepen their content knowledge and support their second language reading and writing skills. Clearly, you are the main role model for appropriate English usage, word choice, intonation, fluency, and the like, but do not discount the value of student–student interaction. In pairs and small groups, English learners practice new language structures and vocabulary that you have taught as well as important language functions, such as asking for clarification, confirming interpretations, elaborating on one's own or another's idea, and evaluating opinions.

Don't forget that sometimes the interaction patterns expected in an American classroom differ from students' cultural norms and prior schooling experiences. You will want to be sensitive to sociocultural differences and work with students to help them become competent in the culture you have established in your classroom, while respecting their values.

6. Practice & Application

Practice and application of new material is essential for all learners. Our research on the SIOP® Model found that lessons with hands-on, visual, and other kinesthetic tasks benefit ELs because students practice the language and content knowledge through multiple modalities. As a SIOP® teacher, you want to make sure your lessons include a variety of activities that encourage students to apply both the English-language arts content and the English language skills they are learning. As an ELA teacher, it is obvious that all of your students will engage in reading, writing, listening, and speaking. For English learners, however, it is imperative that they practice and apply these literacy and language processes in each and every lesson.

7. Lesson Delivery

If you have delivered a successful SIOP® lesson, that means that the planning you did worked—the content and language objectives were met, the pacing was appropriate, and the students had a high level of engagement. We know that lesson preparation is crucial to effective delivery, but so are classroom management skills. We encourage you to set routines, make sure students know the lesson objectives so they can stay on track, and introduce (and revisit) meaningful activities that appeal to students. Don't waste time, but be mindful of student understanding so that you don't move a lesson too swiftly for students to grasp the key information.

8. Review & Assessment

Each SIOP® lesson needs time for review and assessment. You will do your English learners a disservice if you spend the last five minutes teaching a new concept rather than reviewing what they have learned so far. Revisit key vocabulary and concepts with your students to wrap up each lesson. Check on student comprehension frequently throughout the lesson period so you know whether additional explanations or reteaching are needed. When you assess students, be sure to provide multiple measures for students to demonstrate their understanding of the content. Assessments should look at the range of language and content development, including measures of vocabulary, grammar, comprehension skills, and content concepts.

WHY IS THE SIOP® MODEL NEEDED NOW?

We all are aware of the changing demographics in our U.S. school systems. English learners are the fastest growing subgroup of students and have been for the past two decades. According to the U.S. Department of Education in 2006, English learners numbered 5.4 million in U.S. elementary and secondary schools, about 12% of the student population, and they are expected to comprise about 25% of that population by 2025. In several states, this percentage has already been exceeded. The educational reform movement, and the No Child Left Behind (NCLB) Act in particular, has had a direct impact on English learners. States have implemented standards-based instruction and high-stakes testing, but in many content classes, little or no accommodation is made for the specific language development needs of English learners; this raises a significant barrier to ELs' success because they are expected to achieve high academic standards in English. In many states, ELs are required to pass end-of-grade tests in order to be promoted and/or exit exams in order to graduate.

Unfortunately, teacher development has not kept pace with the EL growth rate. Far too few teachers receive an undergraduate education that includes coursework in English as a second language (ESL) methodologies, which can be applied in content classes through sheltered instruction, and in second language acquisition theory, which can help teachers understand what students should be able to accomplish in a second language according to their proficiency levels, prior schooling, and sociocultural backgrounds. At the end of 2008, only four states—Arizona, California, Florida, and New York—required some undergraduate coursework in these areas for all teacher candidates.

Some teachers receive inservice training in working with ELs from their schools or districts, but it is rarely sufficient for the task they confront. Teachers are expected to teach ELs the new language, English, so the ELs can attain a high degree of proficiency, and in addition, instruct them in all the topics of the different grade-level content courses (more often than not taught in English). A survey conducted by Zehler and colleagues (2003) in 2002 found that approximately 43% of elementary and secondary teachers had ELs in their classrooms, yet only 11% were certified in bilingual education and only 18% in English as a second language. In the five years prior to the survey, teachers who worked with three or more ELs had received on average four hours of inservice training in how to serve them—hardly enough to reach a satisfactory level of confidence and competence.

Even teachers who have received university preparation in teaching English learners report limited opportunities for additional professional development. In a recent survey that sampled teachers in 22 small, medium, and large districts in California, the researchers found that during the previous five years, "forty-three percent of teachers with 50 percent or more English learners in their classrooms had received no more than one inservice that focused on the instruction of English learners" (Gandara, Maxwell-Jolly & Driscoll, 2005, p. 13). Fifty percent of the teachers with somewhat fewer students (26%–50% English learners in their classes) had received either no such inservice or only one. The result of this paucity of professional development is that ELs sit in classes with teachers and other staff who lack expertise in second language acquisition, multicultural awareness, and effective, research-based classroom practices.

It is not surprising, then, that ELs have experienced persistent underachievement on high-stakes tests and other accountability measures. On nearly every state and national assessment, ELs lag behind their native-English speaking peers and demonstrate significant achievement gaps (Kindler, 2002; Kober, et al., 2006; Lee, Grigg & Dion, 2007; Lee, Grigg & Donahue, 2007). In addition to having underqualified teachers, ELs are also more likely to be enrolled in poor, majority-minority schools that have fewer resources and teachers with less experience and fewer credentials than those serving English-proficient students (Cosentino de Cohen, Deterding & Clewell, 2005).

Lower performance on assessments is also the result of education policy. Although research has shown that it takes several years of instruction to become proficient in English (four to nine years, depending on a student's literacy level in the native language and prior schooling) (Collier, 1987; Cummins, 2006; Genesee, Lindholm-Leary, Saunders, & Christian, 2006), current NCLB policy forces schools to test ELs in reading after one year of U.S. schooling in grades 3–8 and one grade in high school. English learners are supposed to take the tests in mathematics and science from the start. Adding to the disconnect between research and policy is the fact that these tests have been designed for native

English speakers, rendering them neither valid nor reliable for ELs (AERA, APA, & NCME, 2000). By definition, an English learner is **not** proficient in English; as most of these state assessments are in English, the majority of ELs score poorly on them and are unable to demonstrate their real level of understanding of the subject matter.

Even though it is hard to turn around education policy, teachers, schools, districts, and universities do have opportunities to enact changes in professional development and program design. With this book we hope to help English-language arts teachers grow professionally and develop appropriate skills for working with English learners. There are many approaches and numerous combinations of techniques that can be applied to the delivery of sheltered content instruction. Currently, however, the SIOP® Model is the only scientifically validated model of sheltered instruction for English learners, and it has a growing research base (Center for Applied Linguistics, 2007; Echevarria, Richards & Canges, in press; Echevarria & Short, in press; Echevarria, Short & Powers, 2006; Short & Richards, 2008). The SIOP® Model is distinct from other approaches in that it offers a field-tested protocol for systematic lesson planning, delivery, and assessment, making its application for teaching English learners transparent for both preservice candidates preparing to be teachers and practicing teachers engaged in staff development. Further, it provides a framework for organizing the instructional practices essential for sound sheltered content instruction.

appendix b: The Sheltered Instruction Observation Protocol (SIOP®)

Observer(s): _____   Teacher: _____

Date: _____   School: _____

Grade: _____   Class/Topic: _____

ESL Level: _____   Lesson: Multi-day   Single-day   (*circle one*)

Total Points Possible: 120 (Subtract 4 points for each NA given: _____)

Total Points Earned: _____   Percentage Score: _____

Directions: Circle the number that best reflects what you observe in a sheltered lesson. You may give a score from 0–4 (or NA on selected items). Cite under "Comments" specific examples of the behaviors observed.

LESSON PREPARATION

4	3	2	1	0
1. **Content objectives** clearly defined, displayed and reviewed with students		**Content objectives** for students implied		No clearly defined **content objectives** for students

Comments:

4	3	2	1	0
2. **Language objectives** clearly defined, displayed and reviewed with students		**Language objectives** for students implied		No clearly defined **language objectives** for students

Comments:

4	3	2	1	0
3. **Content concepts** appropriate for age and educational background level of students		**Content concepts** somewhat appropriate for age and educational background level of students		**Content concepts** inappropriate for age and educational background level of students

Comments:

4	3	2	1	0
4. **Supplementary materials** used to a high degree, making the lesson clear and meaningful (e.g., computer programs, graphs, models, visuals)		Some use of **supplementary materials**		No use of **supplementary materials**

Comments:

(Echevarria, Vogt, & Short, 2000; 2004; 2008)

152

4	3	2	1	0	NA

5. **Adaptation of content** (e.g., text, assignment) to all levels of student proficiency

Some **adaptation of content** to all levels of student proficiency

No significant **adaptation of content** to all levels of student proficiency

Comments:

4	3	2	1	0

6. **Meaningful activities** that integrate lesson concepts (e.g., interviews, letter writing, simulations, models) with language practice opportunities for reading, writing, listening, and/or speaking

Meaningful activities that integrate lesson concepts but provide few language practice opportunities for reading, writing, listening, and/or speaking

No **meaningful activities** that integrate lesson concepts with language practice

Comments:

BUILDING BACKGROUND

4	3	2	1	0	NA

7. **Concepts explicitly linked** to students' background experiences

Concepts loosely linked to students' background experiences

Concepts not explicitly linked to students' background experiences

Comments:

4	3	2	1	0

8. **Links explicitly made** between past learning and new concepts

Few links made between past learning and new concepts

No links made between past learning and new concepts

Comments:

4	3	2	1	0

9. **Key vocabulary** emphasized (e.g., introduced, written, repeated, and highlighted for students to see)

Key vocabulary introduced, but not emphasized

Key vocabulary not introduced or emphasized

Comments:

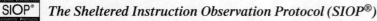

COMPREHENSIBLE INPUT

4	3	2	1	0

10. **Speech** appropriate for students' proficiency levels (e.g., slower rate, enunciation, and simple sentence structure for beginners)

Speech sometimes inappropriate for students' proficiency levels

Speech inappropriate for students' proficiency levels

Comments:

4	3	2	1	0

11. **Clear explanation** of academic tasks

Unclear explanation of academic tasks

No explanation of academic tasks

Comments:

4	3	2	1	0

12. **A variety of techniques** used to make content concepts clear (e.g., modeling, visuals, hands-on activities, demonstrations, gestures, body language)

Some **techniques** used to make content concepts clear

No **techniques** used to make concepts clear

Comments:

STRATEGIES

4	3	2	1	0

13. Ample opportunities provided for students to use **learning strategies**

Inadequate opportunities provided for students to use **learning strategies**

No opportunity provided for students to use **learning strategies**

Comments:

4	3	2	1	0

14. **Scaffolding techniques** consistently used, assisting and supporting student understanding (e.g., think-alouds)

Scaffolding techniques occasionally used

Scaffolding techniques not used

Comments:

4	3	2	1	0
15. A variety of **questions or tasks that promote higher-order thinking skills** (e.g., literal, analytical, and interpretive questions)		Infrequent **questions or tasks that promote higher-order thinking skills**		No **questions or tasks that promote higher-order thinking skills**

Comments:

INTERACTION

4	3	2	1	0
16. Frequent opportunities for **interaction** and discussion between teacher/student and among students, which encourage elaborated responses about lesson concepts		**Interaction** mostly teacher-dominated with some opportunities for students to talk about or question lesson concepts		**Interaction** teacher-dominated with no opportunities for students to discuss lesson concepts

Comments:

4	3	2	1	0
17. **Grouping configurations** support language and content objectives of the lesson		**Grouping configurations** unevenly support the language and content objectives		**Grouping configurations** do not support the language and content objectives

Comments:

4	3	2	1	0
18. Sufficient **wait time for student responses** consistently provided		Sufficient **wait time for student responses** occasionally provided		Sufficient **wait time for student responses** not provided

Comments:

4	3	2	1	0	NA
19. Ample opportunities for students to **clarify key concepts in L1** as needed with aide, peer, or L1 text		Some opportunities for students to **clarify key concepts in L1**		No opportunities for students to **clarify key concepts in L1**	

Comments:

PRACTICE & APPLICATION

4	3	2	1	0	NA
20. **Hands-on materials and/or manipulatives** provided for students to practice using new content knowledge		Few **hands-on materials and/or manipulatives** provided for students to practice using new content knowledge		No **hands-on materials and/or manipulatives** provided for students to practice using new content knowledge	

Comments:

4	3	2	1	0	NA
21. Activities provided for students to **apply content and language knowledge** in the classroom		Activities provided for students to **apply** either **content or language knowledge** in the classroom		No activities provided for students to **apply content and language knowledge** in the classroom	

Comments:

4	3	2	1	0
22. Activities integrate all **language skills** (i.e., reading, writing, listening, and speaking)		Activities integrate some **language skills**		Activities do not integrate **language skills**

Comments:

LESSON DELIVERY

4	3	2	1	0
23. **Content objectives** clearly supported by lesson delivery		**Content objectives** somewhat supported by lesson delivery		**Content objectives** not supported by lesson delivery

Comments:

4	3	2	1	0
24. **Language objectives** clearly supported by lesson delivery		**Language objectives** somewhat supported by lesson delivery		**Language objectives** not supported by lesson delivery

Comments:

4	3	2	1	0

25. **Students engaged** approximately 90% to 100% of the period

Students engaged approximately 70% of the period

Students engaged less than 50% of the period

Comments:

4	3	2	1	0

26. **Pacing** of the lesson appropriate to students' ability levels

Pacing generally appropriate, but at times too fast or too slow

Pacing inappropriate to students' ability levels

Comments:

REVIEW & ASSESSMENT

4	3	2	1	0

27. Comprehensive **review of key vocabulary**

Uneven **review of key vocabulary**

No **review of key vocabulary**

Comments:

4	3	2	1	0

28. Comprehensive **review of key content concepts**

Uneven **review of key content concepts**

No **review of key content concepts**

Comments:

4	3	2	1	0

29. Regular **feedback** provided to students on their output (e.g., language, content, work)

Inconsistent **feedback** provided to students on their output

No **feedback** provided to students on their output

Comments:

4	3	2	1	0

30. **Assessment of student comprehension and learning** of all lesson objectives (e.g., spot checking, group response) throughout the lesson

Assessment of student comprehension and learning of some lesson objectives

No **assessment of student comprehension and learning** of lesson objectives

Comments:

(Reproduction of this material is restricted to use with Echevarria, Vogt, and Short (2008), *Making Content Comprehensible for English Learners: The SIOP® Model.*)

The Sheltered Instruction Observation Protocol (SIOP®)

(Echevarria, Vogt, & Short, 2000; 2004; 2008)

Observer(s): _____   Teacher: _____

Date: _____   School: _____

Grade: _____   Class/Topic: _____

ESL Level: _____   Lesson: Multi-day   Single-day   *(circle one)*

Total Points Possible: 120 (Subtract 4 points for each NA given) _____

Total Points Earned: _____   Percentage Score: _____

Directions: Circle the number that best reflects what you observe in a sheltered lesson. You may give a score from 0–4 (or NA on selected items). Cite under "Comments" specific examples of the behaviors observed.

	Highly Evident		Somewhat Evident		Not Evident	
Preparation	**4**	**3**	**2**	**1**	**0**	
1. **Content objectives** clearly defined, displayed, and reviewed with students	❑	❑	❑	❑	❑	
2. **Language objectives** clearly defined, displayed, and reviewed with students	❑	❑	❑	❑	❑	
3. **Content concepts** appropriate for age and educational background level of students	❑	❑	❑	❑	❑	
4. **Supplementary materials** used to a high degree, making the lesson clear and meaningful (e.g., computer programs, graphs, models, visuals)	❑	❑	❑	❑	❑	
5. **Adaptation of content** (e.g., text, assignment) to all levels of student proficiency	❑	❑	❑	❑	❑	**NA** ❑
6. **Meaningful activities** that integrate lesson concepts (e.g., surveys, letter writing, simulations, constructing models) with language practice opportunities for reading, writing, listening, and/or speaking	❑	❑	❑	❑	❑	

Comments:

Building Background	**4**	**3**	**2**	**1**	**0**	**NA**
7. **Concepts explicitly linked** to students' background experiences	❑	❑	❑	❑	❑	❑
8. **Links explicitly made** between past learning and new concepts	❑	❑	❑	❑	❑	
9. **Key vocabulary** emphasized (e.g., introduced, written, repeated, and highlighted for students to see)	❑	❑	❑	❑	❑	

Comments:

Comprehensible Input	**4**	**3**	**2**	**1**	**0**
10. **Speech** appropriate for students' proficiency levels (e.g., slower rate, enunciation, and simple sentence structure for beginners)	❑	❑	❑	❑	❑
11. **Clear explanation** of academic tasks	❑	❑	❑	❑	❑
12. **A variety of techniques** used to make content concepts clear (e.g., modeling, visuals, hands-on activities, demonstrations, gestures, body language)	❑	❑	❑	❑	❑

Comments:

Strategies	**4**	**3**	**2**	**1**	**0**
13. Ample opportunities provided for students to use **learning strategies**	❑	❑	❑	❑	❑

	Highly Evident		Somewhat Evident		Not Evident	
	4	**3**	**2**	**1**	**0**	
14. **Scaffolding techniques** consistently used assisting and supporting student understanding (e.g., think-alouds)	❑	❑	❑	❑	❑	
15. A variety of **questions or tasks that promote higher-order thinking skills** (e.g., literal, analytical, and interpretive questions) *Comments:*	❑	❑	❑	❑	❑	

Interaction	**4**	**3**	**2**	**1**	**0**	
16. Frequent opportunities for **interaction** and discussion between teacher/student and among students, which encourage elaborated responses about lesson concepts	❑	❑	❑	❑	❑	
17. **Grouping configurations** support language and content objectives of the lesson	❑	❑	❑	❑	❑	
18. Sufficient **wait time for student responses** consistently provided	❑	❑	❑	❑	❑	
19. Ample opportunities for students to **clarify key concepts in L1** as needed with aide, peer, or L1 text *Comments:*	❑	❑	❑	❑	❑	**NA** ❑

Practice and Application	**4**	**3**	**2**	**1**	**0**	**NA**
20. **Hands-on materials and/or manipulatives** provided for students to practice using new content knowledge	❑	❑	❑	❑	❑	❑
21. Activities provided for students to **apply content and language knowledge** in the classroom	❑	❑	❑	❑	❑	❑
22. Activities integrate all **language skills** (i.e., reading, writing, listening, and speaking) *Comments:*	❑	❑	❑	❑	❑	

Lesson Delivery	**4**	**3**	**2**	**1**	**0**
23. **Content objectives** clearly supported by lesson delivery	❑	❑	❑	❑	❑
24. **Language objectives** clearly supported by lesson delivery	❑	❑	❑	❑	❑
25. **Students engaged** approximately 90% to 100% of the period	❑	❑	❑	❑	❑
26. **Pacing** of the lesson appropriate to students' ability level *Comments:*	❑	❑	❑	❑	❑

Review & Assessment	**4**	**3**	**2**	**1**	**0**
27. Comprehensive **review of key vocabulary**	❑	❑	❑	❑	❑
28. Comprehensive **review of key content concepts**	❑	❑	❑	❑	❑
29. Regular **feedback** provided to students on their output (e.g., language, content, work)	❑	❑	❑	❑	❑
30. **Assessment of student comprehension and learning** of all lesson objectives (e.g., spot checking, group response) throughout the lesson *Comments:*	❑	❑	❑	❑	❑

(Reproduction of this material is restricted to use with Echevarria, Vogt, and Short (2008), *Making Content Comprehensible for English Learners: The SIOP® Model.*)

Examples of Academic Language in the English-Language Arts (K–2)

Word Analysis, Fluency, & Vocabulary Development	Reading Comprehension	Literary Response & Analysis	Writing Strategies	Written & Oral English Language Conventions	Listening & Speaking
title page	title	important events	left-to-right	sentence	share information
uppercase & lowercase letters	table of contents	realistic text	top-to-bottom	letter names	describe
letters	predictions	storybooks	words	alphabet	songs
words	retell	poems	sentences	fiction	rhymes
rhyming words	ask questions	newspaper articles	spacing	autobiography	tell about an experience
blend	answer questions	character	focus	description	ask questions
color names	stories	setting	descriptive words	person	stay on topic
title	sequence	important events	print legibly	place	poems
author	who, what, when, where	characters	narrative	event	stories
sentences	main idea	beginning of story	descriptive words	writing process	rhymes
long sounds	chapter headings	middle of story	detail	prewriting	songs
short sounds	author's purpose	end of story	friendly letter	drafting	give directions
syllables	informational text	author	date	revising	follow directions
compound words	facts	illustrator	salutation	complete sentence	speak clearly
contractions	details	compare & contrast	body	incomplete sentence	retell stories
vowels	cause and effect	plot	closing	word order	describe story elements
consonants	diagrams	alternative ending	signature	nouns	report on a topic
abbreviations	charts	rhythm		verbs	
prefixes	graphs	rhyme		commas	
suffixes	informational text	alliteration		periods	
fluency	literature	poetry		quotation marks	
plurals	expository text			capitalize	
				proper nouns	

Vogt, M.E., Echevarria, J., Short, D.J. (2009). *The SIOP Model for Teaching English-Language Arts to English Learners.* Boston: Allyn & Bacon.

Examples of Academic Language in the English-Language Arts (3–5)

Word Analysis, Fluency, & Vocabulary Development	Reading Comprehension	Literary Response & Analysis	Writing Strategies	Writing Applications (Genres)	Written & Oral Language Conventions	Listening & Speaking
word families	glossary	fairy tales	paragraph	concrete details	subjects	retell
regular multisyllabic	index	myths	topic sentence	memorable event	predicates	paraphrase words
pacing	literal information	folktales	supporting facts & details	observations	pronouns	use of appropriate props
intonation	inferred information	legends	cursive writing	recollections	adjectives	fluency
expression	modify predictions	fables	atlas	sensory details	compound words	rhythm
antonyms	main ideas in expository text	theme	encyclopedia	written response to literature	articles	pacing
synonyms	supporting details in expository text	alliteration	rubric	support judgments	past tense	speaker's opinions
homophones	problems & solutions	onomatopoeia	writing narrative	central question	present tense	verifiable facts
context clues	multiple-step written instructions	narrator	writing description	sources of information	future tense	clear diction
dictionary meanings	comprehension strategies	influence of events	writing personal letters	significant details	blends	pitch
prefix meanings	make and confirm predictions	future actions	audience	providing context	contractions	tempo
suffix meanings	prior knowledge	figurative language	purpose	literary work	compounds	tone
word origins	topic sentences	simile	introductory paragraph	writing a summary	double the consonants	elaboration
word derivations	evaluate information	metaphor	body		change ending from -y to -i	giving precise directions
word roots	fact and opinion	hyperbole	concluding paragraph		plurals	details
base words	structural patterns	personification	introductory paragraph		alphabetical order	examples
multiple meaning words	compare & contrast	characteristics of poetry	indentation		simple sentence	anecdotes
thesaurus	cause & effect	characteristics of drama	similarity & difference		compound sentence	modulation

(continued)

Vogt, M.E., Echevarria, J., Short, D.J. (2009). *The SIOP Model for Teaching English-Language Arts to English Learners*. Boston: Allyn & Bacon.

Word Analysis, Fluency, & Vocabulary Development	Reading Comprehension	Literary Response & Analysis	Writing Strategies	Writing Applications (Genres)	Written & Oral Language Conventions	Listening & Speaking
homographs	chronological order	characteristics of fiction	quotations		regular verbs	gestures
Greek roots	proposition	characteristics of nonfictions	paraphrasing		irregular verbs	role of media
Latin roots	support	conflict	citations		prepositional phrases	verbal & nonverbal messages
figurative language	comprehension	character motives	prefaces		adverbs	making inferences from oral report
	monitor	implied theme	appendixes		conjunctions	engaging the audience
	clarify	theme stated directly	reference materials		parentheses	verbal cues
	summarize	imagery	online information		commas in direct quotations	facial expression
	synthesize	symbolism	keyboarding skills		apostrophes	persuasive techniques
	hypothesize	reader perspective	adding text		quotation marks	logical fallacies
	text features		deleting text		appositives	persuasion
	assess evidence		cursor		independent clause	interpretation of events
	draw inferences		software		dependent clause	show rather than tell
	draw conclusions		memory		transitions	informative presentations
	generalizations		disk drive		modifiers	frame questions
			hard drive		colon	establish a controlling idea
			editing			develop the topic
			developing a plot			oral responses to literature
			describing a setting			summarize significant events

Vogt, M.E., Echevarria, J., Short, D.J. (2009). *The SIOP Model for Teaching English-Language Arts to English Learners*. Boston: Allyn & Bacon.

Word Analysis, Fluency, & Vocabulary Development	Reading Comprehension	Literary Response & Analysis	Writing Strategies	Writing Applications (Genres)	Written & Oral Language Conventions	Listening & Speaking
			summarizing ideas & details			use examples to support conclusions
			endnotes			
			bibliographic references			
			passwords			
			pull-down menus			
			word searches			
			spell check			
			revising manuscripts			

Vogt, M.E., Echevarria, J., Short, D.J. (2009). *The SIOP Model for Teaching English-Language Arts to English Learners*. Boston: Allyn & Bacon.

Examples of Academic Language in the English-Language Arts (6–8)

Word Analysis, Fluency, & Vocabulary Development	Reading Comprehension	Literary Response & Analysis	Writing Strategies	Writing Applications (Genres & their Characteristics)	Written & Oral Language Conventions	Listening & Speaking
figurative language	structural features of popular media	character qualities (e.g., courage or cowardice)	forms of writing (e.g., letter to editor, review, poem)	fictional narrative	modifiers	word choice
shades of meaning (e.g., *softly & quietly*)	compare-and-contrast organizational pattern	influence of setting	state a clear purpose	stem & leaf plot	active voice	pitch
idioms in prose/poetry	outlines	problem	visual image	plot line	infinitives	feeling
analogies in prose/poetry	logical notes	resolution	organization by categories	beginning	participles	tone
metaphors in prose/poetry	summaries	tone	spatial order	conflict	mechanics of writing	posture
similes in prose/poetry	reports	sentence structure	climactic order	rising action	dependent clauses	gesture
clarify word meanings through definition	applications (e.g., for library card, savings account)	line length	organizational features of electronic text	climax	pronoun references	mood
clarify word meanings through example	evidence for author's conclusion	punctuation	margins	denouement	hyphens	emotion
clarify word meanings through restatement	supporting citations	rhyme	tabs	point of view	dashes	select a focus
clarify word meanings through contrast	unsupported inferences	repetition	spacing	interpretations of literary work	brackets	point of view
Greek & Latin affixes	fallacious reasoning	rhythm	columns	semicolons	semicolons	vocal modulation
historical influences on English word meanings	persuasion	first-person narrative	page orientation	bases	bases	nonverbal
	propaganda	third-person narrative	consistency of ideas within & between paragraphs	affixes	affixes	sustain audience attention
	cause-and-effect organizational pattern	autobiography	effective transitions	state a clear position	parallelism	rhetorical devices
	author's argument	biography	anecdotes	relevant dialogue	written discourse	cadence

Vogt, M.E., Echevarria, J., Short, D.J. (2009). *The SIOP Model for Teaching English-Language Arts to English Learners.* Boston: Allyn & Bacon.

Word Analysis, Fluency, & Vocabulary Development	Reading Comprehension	Literary Response & Analysis	Writing Strategies	Writing Applications (Genres & their Characteristics)	Written & Oral Language Conventions	Listening & Speaking
	author's point of view	actions	descriptions	support judgments	subordination	repetitive patterns
	perspective	images	facts & statistics	thesis statement	coordination	use of onomatopoeia
	bias	symbolism	specific examples	primary sources	apposition	persuasive techniques
	stereotyping	credibility of characterization	notetaking	secondary sources	edit written manuscripts	propaganda techniques
	author's evidence	fact-fantasy in historical fiction	outlining	direct quotations	spelling conventions	false or misleading information
	word origins	short story	summarizing	documents		probing questions
		novel	inquiry	formatting		claims and conclusions
		novella	investigation	headings		questions, challenges, affirmations
		essay	research	fonts		voice modulation
		foreshadowing	quoted information			inflection
		recurring themes (e.g., bravery, loyalty, friendship)	paraphrased information			tempo
		contrast first and third person	bibliography			enunciation
		contrast points of view	methodology for citations			eye contact
		contrast limited & omniscient	word-processing skills			constructive feedback
		contrast subjective & objective	databases			electronic journalism
		responses to literary work	spreadsheets			oral interpretations
		ballad	revision			paraphrase
		lyric	word choice			expression

(continued)

Vogt, M.E., Echevarria, J., Short, D.J. (2009). *The SIOP Model for Teaching English-Language Arts to English Learners*. Boston: Allyn & Bacon.

Word Analysis, Fluency, & Vocabulary Development	Reading Comprehension	Literary Response & Analysis	Writing Strategies	Writing Applications (Genres & their Characteristics)	Written & Oral Language Conventions	Listening & Speaking
		couplet	precision of vocabulary			transitions
		epic				previews
		elegy				body
		ode				summaries
		sonnet				conclusion
		subplots				credibility of speaker
		parallel episodes				hidden agendas
		climax				biased
		plot development				dialogue
		conflict				physical description
		motivation				interpret a reading
		irony				well-defined thesis
		dialect				differentiate fact and opinion
		heritage of author				counterarguments

Vogt, M.E., Echevarria, J., Short, D.J. (2009). *The SIOP Model for Teaching English-Language Arts to English Learners*. Boston: Allyn & Bacon.

Examples of Academic Language in the English-Language Arts (9–12)

Word Analysis, Fluency, & Vocabulary Development	Reading Comprehension (focus on informational materials)	Literary Response & Analysis	Writing Strategies	Writing Applications (Genres & their Characteristics)	Written & Oral Language Conventions	Listening & Speaking
literal meanings	rhetorical devices	comedy	coherent thesis	biographical narrative	main clauses	formulate judgments
figurative meanings	public documents	tragedy	consistent tone	autobiographical narrative	subordinate clauses	media genres
denotative meanings	policy statements	drama	precise language	short story	phrases	patterns of organization
connotative meanings	speeches	dramatic monologue	action verbs	sequence of events	gerunds	chronological
connotative power of words	debates	compare & contrast genres	sensory details	sensory details	infinitives	topical
Greek myths and word meanings	platforms	interactions of main characters	appropriate modifiers	interior monologue	participial phrases	cause and effects
Roman myths and word meanings	hierarchical structures	subordinate characters	active voice	shifting perspectives	semicolons	introduction
Norse myths and word meanings	repetition	internal conflicts	passive voice	stylistic devices	colons	conclusion
etymology of terms in political science	syntax	external conflicts	research questions	ambiguity	ellipses	literary quotations
etymology of terms in history	workplace documents	motivations	research methods	nuance	hyphens	inform
Greek roots	consumer documents	relationships between characters	body of composition	complexity	parallel structure	persuade
Latin roots	public documents	character traits	supporting evidence	primary sources	subordination	classical speech forms
analogies	reasonable assertions about author's arguments	narration	scenarios	secondary sources	modifiers	credibility
	defend interpretations	dialogue	commonly held beliefs	assertions	consistency of verb tenses	validity
	clarify interpretations	soliloquy	hypotheses	appeal to logic, emotion, ethical belief	diction	relevance
	author's explicit philosophical assumptions	universal themes	synthesize information	personal anecdote	syntax	extemporaneous delivery

(continued)

Vogt, M.E., Echevarria, J., Short, D.J. (2009). The SIOP Model for Teaching English-Language Arts to English Learners. Boston: Allyn & Bacon.

Word Analysis, Fluency, & Vocabulary Development	Reading Comprehension (focus on informational materials)	Literary Response & Analysis	Writing Strategies	Writing Applications (Genres & their Characteristics)	Written & Oral Language Conventions	Listening & Speaking
	author's implicit philosophical assumptions	time and sequence	flow of ideas	case study	pagination	rhetorical devices
	validity of arguments	literary devices	conventions for documentation	analogy	in-text citations	mood and tone
	truthfulness of arguments	flashback	style manuals	expert opinions	direct quotations	historically significant speeches
	friendly audiences	foreshadowing	publishing software	address the audience		clarity
	hostile audiences	figurative language	publishing graphics	technical documents		quality
	claims	imagery	logic	scenarios		effectiveness
	counterclaims	allegory	coherence	narration		coherence
	appeal to reason	symbolism	perspective	description		causation
	appeal to authority	ambiguities	precision of word choice	exposition		analogy
	appeal to pathos	subtleties	audience	persuasion		authority
	appeal to emotion	contradictions	purpose	historical investigation		emotion
		ironies	formality of context	argumentation		logic
		incongruities	elements of discourse	validity & reliability of sources		aesthetic effects
		voice	narrative writing	résumés		interviewing techniques
		persona	expository writing	job applications		stylistic devices
		choice of narrator	persuasive writing	multimedia presentation		advertisements
		dialogue	descriptive writing			perpetuation of stereotypes
		scene design	parallelism			visual representation
		asides	repetition			special effects
		literary criticism	analogy			rhetorical questions

Vogt, M.E., Echevarria, J., Short, D.J. (2009). *The SIOP Model for Teaching English-Language Arts to English Learners*. Boston: Allyn & Bacon.

Word Analysis, Fluency, & Vocabulary Development	Reading Comprehension (focus on informational materials)	Literary Response & Analysis	Writing Strategies	Writing Applications (Genres & their Characteristics)	Written & Oral Language Conventions	Listening & Speaking
		asthetic approach	call for action			parallel structure
		historical approach	field studies			concrete images
		rhetorical purpose	oral histories			figurative language
		aesthetic purpose	interviews			characterization
		satire	experiments			irony
		parody	electronic sources			dialogue
		pastoral	anecdotal scripting			classical logical arguments
		author's style	annotated bibliographies			contemporary logical arguments
		personification	subtlety of meaning			inductive & deductive reasoning
		figures of speech				syllogisms
		genres				analogies
		historical periods in American literature				logical fallacies
		archetypes				false causality
		major literary periods				"red herring"
		Homeric Greece				overgeneralization
		medieval				bandwagon
		romantic				propositions of fact, value, problem, or policy
		neoclassic				dramatic soliloquy
		modern				

Vogt, M.E., Echevarria, J., Short, D.J. (2009). *The SIOP Model for Teaching English-Language Arts to English Learners*. Boston: Allyn & Bacon.

appendix d: Unit Activities and SIOP® Components

The purpose of this chart is to illustrate how the SIOP® components map onto the various activities in the K–2, 3–5, 6–8, and 9–12 units. Note that nearly all the activities promote interaction when students work together on the tasks, and/or orally share their work with partners or group members. The activities are listed in the approximate order that they appear throughout the Chapters 4–7.

	Lesson Preparation*	Building Background	Comprehensible Input**	Strategies	Interaction	Practice & Application	Lesson Delivery***	Review & Assessment	Chapter(s)
Anticipation/Reaction Guide		X	X	X	X	X		X	3, 4, 5, 6, 7
Semantic Feature Analysis		X	X	X	X	X		X	3, 4, 5, 6, 7
Conga Line		X	X	X	X	X		X	3, 4, 5, 6,
Adapted Conga Line:									
Mix-Mix-Trade		X	X	X	X	X		X	7
4-Corners Vocabulary Poster		X	X	X	X	X		X	4, 5, 6
Response Boards		X	X		X	X		X	6
Outcome Sentences				X	X	X		X	3, 4, 5, 6
Signal Words Chart		X	X	X		X			4, 6, 7
Split Decision				X	X	X		X	4, 6
Word-Definition-Picture Chart		X	X	X	X	X		X	4
Sentence Frames		X	X	X	X	X		X	3, 4, 5, 6, 7
T-Chart		X	X	X	X	X		X	3, 4, 5, 6
Stop and Think				X		X			5
Quickwrite		X		X		X		X	6
Tickets Out		X		X		X		X	6

	Lesson Preparation*	Building Background	Comprehensible Input**	Strategies	Interaction	Practice & Application	Lesson Delivery***	Review & Assessment	Chapter(s)
Character Map		X		X	X	X		X	7
Word Web		X		X		X		X	7
Discussion Web		X		X	X	X		X	7
Bio-Pyramid		X		X	X	X		X	7
Dinner Party		X		X	X	X		X	7

*All of the activities are selected during Lesson Preparation to provide practice and application of key concepts and vocabulary.

**While the teacher provides comprehensible input throughout a lesson, certain activities also make concepts more comprehensible because they break them down into more manageable parts.

***Students participate in the activities during Lesson Delivery.

appendix e: Blackline Masters for Activities

1 anticipation/reaction guide (Adapted from Buehl, 2009)

Directions: Next to each statement write an ìX" in the appropriate column. Be ready to discuss your opinion with the class.

Before Reading		Statements	After Reading	
Agree	Disagree		Agree	Disagree
☺	☹		☺	☹

For use with Vogt, Echevarria & Short (2010). *The SIOP® Model for Teaching English-Language Arts to English Learners.* Boston: Allyn & Bacon.

anticipation guide + why (Adapted from Buehl, 2009)

Directions: Next to each statement write an "X" in the appropriate column. Be ready to discuss your opinion with the class.

Before Reading		Statements	After Reading	
Agree	Disagree		Agree	Disagree
Why?		Why?		
Why?		Why?		
Why?		Why?		
Why?		Why?		
Why?		Why?		

For use with Vogt, Echevarria & Short (2010). *The SIOP® Model for Teaching English-Language Arts to English Learners.* Boston: Allyn & Bacon.

Name of the person.

Two words describing the person.

Three words describing childhood.

Four words indicating problem overcome.

Five words stating one accomplishment.

Six words stating a second accomplishment.

Seven words stating a third accomplishment.

Eight words stating how people benefited from accomplishments.

For use with Vogt, Echevarria & Short (2010). *The SIOP® Model for Teaching English-Language Arts to English Learners.* Boston: Allyn & Bacon.

character map (Macon, Bewell, & Vogt, 1991)

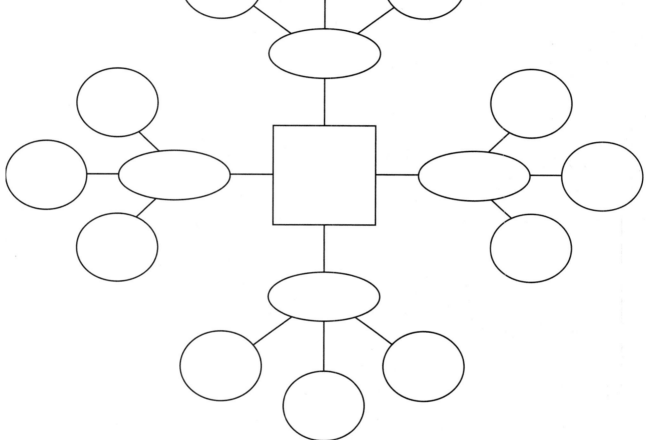

For use with Vogt, Echevarria & Short (2010). *The SIOP® Model for Teaching English-Language Arts to English Learners*. Boston: Allyn & Bacon.

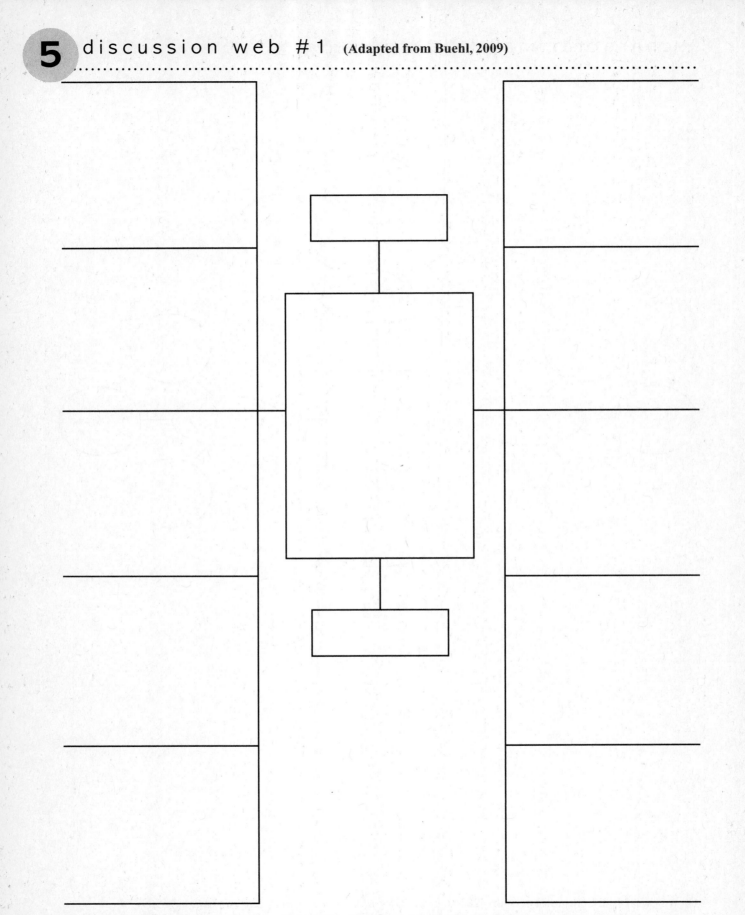

For use with Vogt, Echevarria & Short (2010). *The SIOP® Model for Teaching English-Language Arts to English Learners*. Boston: Allyn & Bacon.

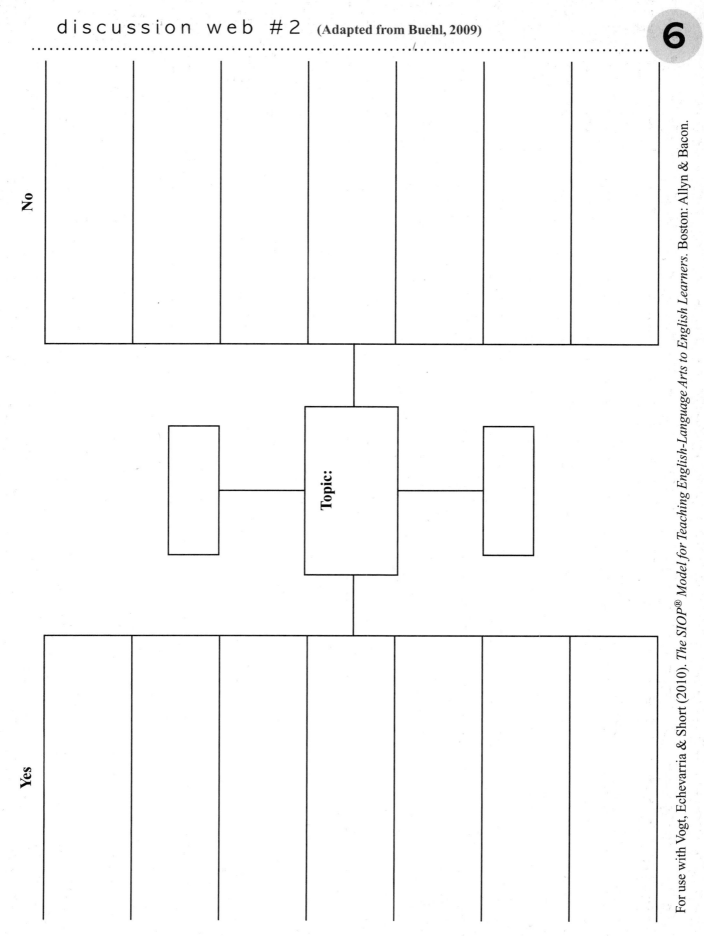

No

Topic:

Yes

For use with Vogt, Echevarria & Short (2010). *The SIOP® Model for Teaching English-Language Arts to English Learners.* Boston: Allyn & Bacon.

1. **Illustration**	3. **Sentence**
2. **Definition**	4. **Vocabulary Word**

For use with Vogt, Echevarria & Short (2010). *The SIOP® Model for Teaching English-Language Arts to English Learners.* Boston: Allyn & Bacon.

Steps for a Portrait Poem	Example
1. The first line is "Who am I?"	
2. Then skip a line and write "I am…"	
3. On the next five lines write down family relationships.	
4. Then skip a line and write "I am…"	
5. On the next four lines write down "job titles" that describe you.	
6. Then skip a line and write "I am…"	
7. On the next three lines write a word that physically describes you.	
8. Then skip a line and write "I am…"	
9. On the next two lines write down a characteristic of yours.	
10. Then skip a line and write "I am…"	
11. And finally the word "me."	

For use with Vogt, Echevarria & Short (2010). *The SIOP® Model for Teaching English-Language Arts to English Learners.* Boston: Allyn & Bacon.

Features

Words

For use with Vogt, Echevarria & Short (2010). *The SIOP® Model for Teaching English-Language Arts to English Learners.* Boston: Allyn & Bacon.

For use with Vogt, Echevarria & Short (2010). *The SIOP® Model for Teaching English-Language Arts to English Learners.* Boston: Allyn & Bacon.

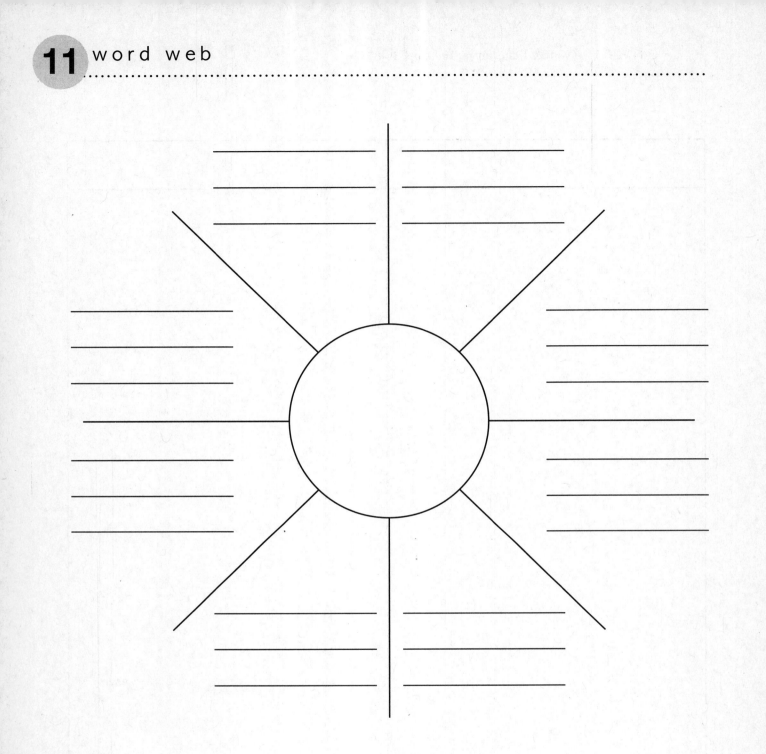

For use with Vogt, Echevarria & Short (2010). *The SIOP® Model for Teaching English-Language Arts to English Learners*. Boston: Allyn & Bacon.

references

. . . .

American Educational Research Association (AERA), American Psychological Association (APA), & National Council on Measurement in Education (NCME). (2000). Position statement of the American Educational Research Association concerning high-stakes testing in pre-K–12 education. *Educational Researcher, 29,* 24–25.

August, D., & Shanahan, T. (Eds.). (2006). *Developing literacy in second-language learners: A report of the National Literacy Panel on Language-Minority Children and Youth.* Mahwah, NJ: Erlbaum.

Aukerman, M. (2007). A culpable CALP: Rethinking the conversational/academic proficiency distinction in early literacy instruction. *The Reading Teacher, 60*(7), 626–635.

Bailey, A. L. (Ed.). (2007). *The language demands of school: Putting academic English to the test.* New Haven, CT: Yale University Press.

Baumann, J., Jones, L., & Seifert-Kessell, N. (1993). Using think-alouds to enhance children's comprehension monitoring abilities. *The Reading Teacher, 47*(3), 184–193.

Belliveau, A. *Who am I?* From the Sun Belt Writing Project. Retrieved from http://www.tnellen.com/cybereng/portrait.html, on July 25, 2008.

Biancarosa, G., & Snow, C. (2004). *Reading next: A vision for action and research in middle and high school literacy.* Report to the Carnegie Corporation of New York. Washington, DC: Alliance for Excellent Education.

Buehl, D. (2009). *Strategies for interactive learning* (3rd ed.). Newark, DE: International Reading Association.

California Department of Education. (1998). *English-language arts content standards for California public schools.* Sacramento: Department of Education. Retrieved from cde.ca.gov/be/st/ss/documents/elacontentstnds.pdf. December, 2008.

Castillo, M. (2008). *Reviewing objectives with English language learners.* Presented at SEI Seminar, Phoenix, AZ.

Cazden, C. (1976). How knowledge about language helps the classroom teacher—or does it? A personal account. *The Urban Review, 9,* 74–91.

Cazden, C. (1986). Classroom discourse. In M. D. Wittrock (Ed.), *Handbook of research on teaching* (3rd ed., pp. 432–463). New York: Macmillan.

Cazden, C. (2001). *Classroom discourse: The language of teaching and learning* (2nd ed.). Portsmouth, NH: Heinemann.

Center for Applied Linguistics. (2007). *Academic literacy through sheltered instruction for secondary English language learners.* Final Report to the Carnegie Corporation of New York. Washington, DC: Center for Applied Linguistics.

Chamot, A. U., & O'Malley, J. M. (1994). *The CALLA handbook: Implementing the cognitive academic language learning approach.* Reading, MA: Addison-Wesley.

Collier, V. (1987). Age and rate of acquisition of second language for academic purposes. *TESOL Quarterly 21*(3), 617–641.

Cosentino de Cohen, C., Deterding, N., & Clewell, B. C. (2005). *Who's left behind: Immigrant children in high and low LEP schools.* Washington, DC: Urban Institute. Retrieved January 2, 2009 at http://www.urban.org/UploadedPDF/411231_whos_left_behind.pdf

Coxhead, A. (2000). A new academic word list. *TESOL Quarterly, 34*(2), 213–238.

Cummins, J. (1979). *Cognitive/academic language proficiency, linguistic interdependence, the optimum age questions, and some other matters.* Working Papers on Bilingualism, No. 19, 121–129. Toronto: Ontario Institute for Studies in Education.

Cummins, J. (2000). *Language, power, and pedagogy: Bilingual children in the crossfire.* Clevedon, UK: Multilingual Matters.

Cummins, J. (2006). How long does it take for an English language learner to become proficient in a second language? In E. Hamayan & R. Freeman (Eds.), *English language learners at school: A guide for administrators* (pp. 59–61). Philadelphia: Caslon Publishing.

Dutro, S., & Moran, C. (2003) Rethinking English language instruction: An architectural approach. In G. Garcia (Ed.), *English learners: Reaching the highest level of English literacy* (pp. 227–258). Newark, NJ: International Reading Association.

Echevarria, J. (1995). Interactive reading instruction: A comparison of proximal and distal effects of instructional conversations. *Exceptional Children, 61*(6), 536–552.

Echevarria, J., & Graves, A. (2007). *Sheltered content instruction: Teaching English language learners with diverse abilities* (3rd ed.). Boston: Allyn & Bacon.

Echevarria, J., Richards, C., & Canges, R. (in press). The role of language in the acquisition of science concepts. *Journal of Research on Educational Effectiveness.*

Echevarria, J., & Short, D. J. (2009). Programs and practices for effective sheltered content instruction. In D. Dolson & L. Burnham-Massey (Eds.), *Improving education for English learners: Research-based approaches.* Sacramento, CA: California Department of Education.

Echevarria, J., Short, D., & Powers, K. (2006). School reform and standards-based education: An instructional model for English language learners. *Journal of Educational Research, 99*(4), 195–211.

Echevarria, J., Short, D., & Vogt, M.E. (2008). *Implementing the SIOP® model through effective professional development and coaching.* Boston, MA: Pearson/Allyn & Bacon.

Echevarria, J., & Silver, J. (1995). *Instructional conversations: Understanding through discussion.* [Videotape]. National Center for Research on Cultural Diversity and Second Language Learning.

Echevarria, J., Vogt, M.E., & Short, D. J. (2008). *Making content comprehensible for English learners: The SIOP® Model* (3rd ed.). Boston: Allyn & Bacon.

Echevarria, J., Vogt, M.E., & Short, D. J. (2010). *The SIOP® Model for teaching mathematics to English learners.* Boston: Allyn & Bacon.

Echevarria, J., Vogt, M.E., & Short, D. (2010a). *Making content comprehensible for elementary English learners: The SIOP™ Model.* Boston: Allyn & Bacon.

Echevarria, J., Vogt, M.E., & Short, D. (2010b). *Making content comprehensible for secondary English learners: The SIOP™ Model.* Boston: Allyn & Bacon.

Fisher, D., & Frey, N. (2008). *Wordwise & content rich: Five essential steps to teaching academic vocabulary.* Portsmouth, NH: Heinemann.

Flynt, E. S., & Brozo, W. G. (2008). Developing academic language: Got words? *The Reading Teacher, 61*(6), 500–502.

Gandara, P., Maxwell-Jolly, J., & Driscoll, A. (2005). *Listening to teachers of English language learners: A survey of California teachers' challenges, experiences, and professional development needs.* Santa Cruz, CA: The Center for the Future of Teaching and Learning.

Garcia, G., & Beltran, D. (2003). Revisioning the blueprint: Building for the academic success of English learners. In G. Garcia (Ed.), *English learners: Reaching the highest levels of English literacy* (pp. 197–226). Newark, DE: International Reading Association.

Garcia, G. E., & Godina, H. (2004). Addressing the literacy needs of adolescent English language learners. In T. Jetton & J. Dole (Eds.), *Adolescent literacy: Research and practice* (pp. 304–320). New York: The Guildford Press.

Genesee, F., Lindholm-Leary, K., Saunders, W., & Christian, D. (2006). *Educating English language learners: A synthesis of research evidence.* New York: Cambridge University Press.

Gersten, R., Baker, S. K., Shanahan, T., Linan-Thompson, S., Collins, P., & Scarcella, R. (2007). *Effective literacy and English language instruction for English learners in the elementary grades: A practice guide* (NCEE 2007-4011). Washington, DC: National Center for Education Evaluation and Regional Assistance, Institute of Education Sciences, U.S. Department of Education. Retrieved from http://ies.ed.gov/ncee.

Goldenberg, C. (2008). Teaching English language learners: What the research does—and does not—say. *The American Educator, 32*(2), 8–23.

Graham, S., & Perin, D. (2007). *Writing next: Effective strategies to improve writing of adolescents in middle and high schools.* A report to the Carnegie Corporation of New York. Washington, DC: Alliance for Excellent Education.

Hiebert, E. H. (2005). *Word Zones™: 5,586 most frequent words in written English.* Available at www.textproject.org.

Hiebert, E. H. (2005). *1,000 most frequent words in middle-grades and high school texts.* Available at www.textproject.org.

Holt Literature & Language Arts (Fourth Course: Grade 10). Austin, TX: Holt, Rinehort and Winston, 73–145.

Kagan, S. (1994). *Cooperative learning.* San Clemente, CA: Kagan Publishing.

Kindler, A. (2002). *Survey of the states' limited English proficient students and available educational programs and services. 2000–01 summary report.* Washington, DC: National Clearinghouse for English Language Acquisition.

Kober, N., Zabala, D., Chudowsky, N., Chudowsky, V., Gayler, K., & McMurrer, J. (2006). *State high school exit exams: A challenging year.* Washington, DC: Center on Education Policy.

Krashen, S. (1985). *The input hypothesis: Issues and implications.* London: Longman.

Lee, J., Grigg, W., & Dion, P. (2007). *The nation's report card: Mathematics 2007.* (NCES 2007-494). U.S. Department of Education, Institute of Education Sciences, National Center for Education Statistics. Washington, DC: U.S. Government Printing Office.

Lee, J., Grigg, W., & Donahue, P. (2007). *The nation's report card: Reading 2007.* (NCES 2007-496). U.S. Department of Education, Institute of Education Sciences, National Center for Education Statistics. Washington, DC: U.S. Government Printing Office.

Lee, O. (2005). Science education with English language learners: Synthesis and research agenda. *Review of Educational Research, 75*(4), 491–530.

Macon, J. M., Bewell, D., & Vogt, M.E. (1991). *Responses to literature: Grades K–8.* Newark, DE: International Reading Association.

Mehan, H. (1979). *Learning lessons.* Cambridge: Harvard University Press.

National Center for Education Statistics. (2002). *Schools and staffing survey, 1999–2000: Overview of the data for public, private, public charter, and Bureau of Indian Affairs elementary and secondary schools.* (NCES 2002–313). Washington, DC: U.S. Department of Education, National Center for Educational Statistics.

National Institute of Child Health and Human Development (NICHD). (2000). *Report of the National Reading Panel, Teaching children to read: An evidence-based assessment of the scientific research literature on reading and its implications for reading instruction.* (NIH Publication No. 00-4769). Washington, DC: U.S. Department of Health and Human Services.

Oczkus, L. (2009). *Interactive think-aloud lessons: 25 surefire ways to engage students and improve comprehension.* New York: Scholastic, and Newark, DE: International Reading Association.

Parish, T., Merikel, A., Perez, M., Linquanti, R., Socias, M., & Spain, M. (2006). *Effects of the implementation of Proposition 227 on the education of English learners, K–12: Findings from a five-year evaluation.* Palo Alto, CA: American Institutes for Research.

Pittelman, S. D., Heimlich, J., Berglund, R., French, M., & Heimlich, J. E. (1991). *Semantic feature analysis: Classroom application.* Newark, DE: International Reading Association.

Read-Write-Think. *Sample Character Traits.* Retrieved on January 24, 2009 at http://readwritethink.org/lessons/lesson_view.asp?id=175. Newark, DE: International Reading Association; National Council of Teachers of English.

Reiss, J. (2008). *102 content strategies for English language learners.* Upper Saddle River, NJ: Pearson/Merrill Prentice Hall.

Ruddell, M. R. (2007). *Teaching content reading and writing* (5th ed.). New York: John Wiley & Sons.

Saunders, W., & Goldenberg, C. (2007). The effects of an instructional conversation on English Language Learners' concepts of friendship and story comprehension. In R. Horowitz (Ed.), *Talking texts: How speech and writing interact in school learning* (pp. 221–252). Mahwah, NJ: Erlbaum.

Saunders, W., & Goldenberg, C. (2009). Research to guide English language development instruction. In D. Dolson & L. Burnham-Massey (Eds.), *Improving*

Education for English Learners: Research-Based Approaches. Sacramento, CA: California Department of Education.

Scott, J. A., Jamison-Noel, D., & Asselin, M. (2003). Vocabulary instruction day in twenty-three Canadian upper elementary classrooms. *The Elementary School Journal 103*, 269–286.

Short, D. J., & Richards, C. (2008). *Linking science and academic English: Teacher development and student achievement*. Paper presented at the Center for Research on the Educational Achievement and Teaching of English Language Learners.

Short, D. J., Vogt, M.E., & Echevarria, J. (In press). *The SIOP® Model for teaching history-social studies to English learners*. Boston: Allyn & Bacon.

Short, D. J., Vogt, M.E., & Echevarria, J. (In press). *The SIOP® Model for teaching science to English learners*. Boston: Allyn & Bacon.

Stahl, S. A., & Nagy, W. E. (2006). *Teaching word meanings*. Mahwah, NJ: Lawrence Erlbaum Associates, Inc.

Suarez-Orozco, C., Suarez-Orozco, M. M., & Todorova, I. (2008). *Learning in a new land: Immigrant students in American society*. Cambridge, MA: Harvard University Press.

Tharp, R., & Gallimore, R. (1988). *Rousing minds to life: Teaching, learning and schooling in social context*. Cambridge: Cambridge University Press.

U.S. Department of Education. (2006). *Building partnerships to help English language learners*. Fact sheet. Retrieved January 2, 2008 at http://www.ed.gov/nclb/methods/english/lepfactsheet.html.

Vogt, M.E. (1996). Creating a response-centered curriculum with literature discussion groups. In L. B. Gambrell & J. F. Almasi (Eds.), *Lively discussions! Fostering engaged reading* (pp. 181–207). Newark, DE: International Reading Association.

Vogt, M.E., & Echevarria, J. (2008). *99 ideas and activities for teaching English learners with the SIOP® Model*. Boston: Allyn & Bacon.

Walqui, A. (2006). Scaffolding instruction for English language learners: A conceptual framework. *The International Journal of Bilingual Education and Bilingualism, 9*(2), 159–180.

Watson, K., & Young, B. (1986). Discourse for learning in the classroom. *Language Arts, 63*(2), 126–133.

Zehler, A. M., Fleishman, H. L., Hopstock, P. J., Stephenson, T. G., Pendzik, M. L., & Sapru, S. (2003). *Descriptive study of services to LEP students and to LEP students with disabilities: Policy report: Summary of findings related to LEP and SpEd-LEP students*. Arlington, VA: Development Associates.

Zwiers, J. (2004). *Developing academic thinking skills in grades 6–12*. Newark, DE: International Reading Association.

Zwiers, J. (2008). *Building academic language: Essential practices for content classrooms* (Grades 5–12). San Francisco: Jossey-Bass; Newark, DE: International Reading Association.

index

. . . . ●

193